Making Good

Making Good
Prisons, Punishment and Beyond

Martin Wright

Foreword by Barbara Wootton

Burnett Books

First published 1982 by Burnett Books Limited
Produced and Distributed by
The Hutchinson Publishing Group
17–21 Conway Street
London W1P 6BS

Printed in Great Britain by The Anchor Press Ltd
and bound by Wm Brendon & Son Ltd
both of Tiptree, Essex

British Library Cataloguing in Publication Data

Wright, Martin
  Making good.
  1. Prisons—Great Britain
  I. Title
  365'.941   HV9647

  ISBN 0–09–147220–2
  ISBN 0–09–147221–0 Pbk

For Lisa

Contents

Foreword

Apart from habitual criminals and prison officers, there can be few people in this country who have a more extensive acquaintance with the insides of our prisons than the author of this book in his capacity of Director of the Howard League for Penal Reform. Equipped with this experience and with massive researches into penal policy and practices both at home and abroad, he begins by launching an attack on the institution of imprisonment in general, followed by a devastating picture of the disgusting conditions now prevailing in the over-crowded prisons of contemporary Britain.

At a time when the head of the Prison Department in the Home Office publicly admits, in the introduction to his annual report for 1980 (Cmnd. 8228), that the prison service has become used in many establishments to 'tolerating the intolerable', this book can hardly be accused of exaggeration, although the author might be open to a charge of selectivity, inasmuch as he makes no mention either of our open prisons (in which the accommodation, at least for men, is habitually underoccupied) or of the handful of prisoners who in recent years have gained University degrees during their incarceration. But these are only small islands in the general morass of squalor and misery.

Undoubtedly our prisons are crammed with petty thieves, hooligans, drunks and vandals whose behaviour is consistently anti-social, but who need not be kept behind bars in the interest of public safety. So the first step (as many would agree) is to clear that lot out, and also to shorten the sentences imposed upon many more serious offenders. Experience has amply demonstrated that prison is too often just a school for crime and that the longer a prisoner's sentence, the greater the likelihood that he will return to crime on release although, of course, the occasional shining exception does from time to time emerge from the prison gates.

Such a clearance, however, raises the question of what is to be done both with offenders for whom prison is inappropriate, and also with

11

those who must inevitably be left inside. In its initial approach to the former of these problems, this book presents a fairly conventional account of the reforms that have been proposed or introduced. Among the available alternatives community service is sympathetically outlined, and it is also suggested that probation might be supplemented by a more exacting form of supervision. Much more space is, however, given to the ingenious system adopted in California, under which probation officers are rewarded by the grant of additional funds for their work every time they persuade a court to impose a probation order in preference to a sentence of imprisonment – a form of bribery which I can hardly imagine operating in this country with its rigid classification of expenditure into non-transferable categories.

As to the treatment of those who are thought to be too dangerous to be left at liberty in the community, we are presented with a sketch of a self-governing regime in which life within the secure prison compound would be almost as free as, and nearly indistinguishable from, life in the community outside the wall. If that seems impossibly idealistic for a residual population entirely composed of prisoners with a history of violence serving long sentences, we are reminded of the Special Unit in Glasgow's Barlinnie prison which did in fact make a considerable success of that kind of system with just such a population, so long as it remained under sympathetic management.

Finally the author reviews the well-worn themes of deterrence versus rehabilitation on which both the existing system and the familiar reformist arguments are based; but instead of supporting either the rehabilitative ideal or a return to punishment, he relegates both to a subsidiary position and reveals the really radical project which he has been keeping up his sleeve, prefaced by a (probably counter-productive) expression of hope that readers will not read his last chapter first. At this point we revert to the good old notion that the primary objective of penal policy should be to make the offender, as far as possible, repair the damage that he has done to an individual victim, or to the community.

The difficulties in applying this principle in a complex modern community with complex modern criminals are obvious enough, but the author quotes to good effect the work of the Dispute Center established in New York by the Institute for Mediation and Conflict Resolution, which has introduced a procedure under which many criminal cases are treated virtually as civil torts. In the first instance the offender and victim are brought together by a mediator, and if this does not produce an agreed result, recourse may be had to an arbitrator, whose decision is binding and enforceable by the judgement of a civil court.

Of course a single chapter at the end of a long book will not immediately reconcile the victim of a burglary to the prospect of negotiating reparation with the perpetrator thereof, or convince him that any agreement reached will in fact be honoured. This chapter has, however, succeeded in producing a penological proposal which has not already been flogged to death, but is so revolutionary as to require a whole book to itself. Does it not follow that Martin Wright, or colleagues who are thinking along the same lines, must either get to work on such a book forthwith, or expect to see this cherished project dismissed as an idealist's dream?

Barbara Wootton
May, 1981

Introduction

Throughout the world there are people either in prison cells or undergoing other forms of punishment. Those who stop to think, and to find out from people with first-hand knowledge, have been uneasy about prisons for a long time; religious codes speak of tempering justice with mercy, penal codes often attempt to combine it with rehabilitation. But the prisons persist – some with tolerable physical conditions, others ranging from the primitive and overcrowded to those which apply modern technology to the ancient practice of immuring people.

Reformers have worked over the years to remove the worst barbarities of the penal system: capital punishment, torture, mutilation, flogging and other cruel, inhuman and degrading punishments. (This book is concerned with the legitimized punishment of those who break the criminal law, rather than the illicit torture practised by political oppressors, although of course the dividing line between the two is not always clear-cut.) The reformers have also tried to remove the worst abuses in prisons, often helped by humane members of the prison service. Sometimes their ideas have led down blind alleys, in the hope of imposing penitence or rehabilitation; sometimes they have resulted in cruelty, such as solitary confinement, or hypocrisy, such as the attempt to change the offender with no corresponding change in the society in which he is expected to survive. (I hope I shall be forgiven for using 'he' throughout instead of the cumbersome 'he or she'; wherever possible I have used 'people' rather than 'men'.) Efforts to reform the penal system have never succeeded, however, in resolving the basic problem of grafting rehabilitative ideals on to an essentially punitive and rejecting tree.

My starting point in writing this book, after a short look (in Chapter One) at these traditional attitudes, is the prison. This is the severest punishment in most 'developed' countries and in the few third world countries which have abolished capital punishment. The early chapters show the harmful and damaging effects of prisons,

15

which must be set against any benefits they are supposed to provide (Chapters Two and Three); then I describe a selection of sanctions which involve only partial deprivation of liberty. In some ways they offer more advantages and fewer drawbacks than prisons (Chapters Four and Five). For the prisons that remain, a reformed régime is proposed (Chapter Six). Thus far the case presented is an orthodox reformist one. A major question is why, given the wide support for it, putting it into effect takes so long. This seems to be due not only to the punitive attitudes mentioned in Chapter One, but to the system's structure, financing and divisions of responsibility: ways of restructuring it so that it might be more receptive to change are suggested in Chapter Seven.

But like others who have worked to advocate reforms along these lines, I have come to feel that there is something missing. The theoretical contradictions have not been resolved. To begin with, it is necessary to be clear about the nature of crime. It is a complex question which this book will not attempt to discuss in detail, but it needs to be borne in mind that the word can be used in different ways. Firstly, the term 'crime' can mean the total sum of all acts prohibited by law, from the businessman's tax evasion to the homeless man's theft of a bottle of milk. Secondly, many people, although they would accept the above definition if pressed, tend to use the word to refer to the more visible and anxiety-provoking offences including 'street crimes', robbery, burglary and violent offences. But, thirdly, referring to the amount of crime, as in 'the total volume of crime has declined for two years running,' it is used to mean the number of offences recorded by the police. This, as criminologists have repeatedly pointed out, bears no necessary relationship to the actual number of crimes committed: more will be recorded if the public becomes less tolerant of a certain form of crime, or if the police put a special effort into pursuing it – and conversely. Lastly, the word is sometimes used in the general sense of 'harmful acts', regardless of whether they are actually illegal, as in 'the way some employers treat their employees is criminal.' Some of the most harmful acts, damaging to health, life and livelihood, have so far escaped being defined as criminal in the narrow legal sense; some crimes harm no one, or only the offender himself. I hope the context will show in which sense the word is being used; in the last chapters the emphasis is increasingly on harmful acts, whether or not they are prohibited and recorded.

A society naturally wants to minimize harmful acts, but the criminal law is in theory concerned with crime in the first of the above senses. The possible aims of the criminal law are generally taken to include: (1) imposing retribution; (2) expressing condemnation of the criminal act; (3) reducing the amount of crime and the anxiety and fear which it causes, bringing as many offenders as possible to justice, and giving the public adequate protection; and (4) making good the harm done to the victim or to society. The first two are symbolic in intention, the latter two practical. The third of these aims, however, the use of criminal justice procedures to try to reduce crime, contains the contradiction which is at the root of the malaise of the present-day penal system (examined in Chapter Eight): the attempt to rehabilitate individual offenders, besides not being strikingly successful (though criticisms may have been overdone), conflicts with the effects of punishment. Punishment, on the other hand, achieves the first and second of the above aims, and is widely assumed to achieve the third, through deterrence. It is hardly too much to say that what rehabilitates does not deter, what deters does not rehabilitate, and what compromises does neither. What is often forgotten is that punishment is probably impossible to apply fairly and has very damaging side-effects; as long as it is unquestioningly accepted, it will inhibit the search for a more satisfactory theoretical foundation on which to build more constructive methods.

The last two chapters are an attempt to outline such a basis. This is not intended to include the first of the above aims, retribution; but the others, it is suggested, could well be achieved rather more effectively than at present, and with beneficial side-effects that would extend beyond the confines of criminal justice.

At first sight this proposal may seem revolutionary, but this is only in the sense that a wheel completes a full revolution: the idea of making good the harm done is a very ancient and widespread one. Nor would the existing system be suddenly swept away: new approaches could gradually be introduced within or alongside it, for the less serious crimes at first, while they gained public confidence.

I want to make it clear that, although many of the ideas and proposals have been put forward by the Howard League for Penal Reform, this is by no means true of all of them; the book is written in my personal capacity, and should not necessarily be taken as reflecting the views of the League or its members.

Acknowledgements

I should like to thank the Council of the Howard League for allowing

me to work part-time for a year while this book was in preparation.
Several people have read various portions and made helpful comments, although of course responsibility for the final version and the
views expressed is mine: my thanks to Keith Bottomley, Marjorie
Jones, Rod Morgan, and Ken Pease, as well as to Farrell Burnett who
has been consistently helpful – and patient. The library of the Cambridge Institute of Criminology was invaluable, and I am grateful to
my Howard League colleagues Madge Elliott and Vicky Packham for
numerous small chores. Mlle Yvonne Marx of the Centre Français de
Droit Comparé kindly provided details of recent French legislation.
Margaret Jones and Joyce Bennett helped by typing the text ef-
ficiently and quickly. I am extremely grateful to Barbara Wootton,
who has contributed so much to humane and rational thinking about
the administration of justice, for making time among her many other
continuing activities to write the Foreword.

The quotation from 'Little Gidding' in T. S. Eliot's *Four Quartets*
is reproduced by permission of Faber and Faber Ltd., London; and
Harcourt Brace Jovanovich Inc., New York.

Above all I owe more than I can say to my wife, Lisa, and my
family for their prolonged forbearance and encouragement.

1. Prisons, Punishment and the Public

Many aspects of imprisonment are ineffective and inhumane. It isolates people from their families, and deprives them of their jobs, if they have any; the work provided in prison is frequently low-grade and insufficient to fill the working week, and sometimes there is none at all. Physical conditions are often deplorable, and safeguards against ill-treatment unsatisfactory. There should be revulsion at the way millions of human beings are treated in prisons throughout the world (no one knows how many prisoners there are, but the number is probably at least five million, perhaps ten). Many are already poor and under-privileged, and prison makes them more so; many have committed only minor offences. Are there compensating advantages to explain why such a system has taken root so firmly? It is perhaps significant that those countries which have the best general records for welfare tend to make least use of imprisonment; but what has held them back from reducing it still further? Reformers have in the past set themselves the ideal of improving prisons, but it is time to ask more fundamental questions both about prisons and about the principles on which the penal system as a whole is based. This introductory chapter will consider some of the reasons why the public has not yet rejected imprisonment as a standard punishment; it will then briefly look at some of the punishments replaced by prisons, and at public attitudes to punishment in general.

Why are Prisons Tolerated?

Prisons are accepted and believed to be necessary partly for negative reasons: the public knows little about the kinds of people who are sent to them, or how they are treated in them. The number of people who have been 'inside', or know someone who has been, is much smaller than the number, say, questioned by the police; and those who have had the experience are not always ready to talk about it. So prison tends to be something that happens to somebody else. As La Rochefoucauld said, *'Nous avons tous assez de force pour supporter les maux d'autrui'*: everyone can endure with equanimity the punishments inflicted on other people's husbands or sons. Relatives who contact the Howard League often say that they never imagined that people could be treated in such a way in British prisons until it happened to someone they knew – and to themselves when they started to come up against the regulations about such things as visits and letters. The theme, over and again, is: 'I know he (or she) has done wrong and deserves to be punished, but this is too much.' Although in some areas of big cities there is a higher proportion of people with direct or indirect knowledge of prisons, they tend not to believe that they can do anything about it; generally, it seems, they accept it as a fact of life, as one more reason for their cynicism towards the authorities.

It is difficult for the media to inform the public about what happens in prisons. In England, although the Home Office has recently adopted a slightly less restrictive policy toward access by journalists, prisoners are still restricted in what they may write for publication. It is consequently difficult to document, let alone prove, the malpractices and brutality which undoubtedly occur; and the other great scandal of prison, the stultifying boredom and waste of human lives, does not lend itself to making news stories. There have been some fictional representations of prison life. The comedy series 'Porridge' gave a somewhat cosy impression, though it did convey that one of the principal occupations of prisoners is outwitting the authorities; others, like the television programmes 'Law and Order' and the film 'Scum', although based on fact, presented such a one-sidedly brutal and corrupt picture as to undermine their own credibility. While some television features and serious newspapers have partly redressed the balance between these extremes (in particular, Rex Bloomstein's eight-part television documentary series 'Strangeways' in late 1980 gave a restrained and thorough picture of the pointlessness and injustice of prison life), in general the media have achieved little more than a slight and occasional public awareness that all is not well with the penal system. Some aspects of the public shortsightedness which results from this lack of information are described by a Canadian parliamentary committee:

Many in the community have the misconception that, once the offenders are sentenced, that is the end of it; they are out of sight and out of life . . .

The reality is that all – except those who die in prison – come out legally on expiration of their sentence. . . .

When they come out they are the people who move into the house or apartment next door, who ride buses with you, eat in the next booth in restaurants, walk on the same streets, sell papers, deliver groceries, fill your gas tanks, and talk about the weather with you in the theatre line-up.

Therefore it is apparent that the community is safer if the person who shares their freedom is not more dangerous when he joins them in life on the outside. Prisons, as they now exist, protect society only during the 2, 3, 10 or 20 years the inmate is in there; but if the institutions are boring, oppressive and lack programmes preparing the inmates for release, they come out angry, vindictive, frustrated, . . . Many are released onto the streets directly from maximum security institutions, unadjusted, unprepared, with fear, tension and paranoia that spell danger to the community. (Canada 1977, paras. 75–78)

Nor is much research published which might percolate into the public consciousness to set the record straight. Part of the reason for this must surely be that social scientists, anxious to achieve some worthwhile research, tend to look to areas where there are not so many obstacles, raised by an over-cautious bureaucracy, to obtaining permission and the necessary access to institutions. What information we have tends therefore to come from the Prison Department and its staff (insofar as they are not inhibited by the Official Secrets Act and civil service rules) and from ex-prisoners, neither of whom can be regarded as impartial sources. Prison administrations have their own reasons for being secretive. Partly it is for the laudable purpose of protecting prisoners from the intrusion of the less scrupulous sections of the media (although the secrecy itself adds to the scarcity value of stories about prison life), but partly it is to protect the Prison Service and its staff against criticism – ostensibly against unjust criticism, but in fact it also serves to keep the volume of justified criticism down to manageable proportions.

In practice secrecy has the subsidiary result of enabling prisons to continue, for reasons explained by Bernard Shaw (1922) in his preface to the Webbs' *English Prisons Under Local Government*:

The public conscience would be far more active if the punishment of imprisonment were abolished, and we went back to the rack, the stake, the pillory, and the lash at the cart's tail. . . . [People] can be shamed at last into recognizing that such exhibitions are degrading and demoralizing . . . We have then to find some form of torment which can give no

21

sensual satisfaction to the tormentor, and which is hidden from public view. That is how imprisonment, being just such a torment, became the normal penalty. . . . It would be far better for [the prisoner] to suffer in the public eye; for among the crowd of sightseers there might be a Victor Hugo or a Dickens, able and willing to make the sightseers think of what they are doing and ashamed of it. The prisoner has no such chance. . . . the secrecy of his prison makes it hard to convince the public that he is suffering at all.

Obsolete Punishments

Thus as more primitive punishments have been done away with, prisons, as the next worst thing, are accepted *faute de pire*. The process was clearly seen in the case of corporal punishment: the legislators who drew up the Criminal Justice Act 1948 considered that the only way to secure its abolition as a judicial penalty was to introduce a new 'short, sharp' custodial sentence in institutions with a specially strict régime – detention centres. Some people remain unthinkingly in favour of corporal punishment as a 'solution'; others regretfully admit that it would be undesirable to reintroduce it, if only because the delay in bringing offenders to trial means that it cannot be inflicted promptly. A persistent mythology surrounds birching and flogging: it is asserted, for example, that no one ever risked a second dose of the cat o' nine tails. Comprehensive Home Office research over three decades showed, however, not merely that this is untrue but that those who had been flogged were if anything more likely to commit further violent offences; the Advisory Council on the Treatment of Offenders (1960) examined the records of 3,023 persons convicted from 1921 until abolition in 1948. Of offenders who had no previous serious convictions, 38.8% of those who were flogged were reconvicted for a major offence, including violence in some cases, but only 33.1% of those not flogged. Where offenders did have a serious criminal record, reconvictions of those flogged amounted to 68.5%, of those not flogged 66.9%. The degrading nature of the ceremony is described in the Advisory Council's report (pp.23–24): the victim was strapped to a triangular frame, with his hands above his head, with leather belts to protect sensitive parts of his body; for juveniles, sometimes one police constable would take the boy on his back, with another holding his feet. It is often assumed that flogging was imposed for a range of offences, but in fact since the Larceny Act of 1916, it had been permissible only for robbery with violence and related offences – and after abolition in 1948 the numbers sentenced for this offence declined for seven consecutive years (Howard League, 1961). Moreover, within penal establishments in this country corporal punishment was abolished in 1967, because it was found to be not merely ineffective but also counter-productive. Nevertheless, proponents of corporal punishment appear to ignore the possibility that any other response might be more appropriate and more effective. Speakers like Mr Teddy Taylor, M.P. continue to call for 'the return of corporal punishment for crimes of violence and the imposition of sentences that strike fear into the hearts of potential offenders' (*Daily Telegraph*, 27 August 1975). Sir Keith Joseph, on the other hand, as a former minister for social services and home affairs spokesman, has considered the evidence and concluded that judicial beating is necessarily cold-blooded and would brutalize more than it cured.

The question is enmeshed in atavistic attitudes. In the 1970s it was still possible for a judge to say publicly that he would like to put football hooligans in the stocks (Judge Gwyn Morris, Q.C., in *The Times* 9 August 1975). Another (Judge Hill, 4 February 1978) spoke of cutting a persistent offender's ears off, but said afterwards that he had not been speaking seriously. And there seems to be a kind of horrified admiration for those Muslim countries which do not shrink from the painful task of cutting off the hands of thieves, although the fact that this penalty is accompanied by flogging for dealing in alcohol and public stoning to death or beheading by the sword for adultery conveys a hint that the Islamic code might after all be too rigorous for Western *mores*. Some Muslim writers, it should be noted, are at pains to stress that the injunction 'As for the thief, both male and female, cut off their hands' (*Koran*, 5:38) should be taken in conjunction with the insistence on the mercy of Allah, repeated for example in the very next verse; moreover, the phrase 'cut off their hands' can be interpreted figuratively as 'prohibit the use of their hands', i.e. restrict their free movement or activity (Khan, 1967, pp.74–76). There is, however, nothing figurative about the penal code in, for example, Pakistan, which provides for amputation of the right hand from the joint of the wrist, by an authorized medical officer, unless the left hand or the left thumb or at least two fingers of the left hand are either missing or entirely unserviceable; and similarly, after a second conviction, for the left foot (*Offences against Property (Enforcement of Hudood) Ordinance*, 1979).

Public Attitudes to Punishment

Punishment is a very old and deep-rooted principle; this does not necessarily justify it, although it makes it hard to eradicate. Policy should not be based on badly thought out and ill-informed attitudes merely because they are widespread. As Sir Keith Joseph has said in another context, 'Ideas, generally yesterday's ideas, are the most powerful of all forces' (speech on 3 October 1974). Part of the folk-lore about punishment, for example, is the image of the village bobby who in the good old days gave delinquent youngsters 'a smart cuff' (see, for example, Lord Justice Lawton's Cambridge speech, *Guardian*, 2 September 1978). The assumption here is that better behaviour was induced by the pain of the blow rather than by the talking-to which probably accompanied it. Often no doubt there was a talking-to without a cuff. In any case there is not a shred of evidence as to the relative effectiveness of using one or the other or both; it is astonishing that judges, who insist on evidence in determining guilt, so often disregard it in relation to the choice of punishment. If the legendary bobby had any effect it was probably produced by the fact that action was taken promptly by an adult whom the boy knew and quite possibly respected, and who would be likely to catch him if he repeated his offence. The same applies to beatings at school, which ex-inmates of famous boarding schools often say 'didn't do them any harm'. Nor did they always do much good: the Old Etonian Marquess of Tweeddale told the House of Lords in a debate on law and authority in society (*Hansard* [H.L.] 1 March 1978, col. 511) that he was beaten 27 times and birched twice at school – clearly a case of juvenile recidivism.

While I was writing this I visited Leominster Priory, where a ducking stool is preserved, reputedly the last one used in this country (in 1809). It was used to punish not only scolding women but tradesmen who gave short measure or sold adulterated food. A jokey poem on a postcard gave away the *Schadenfreude* of the whole thing by describing it as 'the joy and terror of the town'. A local Christian gentleman came in; we spoke of penal reform and he summarized, without further prompting, the plain man's theory of penology: it might not be a bad thing if the ducking stool were used occasionally today, things were better when the village policeman etc., and he didn't resent the beatings he had received at school because he had probably deserved them. The assumption that when a person has done wrong he should be made to suffer is deeply ingrained. The prevailing orthodoxy has been lucidly stated by Lord Justice Lawton:

> When sentencing, judges should take into consideration the extent to which what they do is likely to accord with public opinion. If their sentences outrage public opinion by being too severe, the public will not benefit. A criminal who was deserving of punishment may be turned into a martyr overnight and the law will be lowered in the estimation of right thinking people. This latter result tends to follow when sentences are thought by the public to be too lenient. A sentence is the expression of the community's disapproval of crime and if it is either too severe or too lenient the disapproval can shift from the crime to the law and the judges. Judges, however, must not pander to public opinion which may be wrong-headed or sentimental ... In difficult cases the judge may have to lead public opinion to an understanding of what he has done. This he can do by giving reasons for his sentence. (Lawton, 1975.)

But this does not say how judges assess public opinion: by reading the newspapers? If so, which ones? The editorials or the correspondence columns? Listening to phone-ins? In conversation at clubs and dinner parties? If the relatives of a victim call for retribution, does that make it a sound basis for penal policy? Even supposing it could be shown that there was a clear majority of opinion in favour of a particular set of penal policies, and that the judges and magistrates collectively knew what it was, there are difficulties. Firstly, the public is not well educated on either the facts or the moral arguments relating to penal policy. Secondly, this lack of education is shared by judges, with the exception of some who have taken a special interest in criminology or have served on the Parole Board or the Advisory Council on the Penal System. Magistrates' horizons have probably been extended by training, though it is difficult to say how much, and it is to be hoped that the new Judicial Studies Board will do the same for judges. Statistics, which are issued almost daily on economic questions, are published quarterly for recorded crime but only annually for prisons and probation. The probation service is small (less than 6,000), decentralized, and no longer has even a separate department within the Home Office which could spread information about the advantages of non-custodial sanctions. Until reformers succeed in getting a wider range of facts accepted into the 'conventional wisdom' it seems likely that a self-reinforcing process takes place: eminent people express conventional views, are supported by newspaper editorials, take these as a reflection of public opinion and reiterate their original statements. At the same time, some readers of the press also accept these authoritative pronouncements and reflect them back to the speakers personally or in resolutions at conferences, again strengthening their natural belief that they are right.

The question amounts to this: What is the reason for the persistent use of punishment in general and prisons in particular? But first it is necessary to ask: Why do certain types of activity continue to be considered criminal, while other harmful acts do not? Part of the reason, it has been suggested, is that these processes fit in very well with the interests of numerous people or groups within the community, including many who are articulate, influential or powerful. Many who regard themselves as law-abiding discount some offences (and some harmful acts which have not been defined as criminal) which they themselves commit and therefore tolerate: motoring offences and tax evasion are obvious examples. 'Crime' is thought of as comprising a much narrower range of offences, committed by 'them', not by 'people like us'. If individuals offend sufficiently seriously to be sent to prison, this imposes upon them the status of being 'criminals' and hence 'different' (or to use the sociologists' term 'deviant'); if the experience of prison and its aftermath drives them to offend again, they are more likely to be caught, and hence to be regarded as still more deviant. This way of looking at things obscures not only the lawbreaking of 'people like us', but also the fact that many of the legal things we do, including the way we order society, apportion resources and define crime, help to push other people into some of the types of behaviour which we condemn.

There are however some more positive reasons for the public's willingness to tolerate prisons. They will be outlined here and considered in more detail later. Firstly, the justification is often advanced that imprisonment deters individuals from committing crime. Lord Justice Lawton (1975) has expressed this view in all its deceptive simplicity:

> I am convinced that crime will continue to increase as long as the public are bamboozled into thinking that a prime cause of it is bad social conditions and not wickedness. Bad social conditions are contributory factors but the public should realize that criminals are human beings . . . and that like all other human beings of sound mind they will probably respond to rewards and punishments. What may have gone wrong in the past seventy

years is that the State has made the carrots more and more appetizing and the stick (figuratively of course) has been little used.

Almost every sentence of a statement like this contains assumptions, explicit or unspoken, which are open to question. If crime is ascribed to wickedness, that is not of itself a justification for sending people to prison. After jumping from a moralistic to a behaviouristic dimension, Lawton makes no reference to the basic findings of behaviourist psychology, in particular that punishment to be effective must be applied promptly, and that the effects of reward tend to be more long lasting. He assumes that criminals calculate the risks in advance, but many plainly do not; for those who do, the odds against detection may make the risk worthwhile, even if the punishment were doubled. Although environmental effects can be exaggerated, few criminologists would dismiss them so casually, especially since for many people today the rewards offered for law-abiding behaviour are small, and smaller still for most ex-prisoners. It is irrelevant that state benefits are greater than they were seventy years ago, since people compare their conditions with those of their contemporaries, not of their grandfathers.

Prison is, secondly, supposed to protect the public from certain offenders. Many people agree about the extreme cases: those whose violence is serious and likely to be repeated will have to be locked away (although there is less agreement about how they can be defined). But others are by any standards petty offenders, for whom any advantage from 'giving the public a rest from their activities' (in the time-worn judicial phrase) is outweighed by the adverse effects of the prison sentence. It is between these extremes that the problem becomes more difficult: the less serious violence and the more serious property offences. This is where it is most important to ensure that measures intended to protect the public do not, because of the hostility, violence and other effects engendered by prisons themselves, have the contrary result.

The third practical justification for prisons is that they are supposed to rehabilitate. The belief persists that it is possible to impose some form of treatment and training for prisoners during their incarceration, after which, if they offend again, the blame can be placed on them. They are assumed, particularly in the case of 'borstal training', to have been given a chance. It is true that some training does take place, some prisoners are helped by staff, and some do reflect on their misdeeds, regret them and resolve to change. But rehabilitative and

27

educational facilities in prisons are generally limited and in some countries non-existent: not only do most prisoners receive little treatment or training, but when they do its effects are likely to be submerged by the other influences of prison, and by the person's experiences after his return to the community. To justify imprisonment primarily on grounds of education and welfare is specious, for if a person needs help of this kind it should be provided in the community and not combined with the severe punishment of imprisonment, unless such punishment is warranted by the seriousness of the offence. Help should of course be available in prison as well; but it should not form part of the reason for sending anyone there.

In addition to these practical justifications of imprisonment, however, there are deep-seated symbolic ones. As a method of punishment, graduated in periods of time, it marks and denounces the seriousness of the offence. Criminologists have recently focused their attention on the tariff aspect of this denunciation in an attempt to ensure greater consistency between crimes and the penalties they attract. Existing maximum penalties have, however, been fixed haphazardly by Parliament over the years. The Advisory Council on the Penal System (1978) suggested that the actual sentencing practice of the courts bears a closer relationship to seriousness, and should form the basis of a new scale of maxima, with a proviso that the maximum could be exceeded in certain defined cases of exceptional gravity. But if a change is to be made, there is a case for constructing a new tariff: the *relative* seriousness could be assessed by consultation or modern survey techniques, while the length of partial or total deprivation of liberty would be determined on a scale well below the current rate unless any practical reason could be shown for keeping it at its present level.

An entirely new scale, almost eliminating the judge's discretion in sentencing, has been created in the Uniform Determinate Sentencing Act of 1976 in California. Apart from a few exceptionally serious crimes for which an indeterminate sentence of seven years to life is possible, there are 181 offences classified in four 'ranges'; for each of these there is a standard length of prison sentence, with a slightly shorter or longer one if there are mitigating or aggravating circumstances. The court may however impose probation instead of a prison term, except in seven cases where this power is restricted and two, involving firearms, where it is prohibited (McGee, 1978). The objectionable features of this law, however, are its rigidity and the fixed minimum sentence, which lead to greater use of imprisonment.

The justifications of punishment will be further examined in Chapter Eight; meanwhile the effects of imprisonment in practice will be considered in more detail.

2. Prisons: What They Are Like

Imprisonment is used in most countries as a deliberate instrument of law enforcement policy. Like any policy, it should be examined to assess its effects on individuals and on society. Other departments of state exist to promote the health and welfare of all members of society, and can be judged straight-forwardly according to whether they have achieved this, and whether they have had undesirable side-effects such as regimentation, waste or neglect. The penal system is different, since its method of operation is to inflict unpleasantness and even suffering on a selection of those who break the law, and it is the side-effect of this which is supposed to be beneficial: to induce the rest of society to behave correctly. Little attention is given to measuring the extent to which it achieves its aims: the escape of one prisoner makes headlines, but not the fact that 50% of adults imprisoned and up to 80% of juveniles re-offend within two years of release.

'Cruel, inhuman or degrading punishment or treatment' is prohibited by the Universal Declaration of Human Rights. This chapter will argue that the ordinary prison régime is at best counter-productive, at worst contrary to the Declaration; the next will examine abuses and malfunctions of the system.

This book will not be concerned to allocate blame for conditions in prisons, except as necessary to identify those who have it in their power, if they had the will, to make improvements. As regards the prison service itself, the trouble lies largely in the nature of the job it is asked to do. Even the more idealistic prison governors admit that their basic duty is to be jailers. They are liable to more vociferous public censure for an escape or for the smuggling of alcohol into prison than for running a rigid and soul-destroying régime or for the number of prisoners who re-offend after release. Responsibility for these priorities lies with their political masters and, in a democracy, with the public and the less scrupulous press, although many individual governors and prison officers have shown that régimes can be improved within these constraints, and it must be remembered that everyone has the hard duty to refuse to carry out superior orders which would have evil consequences.

Prisons are also at the mercy of the courts, which decide the number and length of prison sentences, and of Parliament, which sets the limits within which the courts can punish. Both courts and MPs regard themselves as being constrained, in turn, by public opinion; but it is part of their job to think more, and know more, than the general public, and to lead opinion rather than follow it – as MPs, to their credit, have repeatedly done in regard to capital punishment.

Under Parliament and the Home Secretary, prisons are run by the Prison Department of the Home Office, which must take a major share of the responsibility. There are pressures towards reform within the Department, but these have to contend with two powerful forces, apart from those already mentioned. The first is the Civil Service tradition of 'protecting the Minister', which is not a recipe for adventurous decisions unless a strong Home Secretary insists on them; the second is the trade union, the Prison Officers' Association (POA). The POA has resisted several important reforms, such as relaxation of censorship and installation of telephones for prisoners; on the other hand it does not appear that the Prison Department has effectively exercised leadership so as to secure acceptance of the policies it believes to be right, and to encourage staff to propose reforms. In the recent dispute the Home Secretary and the Department stood firm on the question of pay; it remains to be seen whether they will do so on the question of reform.

Responsibility for the state of the prisons, then, must be shared by prison officers, governors, the Home Office, the Home Secretary, the courts, Parliament, the press and the public. Examples in this chapter and the next will, however, be taken from other countries also, suggesting that many of the features described are not merely blemishes on this or that prison system, which could be put right if there were enough pressure for reform, but are the intractable result of the nature of closed penal institutions. These chapters will be critical; more positive aspects of prisons will be mentioned in Chapter Six which considers how prisons, while they still exist, can be improved, using proposals most of which are drawn from existing practices.

Isolation

Prisons separate people from the rest of the community, which includes their families and friends. The division of families is one of

31

the most drastic effects of imprisonment. Husbands and wives are separated from each other and from their children; and of course the effect on prisoners' parents should not be forgotten. If the prisoner has children, they are made temporarily fatherless or motherless, while the prisoner loses the relationship with them and his ability to be a parent to them is undermined. John McVicar (1978) records that on his 36-hour pre-parole leave it was in the presence of a friend's children that 'I experienced for the first time the delight of just being ordinary ... There are not only no women in prison, there are no children either: you miss them both, badly, in different ways.' He bluntly describes the effects of sexual deprivation: if this is what it does to a normal man, what must the effect be on sexually abnormal offenders? 'The denial of heterosexuality is the big punishment of imprisonment ... There is probably less homosexuality in long-term prisons than people imagine. Maybe 20% will indulge – perhaps a quarter of these unwillingly. Prison doesn't so much emasculate a guy as impoverish his sexual imagery to the extent that he cannot relate properly to a woman. He masturbates for so long that when he comes out he just masturbates into a woman.' In the United States homosexual rapes in prison are more prevalent, or at least more talked about. In a study in Philadelphia in the mid-1960s, it was found that some 2,000 rapes occured in prisons and sheriffs' vans in a 26-month period. If local jails and youth institutions are added to the prisons, an estimate of 50,000 sexual assaults per year in American prisons would probably not be too high (Davis, 1968, see also Bowker, 1978; Bowker, 1980; Lockwood, 1980). Since of the nearly 70,000 people received into prison under sentence in 1978 in England and Wales there were about 32,000 men and 1,400 women in the sexually active age-group of 17–29, the sexual impact of imprisonment is a serious matter. Wives, of course, also suffer from sexual deprivation when their husbands are in prison – unless they decide not to: among prisoners aged 25 and over, the Home Office Research Unit found that about five times as many were divorced (or widowed) as in the general population. In addition, some 40% of long-term prisoners were divorced or separated during their sentences (*Home Office Research Bulletin*, 1978).

A prisoner's wife is often left with small children to bring up. If she has difficulty in coping, the children may develop behavioural problems and the mother will have a worrying time; if she learns to manage on her own, she and her husband are likely to have an uneasy period of readjustment while he resumes some of the roles which she has been filling in his absence. In a survey of *Prisoners and Their Families* by Pauline Morris (1965), 34% of wives found the management of their children a problem; in addition, 41% had major difficulties with hire purchase commitments, rent arrears, and acute shortage of low-income housing. Sixty per cent of families owed money other than for hire purchase. Money and children were two major limits on visiting their husbands. In addition there was a feeling of isolation from the prison authorities. Almost all felt that a visit from some official at their husband's prison would have been useful; the majority did not even know of the existence of a prison welfare officer. Since Pauline Morris wrote, the position may have improved; the Prison Department claims in *Prisons and The Prisoner* (Home Office 1977, para. 65) that 'when the family visit the prison, the probation officer will often be available to discuss their problems.' A number of prisoners have however expressed dissatisfaction to the Howard League about welfare officers' work, and there is a feeling that some probation officers work reluctantly for a spell in prison in the hope of improving their promotion prospects; it is also reported that probation officers are seldom on duty on Saturdays when most visitors come.

If imprisonment has been imposed, wisely or not, it would seem sensible to do everything possible to allow the prisoner to preserve his links with the outside world to which, in 99.9% of cases, he will return. But powerful forces are ranged on the side of restricting outside contacts. In the United Kingdom letters are strictly rationed, and they are subject to censorship (this rule has been relaxed, but not abolished, in open prisons and some female establishments; attempts to extend the relaxation to four low-security closed prisons have so far been impeded by prison staff). Curt notes are attached telling prisoners or their correspondents they have infringed a regulation. The most objectionable rules were removed in December 1981, under pressure from the European Commission on Human Rights; but censorship remains, restricting *inter alia* length of letters and, significantly, complaints. Before the reform one seventeen-year-old girl, eight-and-a-half months pregnant, with no family to turn to for support, was told, by means of a printed note, not to write so often to her fiancé in prison (Howard League, 1979). Prison authorities can be mean, for example, by quibbling about the extra cost of an air letter to let a New Zealander's relatives know that he was in prison. They claim the right to decide what's best for prisoners and even for people outside. In Wisconsin a prisoner wrote a letter to his sister-in-law by whom he had had an illegitimate child. The prison authorities prohibited correspondence on the grounds that it was 'counter-rehabilitative' for him to continue his friendship with this woman. A court ruled that the State had failed to meet the burden of proof showing specifically how it was that the prisoner's rehabilitation required interference with his rights under the First Amendment (Wilkins, 1974). Authorities are also self-protective: in an Indian prison Mary Tyler wanted to reassure her parents after a shooting incident which had been reported in the British press: 'I tried to write a few lines as if all was well and my life peaceful and pleasant. No doubt the censors were pleased with me. I hated writing half-truths, but I knew that was the only way any news of me at all would reach my family.' And later: 'I was upset by the puzzled and distressed letters I received from my parents, because it was impossible to explain the real situation to them' (Tyler, 1977, p.119). Thus communication between prisoners and their relatives can be interfered with to protect the authorities from embarrassment or, prisoners suspect, as a means of enforcing the rules more rigidly on prisoners who are considered to be making a nuisance of themselves.

But letters are an inadequate way of holding together an intimate relationship with wives and children, or friends, especially for those who are not good at expressing themselves on paper. Prisoners and their families and friends tend to come from less literate sections of the population. Visits are therefore all the more important; but they too are strictly limited. The basic entitlement in English prisons is six and a half hours per *year* (30 minutes every 28 days). Some prisons enforce this; others allow visits of up to about two hours, and 'privilege visits' between the four-weekly ones, but often these must be taken on weekdays to ease the pressure on visiting rooms at weekends. Many wives do not take up their entitlement, because of the cost (the Supplementary Benefits Commission will only pay travelling costs every four weeks), and the problems of taking time off work and of bringing small children or finding someone to mind them – besides the difficulty of communicating in artificial surroundings within a strict time limit. Some probation services organize coaches or low-cost overnight accommodation, but long journeys are still an ordeal; families living in Northern Ireland find it almost impossible to visit relatives in Durham or the Isle of Wight.

The authorities are aware of the problem, though they have not gone very far towards resolving it. Martin and Webster (1971) found that about one-third of prisoners served their sentences within 30 miles of home, but nearly 40% of those having what could be called a home town spent the longest part of their sentence more than 100 miles away. Married men were twice as likely as single ones to remain within 50 miles of their homes. The chances of being visited were definitely related to distance from home – but this may have been because more of the men imprisoned far away were unmarried, as well as because of the distance. In addition, about 80% of prisoners were moved at least once during their sentences. Many prisons, especially new ones, are far from any major centres of population. In England the staff of nearly 50 out of 120-odd penal establishments qualify for 'inconvenience-of-locality allowances.' (*Hansard* [H. C.] 13 July 1979). This usually means inconvenience of access, especially by public transport. Even by car, long journeys with children are tiring, especially for a single adult, and prisoners' wives are less likely than most to possess their own transport. Nagel (1973, p.48) visited a cross-section of new institutions throughout the United States and found them all rurally located, unable to be reached by public transport, and anything from 30 to 455 miles from the State's largest city from which many of their inmates were likely to be drawn; the average distance was 172 miles.

In England and Wales visits are likely to begin with a wait outside the prison gate, regardless of weather, until official visiting time begins. Visitors are then admitted to a waiting room until the prisoner has been called. The visit itself may take place at individual tables, or a number of prisoners may be seated at one side of a long table with their visitors at the other. Family visits are in the sight and hearing of prison officers, but supervision is perfunctory, except in special circumstances. A visitor who is known to be a journalist may be closely supervised and required to sign a statement that he will not publish information. The visiting room in the women's wing at Durham is so small that the supervising officers can hear every word. Maximum security ('Category A') prisoners' visits are individually monitored by prison officers. Notes made by a visitor may be inspected and confiscated; tape recorders are forbidden. It all helps control complaints. Closed visits, in which the visitor is separated from the prisoner by a wire grille or glass, may be ordered for security reasons, or where a prisoner has been caught trying to smuggle contraband. The security reasons may include the fact that the authorities have chosen to place a Category A prisoner temporarily in an old 'local' prison which does not have facilities for the closely monitored visits. Visitors say that under such conditions they can hear other visitors on either side better than the person they came to see. No one wants to speak of intimate feelings and problems in a raised voice, and the visitor and the prisoner are often faced with the choice of asking for things to be repeated, or just not hearing them. In some countries barriers are usual. In Spain older prisons have a yard-wide walkway between two sets of bars separating prisoners and visitors; newer ones have a single perspex sheet containing microphones. In the United States visits may be 'closed', with either an aperture in the steel mesh or glass through which the voice is barely audible, or telephones which, as in Spain, can be monitored by guards or switched off at the end of permitted visiting times. In some places, not even seats are provided (Nagel, 1973, p.102). In English open prisons visits may be allowed in the open air, weather permitting. In Mississippi families are allowed to visit in the grounds; but these are rare exceptions.

There may be a school of thought which argues that restrictions on visiting are desirable lest imprisonment become 'soft'. Martin and Webster (1971, p.59) conclude that, on the contrary, more frequent visits would make the deprivation of liberty more apparent by bringing home to the prisoners how their sentences were affecting others and what they were missing in family relationships.

At the opposite end of the scale is the prisoner who has no one to visit or write to him. In a small-scale pilot survey of two prisons, the Howard League (1979) found that at Winchester, a short-term prison, 48% of the sample had no contacts at all by letter and 60% received no visitors; at Camp Hill medium-term training prison all received and sent at least one letter, but 29% received no visitors. At both prisons most prisoners sent and received less than one letter a week, and received less than half the permitted number of visits. It is nobody's job to offer help to these prisoners to make contact with someone outside during and after their sentences. They are caught in one of the vicious circles which pervade the criminal justice system: imprisonment isolates them from anyone who might help them when they come out, so they are more likely to drift back into trouble; since they have no one to speak on their behalf in court they are more likely to receive another custodial sentence which only reinforces their isolation.

Homelessness

There are several ways in which imprisonment can play havoc with a prisoner's housing. His wife, as has been seen, often has difficulty in paying the rent, and may be evicted by a tough local authority – or a private landlord, for many are in privately rented, furnished accommodation. To keep up the payments on a mortgage is likely to be still harder; if there are children, and the wife has to give up the house, she will have to find accommodation that will accept them. She may not be able to afford a flat large enough for another adult, so that when her husband is released he has to live separately until a new home can be found. If she leaves her husband, of course, he becomes homeless at a stroke. Most single men, unless they were living with their parents, lose their accommodation when imprisoned. Little is known about these processes; the above examples are based on conversations with social workers and there is no means of estimating how common such situations are. It is not easy to define homelessness, or to assess, while a person is in prison, whether he or she will be homeless on release: is a hostel a home? Does a belief that his brother will give him a bed mean that a man is not homeless? For these reasons Walmsley (1972) used the expression 'quite possibly homeless' in his survey, and found that 58% fell into this category. A Home Office study found that of those with homes, 30% were reconvicted, but of the homeless 69% (*Home Office Research Bulletin*, 1978). Over a tenth of the sample were both homeless and mentally disordered, and their reconviction rate was 72%. It is, not surprisingly, common for men to obtain a poorer standard of accommodation than they enjoyed before going to prison (Corden and others, 1978); this is especially true of those who are already socially isolated. Some ultimately become vagrants and often alcoholics. Their homelessness itself becomes in effect a criminal offence. It is then difficult for them to find a lodging, so they sleep rough, and can hardly avoid committing an offence against the vagrancy laws. They are then sent to prison, directly or in default of paying a fine. When they come out it is difficult for them to find a lodging ... In short the law defines their way of life as criminal, yet makes it almost impossible for them to behave otherwise.

Of course this process is not inevitable, and it is not an argument against ever sending anyone to prison. But it will happen to a proportion of those who are sent to prison for the first time, a higher proportion on the second occasion, and so on: at each stage there is a progressively stronger reason to break the vicious spiral by imposing a sentence other than prison. If a prison sentence is nevertheless imposed, it should be kept to the minimum because the longer it is, the more likely the loss of family or home. At the very least, it is reasonable to ask that these factors should be taken into consideration alongside others in deciding what sentences should be imposed – not out of sympathy with the offender, but because of the possible effects on his future conduct, on his family and on society.

Work, Education and Prisons

Placing a person in prison has drastic effects; are these mitigated or compounded by what takes place within the walls? The conventional wisdom of the 1950s and 60s was to give credence to the good intentions of the prison commissioners when they affirmed that treatment and training were provided in prisons. As late as 1967 the Minister of State said in the debate on the second reading of the Criminal Justice Bill that longer sentences were better than very short ones for this reason (Stonham, 1967) and the first edition of the official handbook for sentencers *The Sentence of the Court* (Home Office, 1964) made the same point.

The first thing prison does to anyone who has a job is to deprive him of it. Prisoners are either kept in complete idleness or, more commonly in this country at least, given too little work to do, and work which is often far below their capabilities. In the nineteenth century useless, soul-destroying work was regarded as part of the deterrent effect of prison. The treadwheel, which could in theory 'turn a mill or other engine', was in fact used to 'grind the wind' by turning a large fan or regulator; the utterly futile crank did nothing but lift sand which was then dropped again; and in shot-drill prisoners were made to move cannon balls weighing 24 pounds for an hour and a quarter at a time (Webb and Webb, 1922; Mayhew and Binney, 1862). Even today rumours surface from time to time of work being made by slitting newly-made mailbags and sending them back to the sewing shop, or in a women's prison of dealing similarly with knitted squares which were to be made into blankets. It is not suggested that this is done from Victorian motives of making prison obnoxious; if the authorities were to admit such practices at all they would doubtless claim that the rejected goods were faulty, or that they were driven to this means of making work as the only way of keeping prisoners out in the workshops rather than 'banged up' in their cells.

The provision of adequate work within closed institutions is inherently difficult. If society requires of a person who has broken the law that he should work, it would be much easier to arrange this in the community than in prison. Many offenders have jobs already, and if they have not, they can go to find one – it does not have to be brought to them. If there is a shortage of jobs, there is more chance of finding a government-sponsored work scheme outside the prison. In prison problems such as lack of employment are found, just as they are outside, but in addition there are extra ones such as the remoteness of many institutions, the high turnover of the workforce, and the requirements of security. As elsewhere in industrial societies there is a shortage of work, much of the work is boring and trivial, and these factors are aggravated by mechanization. Efforts are being made to eliminate mailbag sewing, which is not only a tedious occupation but has strong emotional associations with all that is soul-destroying about prison life. But mechanization brings problems too. The story is told that at Wormwood Scrubs prison a few years ago there was a mailbag shop employing about 200 men; an expert came and recommended that it be converted to cutting-out cloth for tailoring, and big tables were brought in, reducing its capacity to a couple of dozen; then another expert introduced machines, cutting the workforce still further and increasing the output beyond the capacity of the other institutions where the garments were sewn. Meanwhile most of the men who might have been sewing mailbags had to be kept in their cells. Situations like this will be eased, but not solved, if the prison population can be reduced: other occupations must be found, including some outside the prison, and some which might fall under the heading of education or craftwork rather than industrial production. It is also said by people in the prison service that some prisoners are incapable of more demanding work; if that were true (which is debatable), prison should help them to acquire skills.

The dilemma of providing enough industrial work is symbolized by a machine in the woodworking shop at Albany prison on the Isle of Wight, which cost many thousands of pounds, and does the work of umpteen men. It is operated by one man. It requires little skill, and makes an earsplitting noise, so that he has to wear protective earmuffs which increase his isolation still further. Is the prison in the furniture business or the people business? What is it doing to that prisoner? If, like many, he has problems such as lack of skills, or difficulty in getting on with workmates or foreman, it is doing nothing to help him to overcome them. If he is an ordinary person who has committed crime out of ordinary motives, it is probably inculcating the lesson that work is a daily grind which can be expected to yield no satisfaction except a pay packet; it may make him want to stay out of prison, but it will do little to make him choose regular monotonous work as his way of life rather than crime, which is usually more adventurous. Yet that machine, unlike the crank, was not specially designed to plague the prisoner: it is not deliberately degrading. Millions of ordinary citizens throughout the industrialized world have to spend their lives at such machines, and prison is the ultimate sanction to keep them from throwing it all up and going thieving. Should the prisoner, who has broken the law, enjoy more satisfying work than they, most of whom have not broken it so seriously or so often?

Thus prison work raises two of the oldest questions in the perennial debate: rehabilitation, and what used to be called the principle of 'less eligibility': the prisoner should not be so well looked after that he would prefer to be inside rather than face the conditions he might expect outside. At least as long ago as 1821 this argument was already being put forward, and refuted: 'There are, I fear, numbers of persons in this country who wear clothes which are insufficient to protect them from the inclemency of the weather, or who inhabit damp and unwholesome situations, or are employed at noxious trades, or work at unreasonable hours, or are subject to other hardships or privations of the like nature; but I have never heard it contended that these evils, *from which it is not in our power to relieve other classes of the community*, are on that account to be imposed on prisoners' (Holford, 1821). The clue lies in the phrase which I have emphasised: we (by which I here mean those members of society who individually or collectively have the power to effect changes) are in complete control of prisoners' environment, and therefore have a moral responsibility to see that it is humane.

The unskilled form a conspicuous part of prison populations but there are also many intelligent, competent people whose skills are usually wasted while they are there (*Home Office Research Bulletin*, 1978). As Martin and Webster point out in *The Social Consequences of Conviction* (1971, p.204) a large part of one's identity, one's associations, reputation and skill, are bound up with one's working life. Although the effects of losing a job may be serious they are generally not irreparable; the loss of the opportunity to practise a skill or profession is more drastic: 'The one affects employment, the other a way of life.' On one day in 1979, out of 32,822 prisoners available for work, 'industry' accounted for 14,270; of these, 2,527 (17.7%) were engaged on 'textiles, heavy' (mainly mailbags) (Home Office, 1980). No less than 7,051 (21.5% of the total workforce) were 'cleaners, etc.', which covers everything from making prison officers' tea to leaning on a mop and looking busy when anyone goes past. It was because of the debilitating effects of the tempo of prison work, with often only a five hour working day, that the Peter Bedford Project chose cleaning as the type of work through which 'unemployable' men would be enabled to get back to employment: office cleaning is normally done in two shifts, morning and evening, and until a man had regained his fitness sufficiently to hold down a full-time job he could begin by working one shift a day only. Prison tasks have included painting toy soldiers and putting the 'gifts' into packets of corn flakes. White-collar workers are seldom able to find suitable work in prison, and while it would be unfair to guarantee middle-class offenders a more comfortable time in prison, no one benefits if their potential is wasted. One whose case was brought to the attention of the Howard League was an electronics expert, the only person in the firm he had worked for who could compile an instruction manual for a new piece of equipment with good export potential; but because this did not fit into the usual pattern of prisoners working together in workshops the firm had difficulty in persuading the prison authorities to accept a contract under which he could complete this job. Two more examples, though trivial in themselves, give a hint of the variety of ability which lies unused in prisons. In its evidence to the May Committee on U.K. prisons, the Howard League mentioned a prisoner with financial expertise who had been asked by a prison officer to help work out the allowances to which the officer was entitled; and at the time of the fifth United Nations Congress on Crime Prevention and Treatment of Offenders, it was announced that an American football team, the Pittsburgh Pirates, would scout in prisons in search of locked up talent (*International Herald Tribune*, 2 September, 1975). Improved sporting facilities are often proposed as one of the means of keeping active young people out of trouble; but after the Winter Olympics of 1980 the Olympic Village at Lake Placid, New York State, was converted not into a sports centre to help keep youngsters *from* offending, but a youth prison to punish them after they *have* offended.

Prisoners include a high proportion with under-average educational achievement; yet educational provision is often lacking. Even in a relatively developed country like England, 29,999 men were received under sentence in 1978 (excluding fine defaulters), but only 739 (2.5%) completed vocational training courses during the year; of the 26,224 males under 21, 1,266 trainees (4.8%) did so (Home Office, 1979, para. 143). From both groups a total of 5,157 (9.2%) sat for examinations (para. 142). During the year 1977 only

98 prisoners and trainees were allowed to attend education centres in the community (Home Office, 1978, para 44) but this number should be increased after a new directive in early 1981. The picture is improved somewhat by evening classes, which were attended by 32.5% of prisoners in one week in October 1977 (*Hansard*, 14 March 1979); though prisoners may only be able to attend one or two classes a week, and only during the usual academic terms. When governments are economizing, education tends to be a victim: in 1977 cuts were made in the number and length of classes. Library services have been considerably improved during the past decade, but they are still not run by qualified librarians, so that prisoners do not receive professional help in finding information or study materials; in the more crowded prisons library use may consist of a ten-minute visit once a fortnight which is hardly long enough to exchange one batch of light fiction for another.

Psychological Effects of Imprisonment

Imprisonment, generally speaking, replaced the physical punishments of the past by psychological ones; if this is a step forward for mankind, it is not a very big one. Charles Dickens (1842) was one of the first to point out that humane intentions are no guarantee of humane results, and that prison causes psychological damage as severe as the old physical tortures. His words are as true of many present-day prisons as they were of the even more gruesome regime of silence and separation inflicted on prisoners in his time, the result of an unholy confluence of the idealistic theories of reformers (penitence, avoidance of contamination) and the practical purposes of the prison authorities (control):

> In its intention, I am well convinced that it is kind, humane and meant for reformation; but I am persuaded that those who devised this system . . . and those benevolent gentlemen who carry it into execution, do not know what it is they are doing. I believe that very few men are capable of estimating the immense amount of torture and agony which this dreadful punishment, prolonged for years, inflicts upon its sufferers. . . . I hold this slow and daily tampering with the mysteries of the brain to be immeasurably worse than any torture of the body; and because its ghastly signs and tokens are not so palpable to the eye and sense of touch as scars upon the flesh, . . . therefore I the more denounce it, as a secret punishment which slumbering humanity is not roused up to stay.

Bernard Shaw in characteristic style makes a similar point in his Preface to St Joan: 'Not even the most sensationally frightful of these atrocities (floggings and the like) inflicted on its victim the misery, degradation and conscious waste and loss of life suffered in our modern prisons, especially the model ones. We have not even the excuse of getting fun out of our prisons as the Middle Ages did out of their stakes and wheels and gibbets.' In the last century the Head of the Home Office, Sir Godfrey Lushington, told the Gladstone Committee on prisons: 'I regard as unfavourable to reformation the status of a prisoner throughout his whole career; the crushing of self-respect; the starving of all moral instinct he may possess; the absence of all opportunity to do or receive a kindness; the continual association with none but criminals, and that only as a separate item among other items also separate; the forced labour and the denial of all liberty. I believe the true mode of reforming a man, or restoring him to society, is in exactly the opposite direction to all of these. . . . But of course this is a mere idea. It is quite impracticable in a prison. In fact, the unfavourable features I have mentioned are inseparable from prison life' (Prisons Committee, 1895, para. 25, quoted in Webb, 1922, p.122). Even the tough-minded chairman of the Prison Commissioners, Sir Edmund Du Cane, described imprisonment as 'an artificial state of existence absolutely opposed to that which nature points out as the condition of mental, moral and physical health.'

The process begins as a person enters the prison; many ex-prisoners have described the routine of stripping off one's clothes, and with them one's identity as a free person; then come the regulation bath and issue of prison uniform and the symbolic prison number. The latter indignity, presumably intended as a safeguard against administrative mistakes, does not seem to be foolproof: Mr. William John Wright was sent from Brixton prison to St. Albans Crown Court but proved to be the wrong Mr. Wright. When the right one was found, the other was told he was 'free' to go back to prison (*Daily Telegraph*, 14 January, 1977). After some statutory interviews the prisoner goes to 'his' cell. If he is in prison for the first time, he will be given some basic instructions, such as to call prison officers 'sir'; but for the majority of receptions this is not necessary, for two thirds of them have been there before.

The psychological effects of imprisonment, as described by prisoners, are an odd mixture of tension and flaccidity. A common phrase is 'winding up', which refers to the way in which one person can deliberately or otherwise drive another into a state of anxiety, frustration and anger. The feelings of impotent hostility which prison engenders are summed up in a wry phrase of the Goons: 'Open the door or I'll break every bone in my fist!' Largely it seems to be the situation itself which winds prisoners up: worry about their families, or about their own future, frustration at the completely enforced subservience to authority, and, particularly at the beginning of a long sentence, fear of becoming a 'cabbage'. Long periods locked up in cells do nothing to improve this: and it should be realized that in local prisons particularly, the period 'banged up' is unlikely to be less than sixteen hours a day, and at times of staff shortage can reach 23 hours. Prisoners complain that even the statutory hour's 'exercise' is not always allowed.

The public, encouraged by the popular press, has a stereotype of prisons as being too soft, with such luxuries as television (which for some reason seems to arouse particular resentment); paradoxically, reformers also consider it too soft, but for different reasons. They defend the television, which helps to keep prisoners in touch with the world they will return to (and which incidentally they can watch only until about 8.30 p.m., perhaps two or three evenings a week, and pay for through deductions from their earnings). They also defend recreation such as sports and table tennis, not because they are indulgent and 'don't grudge it to them' but because recreation is a human necessity and people deteriorate without it. But the softness which really merits criticism is the removal of all responsibility. In most prisons the inmates are told when to get up, wash, and do everything else: even their lights are commonly controlled by an officer from outside the cell. If they have a family, they are not allowed to take responsibility for it; if they have an alcohol problem, they are relieved of any attempt to resist it by the fact that no alcohol is available in prison (apart from a small amount of contraband, or potentially lethal hooch). One ex-prisoner reverted to theft when he got into financial difficulties after earning his living for four years; he wrote: 'I had no intention or thoughts of going thieving again – though no one has ever given me any concrete moral reason for not doing so. . . . I had a chance of getting money, and if I came unstuck – so what? I could go back to the nick without any worries' (Observer, 19 August 1979). Most either have a surfeit of privacy, alone in a cell, or a surfeit of company, 'two'd or three'd up' or in a dormitory, which the authorities find cheaper to provide, but more difficult to supervise in order to check bullying and extortion. In some places the authorities make little attempt to supervise dormitories, which have no staff sleeping in, and only a couple of night patrols, who are neither highly trained nor closely supervised.

What prisons generally require of prisoners is conformity. It is an old prison service truism that the 'good prisoner' is not the most likely to prove a good citizen; yet the system is designed to induce inmates to act like 'good prisoners'. This too is nothing new. When the Reverend Daniel Nihil was governor of Millbank penitentiary in the early nineteenth century, 'As the most successful simulator of holiness became the most favoured prisoner, sanctified looks were, as a matter of course, the order of the day, and the most desperate convicts in the prison found it advantageous to complete their criminal character by the addition of hypocrisy' (Mayhew and Binney, 1862). To some extent a secular version of the same process operates among prisoners eligible for parole; certainly some prisoners have a feeling that as their parole review approaches they had better refrain from making any complaints or claiming rights which they consider to have been denied them for fear of prejudicing their chances of release on licence. In India, similarly, Mary Tyler reports that for fear of losing small privileges, prisoners remained submissive and dared not speak out.

The use of the threat of withdrawal of privileges for purposes of control is to some extent unavoidable, and is preferable to the use of naked force, but it is open to objections. It is essentially authoritarian, not democratic, and embodies the principle that prisoners can only have as much say over their lives as they are allowed, rather than that they should be allowed as much self-determination as is possible within a prison, subject only to controls necessary to preserve order, protect the weak and prevent escape. Secondly, the method always carries the risk that it will be used arbitrarily, and sometimes without authorization. Thirdly, prisons always have a tendency to define as privileges what ought to be regarded as rights. It is fair to say that there has been a tendency over the years to extend the definition of rights; but the authorities have been inclined to resist it, because they see it as depriving them of the tools, not to say weapons, of control. One prison governor defined the distinction to me by saying that what a prisoner was allowed to do yesterday is a privilege, what he was allowed to do last year is a right; it becomes regarded as a right when no one can remember a time when it was not allowed. At Reading prison in the 1840s education was a privilege: it was only 'when the feelings and conduct of an offender give hope of refor-

mation, that instruction, beyond that of teaching to read, is impar-
ted', because the chaplain felt that to impart secular knowledge
'might prove injurious both to the culprit himself and to society'
(Field, 1848, p.158). Religious knowledge, however, was safe, and
prisoners in Maidstone could practise their new skill of literacy on
two volumes of Bishop Wilson's sermons, Bishop Hall's *Comfort to
the Afflicted*, and the like. The Gladstone report (Prisons Committee, 1895) mentioned the 'privilege of talking'. Under the Progressive Stage System the advance from 'hard' to 'useful' labour and
the use of a mattress on a gradually increasing number of nights were
privileges to be earned, and so, as recently as the 1930s, were
increases above the basic allowances of letters, visits and library
books. As Lionel Fox (1934, p.80) conceded, increasing privileges
were made possible only by reducing conditions in the First Stage
below what would now be regarded as tolerable. Similar processes
have occurred in other countries. In Canada, between 1900 and 1960,
'Lighting was provided in cells first for special "good conduct" prisoners, to enable them to read and learn during daylight hours. As a
reward for good conduct, inmates were permitted to write one letter
every three months to their immediate families. They were also
allowed half-hour visits by relatives once a month' – which is still the
official quota for visits in British prisons today (Canada, 1977, paras.
48–49). Similarly in Israel 'Statute does not impose upon the prison
administration any obligations to enable the prisoner to receive
family visits, nor to permit the mailing and the receiving of correspondence, let alone, allow the prisoner to purchase with his private
funds in the prison canteen or through the administration additional
food produce, books, copybooks, clothes or any other item' (Committee for . . . prisoners in Israel, 1978).

Physical Conditions

Overcrowding is often used as the prime example of what is wrong
with prisons. Even many of those not sympathetic to the cause of
reform accept that if the state is to lock people up, it should not herd
them together in inhumane conditions. Prison conditions are certainly a scandal, although it should be remembered that improving them
would relieve only part of the pressures to which prisoners are subjected, and would do nothing to justify imprisoning people more than is
necessary. In England and Wales in 1979 an average of 40,762 men
were housed in 37,233 places, and 1,458 women in 1,261 places. But

the over-crowding is not evenly distributed. 'Local' prisons are the most crowded: in 1978 Oxford was the worst, with up to 370 men in its 143 places, and in February 1979 the governor of Liverpool, with over 1,400 in a nominal 1,036 places, took the unprecedented step of opening the jail to the press to show the discomfort and frustration endured by prisoners (*Daily Telegraph*, *Guardian*, 13 February 1979). It was usual for prisoners to be in their 13ft by 9ft cells for 16 hours a day; industrial action by staff had increased this to 23 hours a day, depriving the prisoners of visits, work, and anything else to relieve the deadening boredom. On top of this the temperatures in the cells were 'Arctic'; the result was an outburst of violence, which led to the declaration of a state of emergency.

The overcrowding is aggravated by the lack of sanitation, which has been a monotonous complaint at least since Hobhouse and Brockway (1922), who pointed out that warders, too, suffer from the stench. Half a century later, conditions in the old prisons have not improved; prisoners are driven to relieving the stench, with two or three pots in a cell instead of one, by throwing their excreta out of the window. Low status prisoners and those whom staff wish to humiliate are drafted into the 'barmy army' to clear it up each morning (reported for example on BBC television, Panorama, 28 February 1977). In some of the newer prisons electronic unlocking makes it possible to allow prisoners to leave their cells for toilet purposes instead of having to use the revolting pots (actually this could happen in old prisons too if prison officers were willing to climb the stairs and unlock the cells); but even then, as Leo Abse (1973, pp.128–129) has commented, an employee of the Home Office retains control over the prisoners' bodily functions. Only in the newest buildings do cells have their own sanitation, as has been the practice in several other countries for some time. In 1974 the director of the North West Metropolitan Blood Transfusion Service criticised the sanitary arrangements and stopped taking blood transfusions from prisoners in Wormwood Scrubs and Pentonville prisons because of the risk of infectious disease (Fitzgerald and Sim, 1979). The following year the Prison Department issued a non-denial by quoting in its Annual Report the senior medical officer of an unnamed, but presumably different prison as saying: 'The Director of the Regional Blood Transfusion Service was kind enough to assure me that the incidence of hepatitis antigen in blood taken from the prison was no higher than that obtaining in blood received from the general public' (Home Office, 1975 para. 209). The Association of Environmental Health

Officers has become concerned about the risk of disease (*Evening Standard*, 2 May 1979). But the general point is undeniable, and the authorities are openly saying so. A member of the Prisons Board, Kenneth Neale, told a Howard League conference that some prisons were a national disgrace (*Times*, 5 April 1978). The Association of First Division Civil Servants made a similar statement to the May Inquiry into the U.K. Prison Services in 1979. The Institute of Professional Civil Servants spoke bluntly of 'penal slums'.

Overcrowding of prisons is of course nothing new. In 1791 proposals were made for convict stations in The Gambia, because the problem of relieving the pressure on the dangerously overcrowded jails of England had for more than a century been a very serious one (Gray, 1940). In the seventeenth century Crown Pardons were granted to condemned felons conditionally on their agreeing to be 'transported beyond the seas' to America, and transportation was introduced as a form of sentence in 1767 (Fox, 1934), but the loss of the American colonies, and in the next century the refusal of the Australians to accept any more convicts, put the pressure back on English prisons. Transportation was abolished by the Penal Servitude Act 1857, and many of to-day's prisons were brought into use at about that time as a result.

Similar conditions are reported from other parts of the world. Mary Tyler (1977, p.107) describes a women's prison in India where 'There were never less than thirty prisoners, and when I finally left Jamshedpur two years later, there were forty-four women and twelve children sharing the fifteen-feet square cage. At night they were packed in rows, unable to turn one way or the other without great difficulty, young and old, sick and healthy, mad and sane, all crammed in together. The single latrine had to be reached by stepping over the bodies of those who had the misfortune to be sleeping in front of it. The drain leading from it ran overground across the yard at the back, and the stench rose through the open bars on three sides.' In Bangkok, it was recently alleged that the prison built for 500 contained 6,000 prisoners; they had to take turns sleeping. Latrines were wood buckets on a raised platform. The punishment cells, called 'dark rooms', had tiny windows high in the walls, but an electric light burned at all times (*Times*, 29 June 1978).

In the United States the president of the National Council on Crime and Delinquency (NCCD), Milton Rector, wrote in an open letter to the Attorney General of inmates in federal and state institutions being packed in tents, corridors, ships, trailers, basements, and other inappropriate spaces. He gave figures showing the main reason for this: the average length of sentence in the United States has been increasing by about one third every decade since the war:

16.5 months in 1945
21.9 months in 1955
33.5 months in 1965
45.5 months in 1975

In England and Wales, similarly, the average length of sentence increased by 50% between 1961 and 1975 (Home Office, 1977, pp.158–159). Rector concluded that even the plans to build 800 new jails and prisons at a cost of $5 billion were unlikely to be adequate: 'We need a new approach.' This has been formulated by the NCCD as follows:

> No new detention or penal institutions should be built before alternatives to incarceration are fully provided for. ... NCCD calls for a halt on the construction of all prisons, jails, juvenile training schools, and detention homes until the maximum funding, staffing and utilization of non-institutional correction has been attained (Rector, 1977, p.18).

The danger is that the vicious circle will be perpetuated: courts over-fill prisons, humanitarians press for more prisons to relieve the over-crowding, and the courts overfill the new prisons as well. In England and Wales, 'In 1958, the gap between prison accommodation and the average number of prisoners was 1,721. In twenty years, 13,741 places have been added (costing, at to-day's prices, some £400 million). The net result is that the shortfall in 1978 had more than doubled, to 3,930' (*Howard Journal*, 1980, vol. 19 no. 3). By late 1980, the shortfall had reached 6,300.

The 'commonsense' assumption is that the prison population can hardly be reduced when the amount of recorded crime is increasing. This assumption has however been tested by William Nagel, director of the Institute of Corrections at the American Foundation, and found to be untenable. Nagel (1977) ranked the fifty states of the USA according to incarceration rates; he found that those who imprisoned a high percentage were not necessarily those with high rates of recorded crime, but were more likely to be politically conservative and to have more black and poor citizens. A high crime rate was not associated with leniency in the use of imprisonment, but with factors such as unemployment and the level of urban population. In studies of this kind cause and effect are difficult to disentangle, but the following findings of Nagel show at least that more prisons cannot be guaranteed to control crime, and a prison cutback does not necessarily unleash a crime wave: Between 1955 and 1975, fifteen states increased the capacity of their adult prison systems by 56%; their prison populations increased by 57%, and their crime rates by 167%. Fifteen other states increased prison capacity by less than 4%; their prison population fell by 9% and the recorded crime increase was 145%.

3. Prisons:
Endemic Abuses

Even when prisons are relatively well run they are, like all human institutions, prone to malfunction. The requirements of control and security develop an inhuman logic which, if not checked, can ignore the very principles which the system is supposed to be upholding. There are five main ways in which prisons tend towards malpractices. Four lie within the prison system: the excessive application of security and control precautions; officially authorized punishments which go beyond humanely tolerable bounds; the illegal harassment or physical brutality which arises among inmates or between inmates and staff; and the restrictions placed on prisoners' opportunity to know the rules and complain about improper treatment, and especially to communicate their complaint to someone outside the prison so as to secure redress. The remaining abuse is one for which blame lies not with prison administrators but with law makers and enforcers: the fact that disproportionate numbers of those sent to prison are those members of society who are already at a disadvantage, although many of their offences are far from being the most serious.

Excessive Security and Control

It is primarily in the name of security that prisoners may have their letters censored and their conversations monitored at visits. The restriction of letters and visits may help prevent escapes by intercepting both implements and messages – but floodlights, television scanners and the other paraphernalia of modern security should really be more than enough. The restrictions admittedly check the flow of drugs and other contraband, and make it more difficult for inmates of different prisons to plan concerted acts of indiscipline or to form a prisoners' union. They also, however, prevent inmates from revealing abuses within prisons and inhibit the assertion of their legal rights; officials and staff claim in reply that it checks the spreading of

51

false and malicious allegations against staff, and litigation by prisoners who have ample time to concoct vexatious lawsuits. Lastly, it is
sometimes justified on welfare grounds: if a prisoner receives bad
news he could become depressed, smash up his cell or even make a
suicide attempt, whereas if the news is broken to him at a suitable
time by the chaplain, he can be helped over the shock. But this is an
intrusive form of welfare, and the lack of privacy is likely to discourage some inmates from expressing their anxieties in their letters.
Opportunities for prisoners to contact welfare services in a crisis need
improving; meanwhile it might be more appropriate to ask *them*
whether they wish someone to read all their letters in case of bad
news.

The official justifications of censorship are not, of course, entirely
without substance, especially if the prison population falls to the
point where it consists mainly of the most serious offenders; but
these arguments exaggerate the extent to which security requires
such restrictions, and minimize the damage which the restrictions
can cause. The nature of censorship is always the same, whether in a
totalitarian state or in the prisons of an otherwise liberal democracy.
It always tempts officials to use it to protect themselves, for example
by forbidding the mention of prison conditions; to save themselves
work, by limiting the permitted number and length of letters; and to
impose unofficial sanctions, such as enforcing the regulations more
strictly against inmates who have stood up for their rights or those of
others. Anyone writing to a prisoner must impose self-censorship, in
case his letter is stopped or the recipient gets into trouble. The
Howard League gives some examples of how these regulations work
in practice, in its report *Losing touch: restrictions on prisoners'
outside contacts* (1979b). Until recently (see p.33) nothing intended
for the media could be sent out, nor offensive remarks about the
Home Secretary or other public figures. Prisoners are not allowed to
make threats of violence, although some of us might prefer to know if
we are being threatened! A friend or former friend of a prisoner can
ask the governor to stop an unwanted correspondence. If a prisoner
wants to start a new correspondence, the recipient may be subject to
police enquiries.

What are the consequences of these restrictions? When prisoners
are deprived of means of communicating contempt for the soul-
destroying system, as the Russian dissident Andrei Sinyavskii says,
one means of doing so is silence: 'A man answers the mute walls with
muteness of his own.' The authorities, he said, were especially sensi-

tive to this insult. In England, when I visited the prisoner control unit which existed from 1974 to 1975 in Wakefield prison, I was shown the record of one prisoner who had refused to speak to the medical officer: his offence was described in a phrase with a mediæval ring, 'mute of malice'. Sometimes the silent communication takes the form of tattoos. Both Sinyavskii (1976) and Anatoly Marchenko (1969) mention prisoners tattooing political slogans on their foreheads. One, Marchenko relates (pp.142–143), had 'Khrushchev's slave' on his forehead. The slogan was cut out and his skin cobbled together. The process was repeated twice more. After the third crude operation his skin was so tightly stretched across his forehead that he could no longer close his eyes. The other prisoners called him 'The Stare'. Sinyavskii reports similar slogans, and says that these people who had turned themselves into 'indelible propaganda' were shot. The executions initially provoked a new wave of equally criminal slogans; only after a second round of executions did the authorities restrain the movement. Tattooing is common in English prisons, too, even among girls. Some brand themselves by tattooing their faces; others put letters on the first joints of their fingers so as to form an obscene message when they clasp their hands; as, for example, L.T.F.C. on the right hand, interspersed with E.S.U.K. on the left. A visitor to a girls' closed borstal reports that there are more tattoos per square inch of arms than in the heaviest male prison; and not just arms, but legs, thighs, backs and breasts are also adorned, the last often with matching word pairs: 'sweet' and 'sour', 'salt' and 'pepper', 'mild' and 'bitter' (Dean, 1978).

The authorities here encourage removal of tattoos for the inmates' own sakes, to allow them to escape from their low estimation of themselves. This is justly claimed (for example in Home Office, 1977a, para. 48) as a humane example of assisting rehabilitation; but without mentioning that some of the tattoos were crudely carried out in prisons and borstals. Depriving people of their liberty and their freedom to communicate is always likely to cause some disturbance of behaviour which contains the seeds of more extreme reactions, and as long as prisons exist it is important that members of society should be aware that this is part of their human cost.

Security involves searches. In his submission to the Chief Inspector of Prisons after the Hull prison riot of 1976 the MP for Hull East, Mr. John Prescott, wrote 'I am keenly aware that in the name of security, particularly over the last three or four years, cell and personal searches at Hull Prison have been stepped up. This has contributed to a heightening of tension which others associated with the prison have noted and have seen fit to comment upon, and which has led me to write to the Home Office on a number of occasions.' (Prescott, 1976, p. 40). Even a rub-down search involves invasion of one's personal space; strip-searches are experienced as degrading. In Northern Ireland prisoners have complained of being made to squat naked over a mirror; the authorities say that anal searches are essential, and that this is the least degrading way of carrying them out. In 1978, women visiting the Crumlin Road jail complained of being searched when wearing sanitary towels.

Cell searches also give rise to similar feelings; if the authorities have been humane enough to allow prisoners to cover their walls with posters, a thorough search involves pulling these down – an occasion for the appearance, and sometimes the reality, of harassment. Prisoners claim that they are being harassed if they are searched more than once in close succession; but the authorities say this is dictated by security: otherwise a cell which had just been searched could be regarded as a safe hiding place. The demands of security are logical; it is a question of whether security logic is to be untrammelled, or tempered with other human considerations.

Perhaps the worst forms of security are the non-human ones. The Howard League (1969, p.3) protested when guard dogs were introduced after the Mountbatten report; there is still no evidence that dogs add significantly to all the other security devices. John Prescott has expressed concern about guard dogs: after one incident in prison he complained that 'a man, on surrendering, was bitten on reaching the ground by the dogs held by a prison officer. This was not denied, and it was explained to me that there were difficulties in handling such dogs. This incident is relevant because it is said that during the latest disturbance a prisoner, on climbing down from the roof before the end of the incident, was bitten by an Alsatian dog. If true, then taken with the earlier incident, this should be investigated' (Prescott, 1976, p. 10).

Non-human in a different way are electronic devices. Visitors to Kumla prison, Sweden, for example, say that there is something menacing about underground corridors where no staff are on duty, and control is exercised by unseen people sitting at a closed-circuit television screen (e.g. Stockdale 1967, p.145); many prisoners would rather be unlocked by a live (even if disliked) prison officer than by the click of a switch. A second such prison, at Österåker, was halted half-built. Another aspect of security is that certain prisoners have lights in their cells day and night: the Standard Minimum Rules do not prohibit this, though they forbid the use of darkened cells.

Prisoners are not allowed to see the records kept concerning them, and therefore cannot challenge their accuracy. A prisoner told the Howard League that by chance he had discovered a report in his file saying: 'W. is a poor specimen of a man, weak and indecisive, and finds it hard to form an opinion,' and another, by a prison medical officer, said that he had refused to co-operate in treatment. He contested both these judgments, especially the second, which he believed made it difficult for him to obtain treatment in prison and may have prejudiced his prospects for parole. His MP received a letter from a Home Office minister stating that he (the prisoner) had not received a hormone implant since his last prison sentence; three years later the Parliamentary Commissioner for Administration confirmed that he had received two implants in his present sentence (*Howard League Newsletter*, 1980 no. 28, p.6). When a person's freedom is at stake, should vital and possibly damaging statements of this kind be concealed from him? Now that the requirements of parole have forced prison documentation to be more efficient, a prisoner is followed round by a dossier; but he has no means of knowing if it contains inaccurate statements. During a mutiny in the top-security wing at Durham in 1968, prisoners were enraged by what they found in their files. One of them, Walter Probyn, says:

> There were cries of dismay as the records were read. The lies and distortions were worse than anyone had been expecting! Reports from welfare staff and the prison chaplain were amongst the most vicious and spurious. The chaplain had written a most adverse report on a man who was an atheist and had therefore no personal contact with the chaplain and had never spoken to him. . . . Many of the reports given by the screws (whose educational level and IQ were often less than average) used psychoanalytical terminology. Some of the reports by screws contained assessments of prisoners in the most bizarre terms, which had obviously been taken straight from a cheap detective story. We all felt that it was a great pity to have to destroy the records; they were a much greater condemnation of those who wrote them than they were of persons about whom they were alleged to be' (Probyn, 1977, pp.119–120).

John McVicar was equally scathing: 'There was no insight into my character, personality or motives . . . These people had housed me . . . for ten years; . . . this analysis was either pedantic or tautologous or just plain wrong' (McVicar, 1974). Before these accounts are written off as biased, it should be noted that just about the only point on which the official report on the Hull riot agreed with versions given by prisoners (PROP, n.d.) was this same anger when prisoners found what was written about them. In the words of the former (Home Office, 1977b, para. 348): 'There is little doubt that, the original alleged assault apart, the acceleration to the wholesale devastation centred around the finding of personal files which were obtained and distributed to prisoners in their wings. Prisoners contend that this resulted in the forfeiture of any confidence there might have been in the staff of the prison and reinforced the feelings of animosity and hostility. Prisoners who were located in their cells were shown copies of their records and immediately joined in the rampage. The discovery of the records was, in my view, a significant point in the riot in the early hours of 1 September.' Characteristically, however, the only official response was to suggest that records should be 'held in conditions of special security' (para. 383), not that there should be any check on their accuracy, let alone that prisoners should be allowed to see them: 'It is inevitable that the records of violent, uncooperative or disaffected prisoners will not please them' (para. 286). This does not consider the possibility that at least some of them would be less disaffected if they were treated differently. Perhaps John McVicar is not exaggerating too much when he sums up the approach which still appears to be prevalent among those in authority in prisons: 'The only method which penal institutions have for dealing with resentment is to suppress it' (McVicar, 1974, p.166).

The boundary between legitimate and excessive control could be overstepped in various ways. One of these is in choosing the prisoners to whom extra control measures are to be applied. They may be tyrannizing or manipulating other prisoners, or resisting the authorities. But they may also be genuinely concerned for the welfare and rights of prisoners whom they believe to have been incorrectly treated by the prison. Concern of this kind has been the trigger for recent riots in Hull, Gartree and Albany prisons. It is wrong, as well as bad management, to treat as 'subversive' (to use a favourite Prison Department word) someone who is standing up for his own or someone else's rights. In such a situation, if one protester is removed, others are likely to emerge to take his place. Thus it is a mistake to act as if there were a type of person who 'is' subversive, violent, disaffected, and so on. Of course some are more likely to act in these ways than others, but whether they do so depends on circumstances. Research in the Prison Department (Grayson, 1979), undertaken for the Working Party on Dispersal and Control after the disturbances in 1972, demonstrated that 'the institutions in which the rate of disciplinary offending was highest were those containing a greater proportion of younger prisoners serving longer sentences. . . . the "mix" of prisoners within an institution can have a major determining influence on the amount of disturbance it suffers' (Marriage, 1973). Forde (1977) also examined the possibility of identifying groups of 'subversive or troublesome prisoners'. Grayson's summary continues: 'His method involved the collection of factual information on a representative sample of dispersal prisoners . . . these data were used to study a group of prisoners identified by the security staff as subversive. In the event, it proved impossible to arrive at a set of rules by which subversives could be identified. Or to put this differently, the types of prisoners identified as subversive by the security staff changed over time.'

The dangers of letting the theory that 'subversives can be identified and eliminated' override ethical considerations are illustrated by the sorry story of the prisoner control units. In English prisons there were widespread demonstrations during the summer of 1972, encouraged by a group of ex-prisoners called PROP (Preservation of the Rights of Prisoners). At the time the authorities handled the situations coolly, by waiting until the prisoners got tired and gave up. But when one of the PROP leaders called for a national prisoners' strike, some of us thought that it would merely provide hard-line members of the prison service with an excuse for strong repressive measures. Whether or not we were right in our assessment, we were certainly wrong to hope that the Home Office would sympathetically consider the root causes of the prisoners' dissatisfaction. It did make a few concessions such as at last abolishing restricted diet (bread and water), but its main response was to set up a top-level secret working party, which devised the control units to deal with troublesome and subversive prisoners. They were to be held in a régime of mind-bending monotony for six months; if they caused trouble they were to revert to the beginning and start the whole process again. Thus an unco-operative or disturbed prisoner could in theory be kept there indefinitely, even for life if he were serving a life sentence. Although the authorities were conscious of the ethical objections, they met these not by introducing procedural safeguards such as allowing the inmate a hearing, or giving him reasons for his placement in the unit, but simply by putting the placement decision in the hands of a committee at a very high level, which is said to have rejected several applications by governors to have prisoners placed in the unit. The opening of the first (and as it turned out the only) control unit, at Wakefield, was announced inconspicuously in a parliamentary Written Answer at a time when there happened to be a strike at the government printer. It became public knowledge when the sister of one of the first three prisoners to be sent there visited the Howard League, which put her in touch with the *Sunday Times* (6 October 1974). She described, among other things, how when she visited her brother a prison officer not only listened to the entire conversation but took notes and even interrupted to tell her brother that any description of conditions within the unit was forbidden. I was allowed to visit the unit and to speak briefly to one of the prisoners alone. He claimed that he had been put there for standing up for the rights of another prisoner, and described the crushing monotony of sitting alone in his cell sewing mailbags, and the oppressive feeling of being accompanied by a group of prison officers every time he left it, for example, to have a bath. Prisoners' actions and even their moods were all logged, and their correspondence (if any) photocopied. All the relevant voluntary organizations and several MPs protested (see for example Howard League Annual Report 1974/75); the Home Secretary at first merely modified the procedures, but in October 1975 the unit was closed.

In the prisons of the world methods of control are as likely to involve the excessive use of physical force as the calculated pychological force of the control unit. One example of this is the 'cage' at Porterfield prison, Inverness, Scotland, which was used to try to subdue prisoners who had been violent. One prisoner, released from prison in 1979, still had vivid memories of his spell in the 'cage' eight years earlier: 'A bare light shone in the cage 24 hours a day. There was no respite from it. You immediately felt like an animal – that's how you were treated. Meals were simply shoved at you through a small space in the bars – just like the feeding of a dog in a kennel.' Eventually he and another prisoner managed to protest by getting up on a roof: 'After that I was chucked back into the cage, completely naked, and left like that for two days. The cage caused nothing but bitter confrontations between prisoners and their keepers. Some of the officers revelled in what they were doing. Others didn't like it. The cage bred nothing but pure hate, and even to this day I am still bitter about my treatment in it' (*Daily Record*, Glasgow, 23 March 1979). Jimmy Boyle vividly describes how he was beaten up and degraded, to such an extent that he would go to extreme lengths to retaliate. In Peterhead prison, for example, he and a friend smeared their bodies in excrement to deter prison officers from beating them up (Boyle, 1977, pp.134 ff.), and on several occasions he assaulted them. It is to the credit of the Scottish prison authorities that they recognised the possibility of using more civilized means of securing the co-operation of resistant prisoners, and in February 1973 opened the Special Unit at Barlinnie Prison, which will be described in Chapter Six.

Punishments Permitted by Law

Since prisons exist as places of punishment (apart from functions such as holding people before trial) it is not surprising that punishment is the main method used to deal with disciplinary offences inside prison, and that in the attempt to make the punishment 'bite', there has always been a tendency to excess. This is part of the pathology to which prisons are prone. In Canada, until 1913, punishments included hosing inmates by a powerful stream of cold water; a ball and chain worn as they worked, until 1933; handcuffing to bars from 8 a.m. to noon, and 1 p.m. to 5 p.m., used in the 1930s (Canada, 1977, para. 50). In India, fetters were still used in the early 1970s as a punishment some 200 years after their condemnation by John Howard, who wrote:

> Loading prisoners with heavy irons, which make their walking, and even lying down to sleep, difficult and painful, is another custom which I cannot but condemn. In some County-Gaols the *women* do not escape this severity: but in London they do: and therefore it is not necessary in the country. The practice must be more tyranny; unless it proceed from avarice; which I rather suspect; because county-gaolers do sometimes grant dispensations, and indulge their prisoners, men as well as women, with what they call "the choice of irons", if they will pay for it.

(Howard, 1777, p.27). Mary Tyler (1977, p.52) records that in India an iron ring was placed round each ankle, attached by rods to the prisoner's waistband, making it impossible to walk, sit, bathe or use the lavatory in the normal manner. In England, corporal punishment in prisons was not abolished until 1967, almost twenty years after its abolition for criminal offences outside (though latterly it had been little used). Dietary punishment continued in Northern Ireland after its abolition in England in 1979.

Solitary confinement is still in use, and the statutory maximum of 56 days continues to be exceeded by the device of interpreting this as

59

permitting consecutive punishments to be 'awarded' on different charges. (A persistent failing of prisons, incidentally, is euphemism. In England, punishments are called 'Awards', and the Prison Department does not agree with the use of the phrase 'solitary confinement', on the ground that prisoners in fact see prison staff in the course of the day. In some countries punishment cells, known to prisoners by such names as 'the hole', 'the block' or 'chokey', are given names like 'security housing unit' or 'adjustment unit'; imprisonment itself is called 'corrections'.) Whether it is solitary or cellular, the punishment is a severe psychological one. It was imposed 4,119 times in England and Wales in 1979 (Home Office, 1980a, tables 9.2–9.6). No statistics are published about the lengths of these punishments, but there are striking variations in their use. In Liverpool, for example, it was used only six times in 1979 among a population averaging 1,500, but in Lincoln, with 500, it was used 202 times. It is not generally realized, however, that the punishment of 'exclusion from work in association', imposed 7,691 times that year, is very similar to cellular confinement. The prisoner remains in a cell all day in both cases. Cellular confinement means being placed in the punishment block of the prison, removing bed and bedding from about 7.00 till 20.00, not having a radio, and not being allowed to talk to other prisoners during the one hour's exercise. Exclusion from work in association varies from one prison to another. In one, the prisoner remains in a cell in the main prison, can keep his radio, and has company on exercise when possible; his bed remains in his cell. But if he is in Security Category 'A' he is not allowed recreational association with other prisoners in the evenings. In another prison he can talk to other category 'A' prisoners on exercise; his bed must be removed only on weekdays, from 8.45 till 15.45. In a third he is placed in the segregation unit, can keep his bed, but bedding must be removed for two hours morning and afternoon on weekdays. In the latter two it appears that he is not allowed to keep his radio (summarized from letter from Lord Harris, 29 June 1978).

Unlawful Violence

Over and above the official punishments, prisons are places where unofficial harassment and brutality may be inflicted by guards or inmates. It is impossible to assess their prevalence but it is virtually certain that they occur in prisons everywhere to some extent. The investigation at Millhaven (Canada, 1977, para. 181) found that 'The worst excesses of staff brutality are now fortunately in the past. Now all that remains is abuse and harassment, with the prisoners responding in kind. The harassment takes the following forms: waking the inmates without necessity during the night by noise and light; delaying or adulterating inmate meals which have to come by truck from the kitchen . . . ; locking the inmates up 10 minutes before the end of a movie or sporting event they have been watching from the beginning; delaying the summoning of inmates when visitors arrive; delaying the responses to inmate requests (two weeks for a reply to a request to send flowers to a sick parent); refusing to give their names to inmates they are abusing; not allowing enough time for all the inmates on the range to shower during shower periods; denial of equipment; denial of privileges; refusal of explanations; continued insults.' Aggravation of prisoners by staff in relation to mail has been alleged to the Howard League in England; this is echoed in America, where 'In one series of incidents personally observed in a maximum security prison an officer systematically withheld mail from an immature volatile offender until he blew up and was "tagged" (given an infraction report). The officer's office was in an open cage, and the mail to be distributed was in full view of the prisoners. When a letter came in for the victim, the officer would just let it sit there after all other mail had been distributed. When the victim had become sufficiently agitated and paranoid, the officer would "suddenly discover" the letter and give it to him. After some time, the prisoner thought there were letters for him in the cage when there really weren't any.' (Bowker, 1978, p.8).

Sex offenders are likely to be tormented by staff or inmates. One of them (Gent, 1978) states that when he was being handcuffed to an officer before being taken to prison, the officer remarked 'Just my luck to be linked up with a dirty pouff.' Together with child-beaters, wife-beaters and informers, he was placed 'on Rule 43' (i.e. isolated for his own protection). 'Some of the acts [against these men] were . . . monstrosities that should never happen to any man, irrespective of what offence he has committed. Pots full of urine were emptied under doors; food was tampered with; missiles of all descriptions were thrown at you. And, of course, if you were unlucky, there were actual physical assaults. . . . Any man on Rule 43 is treated with distaste, contempt and disgust, not only by other inmates but by a large majority of Prison Officers.' It is fair to add that some officers at that prison, and most at another, treated him better. Stratton (1973, pp.68–9) describes how when he found a sex offender unconscious and bleeding, his reaction was to satisfy himself that the man 'had been well and truly obliged in the fashion prescribed [by the inmate code] for child rapists' and then to go upstairs and read the newspaper. The Prison Department does make some attempt to check these practices, for example by moving the men to prisons where they are not known; if this does not work they are placed on Rule 43, despite its stigmatizing effect.

Apparently the uphill task of changing the attitudes of the persecutors is hardly attempted. Other official responses have included the Criminal Injuries Compensation Board's policy of reducing or withholding awards to men injured by other prisoners, on the ground that those who commit crimes must expect to face prison and the practices which take place there. Another, in Scotland, was expected to remain indefinitely in protective custody after being convicted of the murder and rape of a ten-year-old girl. The judge, however, far from regretting this, said: 'It may be that you will suffer in prison for the nature of your crime. But having regard to the nature of that crime I can feel no sorrow for any treatment to which you might be subjected,' ignoring the fact that one of the professed aims of imprisonment is precisely to prevent the populace from taking the law into their own hands. (The judge also pointed to an aspect of the case which advocates of deterrence should consider. He said: 'To gratify your lust you raped this young girl and then, alarmed at what might follow if you were discovered, you proceeded to murder her.') (*Guardian*, 23 June 1978).

Allegations of violence by staff against inmates are a common feature of books by ex-prisoners. The train robbers describe it as an occasional event:

> ... most of them [found] the middle way of life by neither provoking the authorities nor collaborating with them.
>
> There were times when this balance broke down. On one occasion a convict at Parkhurst was dragged away during a visit by his wife because he was swearing. Interference with a visit was a breach of the unwritten rules of the prison, so he barricaded himself in his cell. [Gordon Goody swung some food to him on a line, was seen on television cameras and called before the Governor] which so enraged the other prisoners in the high security block that they too barricaded themselves in their cells.
>
> ... The prison authorities called out the engineers to break down the door.... As each cell was conquered its inmate was given a beating. Roy [James] waited for his turn to come.

... There was only room for two at a time to kick Roy's prostrate body. He managed to crawl under the bed, terrified that they would damage his eyes... From the bed he crawled through the door and down the corridor, being kicked as he went until finally the warders stripped him and flung him naked into an empty cell. He was left there for the night. His eyes were so swollen that he could not open them, and his teeth had cut holes through his lips.

When Roy returned to his cell, he found that his letters and photographs had been torn to pieces; that the wires of his gramophone had been wrenched out and an apple tart stuffed into the mechanism. He was told that he was to be charged with assaulting the warders; when he was brought before the visiting magistrates, he produced his bloodstained clothes and asked how a single man of his stature could have sustained such injuries attacking seven prison officers. He was convicted of assault and lost forty-two days remission with fifteen days on bread and water. (Read, 1978).

Stratton's book *Who Guards the Guards* (1973) is full of such incidents. His racy style makes his account sound as if it might have been embellished, but taken alongside independent accounts of other examples of violence, the essentials of his account are, unfortunately, quite believable. On one occasion, for example, he says that the deputy governor refused a prisoner a privilege which had been allowed by the governor, and there was a demonstration in the security block. Prison officers, he says,

charged into the security wing with their riot sticks. You should bear in mind that all twelve prisoners in the Security wing were locked in their cells at this time and could do no harm to anyone. The cells were opened one at a time by the screws. They went in and battered each con to the floor, wrecking the cells, smashing radios and all other personal possessions that the cons had. Billy Gentry, for one, had to have twenty stitches put into his head which had been well split open by a riot stick. It seems the screws had foiled a mass escape ... during which said escape screws were in great danger from prisoners who were securely locked in their cells anyway. One screw even managed to get his little finger broken in this ferocious battle of good against evil. Suffice to say, the finger was broken by another screw in his excitement when battering some unfortunate prisoner's head.

Stratton goes on to allege that apart from relieving the monotony, the prison officers' action secured them some extra overtime. There is no means of telling how much this account may be biased; as Stratton himself says, 'I have been accused by one publisher of being too bloody-minded in the way I have written most of this book. I won't dispute that it is very one-sided; it could be nothing else under the circumstances.'

But it is interesting to compare his version with an official report from Canada, where the director of the prison 'testified that he knew that there were on his staff several people who were more dangerous than the inmates' (Canada, 1977, para. 124).

The report found that:

Millhaven Institution opened prematurely in May, 1971, in an atmosphere of brutality borrowed from the violence of the Kingston riot in which a group of inmates killed two fellow inmates and severely beat 16 others. Many of the nearly 400 inmates transferred to Millhaven after the riot . . . were made to run a gauntlet of guards who struck them with clubs as they entered the institution . . .

Its early history was marked by the use of clubs, shackles, gas and dogs, often in combination . . . Inmates who were first shackled, sometimes hands and feet together, were then beaten with clubs, made to crawl on the floor and finally gassed (paras. 177–178).

Staff hostility is not confined to inmates. There have been many allegations of intimidation of staff by staff, directed at keeping in line staff members who would treat inmates fairly or do an honest day's job or inform on the sins of their fellows. About 50 staff members are responsible for almost all the trouble, but they exercise a control out of all proportion to their numbers (paras. 177–178, 182).

George Jackson (1970) links staff violence with violence between inmates:

I have seen the 'keeper' slap a man at the food serving line, take his tray, and send him back to his cell without dinner. The man that was slapped may have been old enough to be the keeper's father. The urge to strike out at the 'keeper' will almost always be repressed. In fact, most of the spontaneous fist fights between inmates occur immediately following an encounter between one of the participants of the fight and a 'keeper'.

The Israeli Committee (1978) makes the all-too familiar allegations about prisoners being beaten by warders, either in the isolation cells far from possible witnesses, or sometimes openly in the prison yard.

One way in which the authorities can invite trouble is by putting some inmates in charge of others. In India the 'matine' or trusty, unlike the other women, 'was fat, smooth-skinned and neatly dressed. The source of her prosperity was soon revealed to us. She used to steal and sell the rations entrusted to her for the other prisoners.' Yet from a combination of self-interest, since they were dependent on her goodwill, and solidarity, since she too was a prisoner, the others refrained from reporting her to the authorities (Tyler, 1977, p.34). At Tucker Prison Farm in Arkansas, USA, armed inmate guards were in virtual control when Tom Murton took over in 1967 after the scandal of torture and deaths was discovered. One trusty told him: 'A trusty had underwear because he took it away from a rank man. A trusty occasionally had milk on the table and salt-meat – a rank man had weevils and beans. A trusty was surviving; a rank man was existing.' (Murton and Hyams, 1969, pp.26–27). But the United Nations Standard Minimum Rules lay down that: 'No prisoner shall be employed, in the service of the institution, in any disciplinary capacity.' (Rule 28 (1)).

Examples of abuses in prisons could be multiplied, but after reading a number of prison autobiographies, and meeting ex-prisoners between whom there can have been no collusion, one can be in no doubt that it is daily being demonstrated in many of the world's prisons that if one group of people is put in charge of another, low-status group, hidden from public view, verbal and physical aggression are bound to occur, and can only be kept in check by first-rate staff selection, training, and supervision, and by contact with the outside world.

Such accounts inevitably tend to put prison staff in a bad light. They are not repeated here with any such intention. The impression consistently given by ex-prisoners I have spoken to is that, as might be expected, a minority of prison officers are outstandingly good, the great majority are average, and a minority are bullies. The Canadian parliamentary sub-committee supports this: 'several young guards who were concerned about the situation talked privately to teams of the Sub-Committee saying they want to do the job but there are a few "thugs in the system" who live by brutality, harassment and even invited hostage-taking "so we can negotiate better pay"' (Canada, 1977, para. 123).

In England some staff members have taken industrial action which deliberately worsened the conditions of prisoners – locking them up for long periods, denying them visits, parole interviews, classes and recreation (Prescott, 1976, p.35) – acting in a way that made prison disturbances more likely. Others have tried to find forms of non-co-operation which would not do too much harm to the goodwill of prisoners or the earnings of staff, such as restricting the intake of prisoners and preventing visits from probation officers but not from families; this reduced the prison population to its lowest level for years, but there was no real possibility of avoiding unfairness to prisoners.

Any large organization has its problems, but the secrecy surrounding prisons makes abuses harder to uncover. Some undesirable practices such as overtime rackets affect the management more than the prisoners: at Millhaven, for example, staff deliberately kept minimal or no records so as to escape accountability for the performance of their duties, and inflated the total cost of overtime to 40% on top of basic pay (Canada, 1977, paras. 183–184). Another common allegation is that prisoners do not get back money and valuables they have deposited with prison staff (Tyler, 1977).

Psychological experiments show the effects of pressures on human behaviour. Milgram (1974), for example, found that people are alarmingly willing to inflict pain on others if ordered to do so. Another experimenter, Zimbardo, divided volunteers into two groups, asking one group to play the role of prisoners, the other to act as guards. The 'guards' became autocratic and aggressive, the prisoners withdrawn; some had to be discharged from the experiment because of extreme emotional reactions, and the project was terminated early (Haney, Banks and Zimbardo, 1973). Although these results were obtained in contrived laboratory situations, bearing little relation to the complex structures of a prison, they lend limited support to the view that prison staffs' conduct is influenced by the pressures to which their job exposes them. There is, as J. V. Barry (1958) pointed out in his biography of the nineteenth century reformer and prison governor, Alexander Maconochie, always a danger in entrusting naked power to human beings over an outcast minority.

Restrictions on the Right to Know the Rules

John Howard insistently asked that the table of fees charged by gaolers to prisoners be hung up. Yet in Britain until recently prisoners were provided only with a 'cell card' which does not contain the complete Prison Rules. They still cannot see Standing Orders (except on visits and letters) but now have limited access to the Rules including the catch-all: 'a prisoner shall be guilty of an offence against discipline if he . . . disobeys any lawful order or refuses or neglects to conform to any rule or regulation of the prison [or], in any way offends against good order and discipline' (Prison Rule 47).

Similarly the Committee for . . . prisoners in Israel (1978) quotes the Israeli *Prison Ordinance (new version)* of 1971: disciplinary offences on the part of a prisoner can include 'Refusal to consume his daily food' (which could cover anything from a hunger strike to throwing his food in the waste bin as a protest, or because he considered it uneatable); 'The refusal to engage in labour or the manifestation of laziness, neglect or carelessness in work' (as determined, presumably, by the prison officer); and 'The commission of any action, or any kind of disorderly behaviour or neglect that may damage the good order or discipline such as may not have been detailed in the previous clauses above.' Prison administrators rightly point out that maintaining order is in principle in the interests of prisoners as much as of staff; they see rules of this kind as necessary tools in doing so. Prisoners see them differently; the Israeli Committee says (p.17):

> In short, any action committed by any prisoner could be considered to constitute a disciplinary offence, should any warder so wish. The prisoner depends completely on the arbitrary caprice of the warders and the prison administration [and sometimes the administration's unwillingness to confront the warders' union]. It is sufficient that a certain prisoner should be out of favour with the prison administration (because of, for example, his refusal to compromise his self-respect, his rejection of servility or his courage to demand the respect of his rights as a human person) in order that the administration turn his life into sheer hell by resorting to completely 'legal' means.

Even home leave and parole can be seen as 'whips' if they can be arbitrarily refused.

At one extreme is the State of South Dakota, which gives each inmate a fifty-page book of rules and admonishes him to study them carefully. His hands and face must be clean, his hair combed, and his hands kept out of pockets. He is told how to behave at meals, in the shower, on visits, and at every other occasion, in the same schoolmasterish detail. Inmates from other States, similarly rule-bound, say that even more enraging is the arbitrary way in which the rules are applied by staff (Orland, 1975). Mary Tyler encountered the other extreme in India. As an Englishwoman she thought it natural to ask to see a copy of prison regulations. She was not permitted to go and see it in the jail office. 'Finally, the Jailer came out with it: the Jail manual did not exist. It was out of print, the jail was run by memory. Not having access to any written rules, it was impossible to be sure of our rights or to know which of our needs and demands could be legitimately fulfilled. The attitude of most of the jail staff was that everyone in jail must have committed some crime to be there in the first place and it was a favour on the part of the government, as personified by themselves, to provide any food and shelter at all. People wanting to know rules and talking about "rights" were nothing but a damned nuisance.' True, if they had a grievance they could petition for redress; but 'we had already realized that jail petitions were dished-out as palliatives for prisoners' grievances, and even if dispatched or read, were never acted upon' (p.50). In England, the Howard League (1979a) told the House of Commons Expenditure Committee that petitions had been devalued by excessive use, and that the system should be re-examined. When petitions to the Home Secretary, which should be a last resort when an injustice is believed to have occurred, are routinely used thousands of times a year, and about 80% are rejected (*Hansard* [H.C.] 21 January 1981, col. *165*) the procedure has become a farce; though not so much as in India where, Mary Tyler says, 'Once the Chief Head Warder brought me some spinach wrapped in a piece of paper which, on inspection, I found to be a petition I had written for another woman a week or two before' (p.109).

The Law's Failure to Protect Prisoners

Some people in the prison service have presented a rosy picture of the old days when a governor could resolve quite serious issues by 'a word "off the record" with a particularly notorious prisoner.' But now 'every action of the prison authorities can come under external review': 'every lawful order is under challenge and the officer's status is gradually undermined,' as the then Chief Inspector of Prisons, G. W. Fowler, said in his report on the Hull prison riot (Home Office, 1977b, paras. 253–257). Fowler considers that 'liberalization' is making the job impossible and hence creating difficulties in recruitment to the service; he does not discuss the possibility that the whole authoritarian (or at best paternalistic) structure is an anachronism. He suggests that sophisticated and politically motivated prisoners, with help from outside pressure groups, were causing the trouble; staff made similar charges about 'left-wing radicals' and other troublemakers after the far more serious riot at Attica, New York, in

1971, but there the subsequent inquiry was an independent one, which rejected this explanation (New York State Special Commission, 1972, pp.104 ff).

No doubt Fowler is accurate in his assessment that there are members of the prison service who feel threatened in this way. But as long ago as 1819 it was stated that 'The law must follow the convicted man into the prison where it has sent him' (Decazes, *Rapport au roi sur les prisons,* quoted by Foucault, 1977). This comment is made in the context of deciding whether the convict may be released before the end of his original sentence, but it applies equally to the upholding of prisoners' rights (Zellick, 1977). As Mr. William Whitelaw has affirmed, 'Respect for the law is indivisible' (*Daily Express*, 25 April 1979). The law's application to prisoners is restricted in several ways, however. Each prison has a Board of Visitors, composed of magistrates and others appointed by the Home Secretary to satisfy themselves that the prison is being properly administered. They have power to enter any part of the prison unannounced at any time, and to speak to inmates alone – but not all of them make adequate use of this power. Furthermore, their independence as a safeguard for prisoners' is undermined, especially in the eyes of prisoners, by the fact that they also adjudicate upon prisoners charged with serious disciplinary offences, and can impose heavy punishments – yet prisoners are allowed no representation at the hearing (*Fraser* v. *Mudge, Times,* 13 June 1975). A prisoner can now write to a solicitor, but not to make a complaint unless this has already been made internally to the governor, the Board of Visitors, the regional director or the Home Secretary (which entails not only delay but the risk of punishment for making 'false and malicious allegations'). If he is suspected of putting anything in his letters other than the complaint he has already made, his letters to his solicitor are liable to be opened and read; so are letters relating to an application before the European Commission on Human Rights. If he wishes to make a complaint against a member of staff, or if he is defending himself against a disciplinary charge by saying that he was reacting to provocation or violence by the officer, he will be reminded of Rule 47 (12), which says that if he makes any 'false and malicious allegation against an officer' he is guilty of an offence against discipline, for which he may be punished. Prisoners know that it is often difficult to prove such an allegation against a member of staff, partly because of lack of evidence, partly because Boards of Visitors are reluctant to undermine staff morale; and if it is not proved it is automatically deemed 'false'. If the Board also decides

that it was 'malicious', in proceedings where he is again unrepresen-
ted, he may lose remission, or be given cellular confinement, or both.
If he persists, he may also break Rule 47 (16), which forbids repeated
'groundless' complaints. This can have several undesirable results.
Either the prisoner makes his complaint, is punished (probably by
cellular confinement and loss of remission) and is deterred from any
further attempt to secure redress; or he cuts his losses and withdraws
his complaint, and hence under present regulations loses his entitlement to raise it with a lawyer or MP; or his complaint was in fact
false, but he is able to claim that it was genuine and that he was
deterred by the rules from pursuing it, in which case he acquires the
status of a victim of 'persecution' and the false allegation about the
prison officer can continue to circulate without being openly dis-
proved.

There is no appeal against a decision of a Board of Visitors, except
by way of petition to the Home Secretary; only recently has the principle been established in the Court of Appeal that the procedure of
Boards should be subject to review by the courts (*R.* v. *Hull Prison
Board of Visitors, ex parte* St. Germain and others, [1979] 1 *All E.R.*
701). Lastly, proceedings before Boards of Visitors are held *in
camera*, and the press is denied access. A statement by Lord Justice
Lawton (1975) about courts seems equally applicable to Boards:
'Injustices, unhappily, still occur from time to time. Judges do not
always show the wisdom and commonsense they should; but if the
Press stops reporting cases there is a danger that irregularities and
folly may not be revealed.' The prison system is only too effective in
preventing errors from being revealed. One rare case in which a prisoner was vindicated was that of Mrs. Patricia Ali. She told the governor of Holloway prison about a homosexual attachment between a
prison officer and a prisoner, and 'the next thing she knew' she lost six
months' remission for making allegations against an officer, and was
placed in cellular confinement. Later the prison officer was imprisoned for six years after pleading guilty to conspiring to effect the
prisoner's escape, and the prisoner admitted sending 'messages of
love' to her (*Times*, 2 April 1974, 21 February 1975; *New Society*, 11
April 1974).

The system results in members of Boards, consciously or not,
being involved in a cover-up; the fact is that although Prison Boards
of Visitors are often accused of always supporting the staff and the
governor against the prisoner, this is not necessarily because of preju-
dice against the prisoner, but results from pressures inherent in the

structure. Baroness Wootton (1967, p.261) recounts how similar forces are at work in a completely different setting: the Board of Governors of the BBC.

> Never were we more acutely conscious of this need to listen to the advice of the professionals who knew more about everything than we did, and who, after all, would have to live with our decisions, than when we were called upon to hear appeals from members of the staff who thought that they had been unjustly treated. This right of direct appeal to the Governors was the privilege, as a last resort, of every BBC employee... Such appeals were by no means infrequent; but their chances of success were greatly diminished by our consciousness that, if for example we insisted that a dismissal notice should be cancelled or that someone who had been passed over ought to have been promoted, we should be undermining the authority of the appellant's superior officer. The whole procedure was in fact quite inappropriate to a large organization... In industry, normal practice to-day is for grievances to be dealt with, without loss of face on anybody's part, by discussion between union representatives and management – instead of by the aggrieved person knocking on the door of the directors' Board Room.

The position in which prisoners feel themselves to be is much the same as that of South African citizens who wish to criticize the police or the prisons:

> Any person who publishes any untrue matter in relation to any action by the Force or any part of the Force, or any member of the Force in relation to the performance of his functions..., without having reasonable grounds (the onus of proof of which shall rest on such person) for believing that that statement is true, shall be guilty of an offence and on conviction liable to a fine not exceeding R 10,000 or to imprisonment for a period not exceeding five years or to both... (Section 27A, inserted in the Police Act 1958 by the Police Amendment Act 1979, quoted in *Observer*, 29 July 1979, p.33.)

Prison authorities are upset by description of the Boards of Visitors' adjudications proceedings as 'kangaroo courts' and it is true that in some ways the British system, at least on paper, offers more safeguards than those of some other countries. The fact remains that from the prisoner's point of view the private adjudications, and the slow and usually unsuccessful petitions, directed ostensibly to the Home Secretary, have much in common with Kafka's *The Trial*:

71

One must lie low, no matter how much it went against the grain, and try to understand that this great organization remained, so to speak, in a state of delicate balance, and that if someone took it upon himself to alter the disposition of things around him, he ran the risk of losing his footing and falling to destruction, while the organization would simply right itself by some compensating reaction in another part of its machinery – since everything interlocked – and remain unchanged, unless, indeed, which was very probable, it became still more rigid, more vigilant, severer and more ruthless.

Imprisoning the Disadvantaged

Many thousands of the unfortunate classes of prisoners ought not to be imprisoned, at all, for the petty offences for which they are committed . . . Many of the visiting magistrates, prison governors and warders are men of the greatest humanity, and are not to blame for the evils of the present system. The *principle* of that system is wrong, as many official persons admit; and public attention is not sufficiently directed to the subject.

Every word of this statement in a Howard Association pamphlet *Prison facts* issued about 1870 is true a century later in Britain and probably most other countries of the world.

The people who are sent to prison are, to a disproportionate extent, undereducated, homeless, mentally ill, unemployed. In a survey of adult male prisoners in the south-east of England, Banks and her colleagues found that three quarters had left school at or before the age of fifteen. Only 11% had trade or technical qualifications, some gained in penal institutions previously. There were 21 recorded as completely illiterate, and 5 more were foreigners unable to read or write English. Only about one third of these 26 were attending classes in prison. A further 90 (over a tenth of the sample) were considered to have educational difficulties (*Home Office Research Bulletin*, 1978). Although 30% were assessed as homeless, the proportion ranged from 6% among first offenders to 77% among those with 21 or more convictions (and as has been suggested above, it is probable that imprisonment is a contributory factor in making people homeless). There were 21% assessed as mentally disordered, including personality disorder and psychopathy, psychosis, neurosis, addiction to alcohol or drugs, and smaller numbers of cases of sexual deviance, epilepsy, and mental retardation. A further 46% could not be classified on the basis of their records, but the report states that most of them 'appeared to require medical or perhaps psychiatric treatment', while the remainder were described by various members of prison staff as 'solitary', 'immature', 'institutionalized', or 'withdrawn' etc. This categorization is not very satisfactory, but that in itself illustrates the fact that prisoners do not even receive adequate assessment. Only 33% were 'apparently normal'. The usual occupation of 26% of the prisoners was unskilled (compared with 8% of the general population). Many of these were assessed as mentally disordered, and 84% had 'always unstable' or 'deteriorating' work records. Most, however, worked satisfactorily in prison, and some could probably do so, under the right supportive and motivating conditions, outside. The researchers attempted to assess the number of prisoners who might be 'divertible' from prison, bearing in mind the protection of the public and their suitability for some non-custodial or semi-custodial measures. The main criteria were: no serious offences against the person; no suggestion of considerable gain from crime, or large sums earned during a criminal career; no obvious competence or planning. On this basis it was estimated that one third of the prison population of the south east would be suitable for non-custodial sanctions, if appropriate facilities existed; yet almost half of them were serving sentences of a year or more.

The high rate of illiteracy in prisons has already been referred to. In one detention centre it was found that of 391 receptions in one year, 63 had a reading age lower than 10 years and were judged to be functionally illiterate. Of these, 75% were reconvicted within two years, compared to 65% of the literate. Among the literate youths, those who were reconvicted were, as a group, different from those who were not, in that their attainments in reading and arithmetic were lower (but not their intelligence), and their scores were higher on five out of 28 personality variables, including hostility, suspicion and social non-conformity (McGurk and others, 1977). The tests did not reveal whether these differences were attributable to their experience of the criminal justice system, but they do suggest that the police and prison services should give greater attention to reducing suspicion and hostility, rather than placing their faith primarily in deterrence.

The extent of deprivation among offenders, or rather among those who are convicted and particularly those who are sent to prison and provide researchers with a readily accessible sample, has been described repeatedly. West, in his study of *The Habitual Prisoner* (1963), found for example that 'at a conservative estimate at least a third of the prisoners were suffering from, or had not fully recovered

73

from, mental illness of considerable severity.' Banks and Fairhead (1976, p.16) found a high proportion of petty offenders maladjusted or mentally disturbed; among those who were homeless the proportion reached 80%. Nor are these findings confined to minor offenders: in another study, never published in full but summarized in the report *Régime for Long-Term Prisoners in Conditions of Maximum Security* (ACPS, 1968), West found that a substantial proportion of prisoners in the top security category came from the all-too-familiar background of broken homes and institutional upbringings, and this is borne out by Gunn (1976): half his admittedly small sample of 27 robbers had been to an approved school, only 37% came from an intact family, nearly a third had made at least one suicide attempt and a similar proportion had been to a mental hospital. In his research on juveniles West (1973, p.27 italics in original) found that 'the boys from *poor* families, from *unsatisfactory* housing, from neglected accommodation, and from the *lowest* socio-economic class were, in each case, more prone to delinquency than those rated more favourably'.

In a recent Home Office review of research Gladstone (1979), careful not to overstate the case, says of unemployment:

> Ecological studies have found evidence that areas of high unemployment tend to have relatively high crime rates. But this approach cannot eliminate the possibility that areas of high unemployment suffer from other social problems which could be what is really promoting crime.... Overall it seems that around 40% of people before the courts in England are unemployed but again this cannot be taken as conclusive evidence of a link since it may be that offenders are jobless more because of disinclination for work than from lack of employment opportunities. But perhaps the most convincing evidence comes from "time-series" studies. The pioneering work by Glaser and Rice (1959) showed that over the years the number of adult property offences in America varied directly with the level of unemployment, a conclusion reinforced by the sophisticated econometric analysis of Fleisher (1966).... Greenberg (1977), examining the effect of unemployment on the use of imprisonment, has found a close correlation between prison admissions and the unemployment rate both in the USA and in Canada.

Similarly, in Britain, 'The number of youths aged 17–20 admitted to prisons and borstals in recent years seems to reflect the unemployment figures for late adolescence.' The implication that prisons serve as a means of mopping up unemployment is a profoundly disturbing one. In South Africa this was proposed openly in the Bantu Laws Amendment Bill (and incorporated into Act no. 12 of 1978), by which an 'idle Black', described as any urban Black who is unemployed for more than 122 days in any calendar year, can be penalized by detention in a rehabilitation centre, farm colony 'or similar institution established or approved under the Prisons Act 1959'. At that time 12.4% of the economically active black population were out of work; the Bill would even apply to tens of thousands of Blacks who were 'unlawfully' employed in urban areas (*Times*, 9 February 1978). At the time of writing some changes are proposed (South African Embassy, 1980?, pp.15–16) but it appears that they would merely achieve a similar result by detaining the 'idle and undesirable Blacks' in 'rehabilitation centres' under a different Act – the one providing for the detention and 'treatment' of alcoholics and drug addicts. The South African Embassy informed me that there might be changes after the recent general election, but they are not yet apparent.

We do not do it that way in this country. Yet indirectly the unemployment is correlated with the rate of imprisonment. Of course any individual unemployed person has the choice of queuing up patiently for his social security benefit and keeping within the law; but it is inevitable that a proportion will not. Since a disproportionate number of the unemployed are black, it is not surprising (quite apart from any allegations of police bias) to see many black people when one visits prisons. No official statistics are published in Great Britain confirming this, but unofficial estimates put the figure at 15 to 20%, and much higher in young offender establishments. In the USA, over 40% of inmates in Connecticut in 1973 were black, 43% in Illinois in 1971, 56% in Michigan, 49.9% non-white in California, rising to 62% by 1974. In American state prisons as a whole, some two-thirds are non-white (Orland, 1975, p.56).

One inmate asked the Canadian Sub-committee on the Penitentiary System: 'How do you expect me to be rehabilitated when I never was habilitated?' The Sub-Committee sums up the continual punishment of the already disadvantaged (Canada, 1977, paras. 34–36):

Many who enter prison have never learned how to live as law-abiding citizens. Some have never known the security and training of strong family ties, nor the protection of society experienced by those who are well endowed socially and economically.

The persistent recidivist statistic can be related to the fact that so many in prison have been irreversibly damaged by the time they reach the final storehouse of the Criminal Justice System – the penitentiary. The failure for some began from birth, or even prenatally in homes where parents were deprived, incompetent, or themselves delinquent. It was compounded in schools, foster homes, group homes, orphanages, the juvenile justice system, the courts, the police stations, provincial jails, and finally in the "university" of the system, the penitentiary.

Pain and punishment have become meaningless to many of these people; layers of scar tissue protect them from further pain. Some are so desensitized that they behave almost like zombies when further pain is inflicted.

Many of the bad features of prisons were exemplified at Attica, the American prison where a riot lasting from 9 to 13 September 1971 ended in the deaths of thirty-two prisoners and eleven members of staff, in what the official report called 'With the exception of the Indian massacres in the late 19th century, . . . the bloodiest one-day encounter between Americans since the Civil War.' Although there had been limited reforms, there was censorship; there was dehumanization; there was little training or rehabilitation; there was bullying; there was a disciplinary system that satisfied neither staff nor inmates. But perhaps most significant in the long run is not the régime itself, but the inmates who were sent there: they were largely from depressed urban areas, black or Puerto Rican, bitter at discrimination and poverty, and beginning to be politically conscious. In the late sixties and early seventies, indeed, 'In virtually every aspect of American life there was declining respect for an authority which seemed incapable of fulfilling promises of democracy and equality' (New York State Commission, 1972, pp.xi, 116). Even perfect prisons, if such a thing were possible, would have little relevance to these problems.

4. Keeping More People Out of Prison

What can be done to reduce society's reliance on prisons, given the prevailing ambivalent framework of attitudes which try to combine punishment with rehabilitation? There was a time when reformers believed with reasonable certainty that, given the resources, they could do something about crime. They would be able to treat it and, if they could intervene early enough in the lives of those considered likely to become criminals, even prevent it. But research has cast doubt on these optimistic ideals. Reformers have therefore revised their opinions; it is now recognised that well-intentioned intervention may have more drawbacks than advantages, and that in any case measures involving the minority of offenders who are caught are unlikely to have much effect on the total volume of crime. The message now is that it is more realistic, more economic, and above all more just, to keep intervention to the minimum compatible with public protection.

Some actions regarded as undesirable or deviant are best not dealt with by the criminal law at all. Some are so minor that they are not worth prosecuting; or they merit only a finding of guilt, perhaps with a warning or conditional discharge, but no substantive penalty; or if a sanction is considered necessary, they do not need such a severe one as imprisonment. This chapter will look at what has been called 'the overreach of the criminal law'. For many offences sanctions will continue to be necessary; but wherever possible this should involve not removal to an institution but constructive measures which build on the offender's good qualities and aptitudes, draw on goodwill in the community, and where necessary offer the offender practical help to enable him to choose a law-abiding and rewarding life-style.

Fewer Offences

One basic way of reducing the amount of crime is to reduce the number of offences on the statute book. If a certain type of behaviour is no longer defined as criminal, this obviously affects the number of crimes, although not necessarily the number of times the behaviour occurs (Walker, 1977). It may mean that the State no longer intends to try to prevent it, as with the legalized forms of homosexual behaviour and abortion, or street bookmaking, for which convictions in London fell from 3,814 in the year before the Betting and Gaming Act 1961 to 9 in the year after (*Hansard* [H.C.] 1963 June 20, col. *81*); or that there is still a desire to limit its occurrence, but the threat of criminal sanctions is no longer considered an effective or just way of trying to do so, as with attempted suicide, which ceased to be a crime in 1961. One of the most striking examples was prohibition in the United States between 1920 and 1933. It resulted in much law-breaking: not only the manufacture, sale or transport of intoxicating liquors, but other offences such as corruption, protection rackets, and improper search and seizure by the police (Sinclair, 1962), much of which persisted after the repeal of the prohibition law.

Perhaps the most obvious candidates for 'decriminalization' are public drunkenness and vagrancy. Various attempts have been made to deal with these problems by legislation. In England, for example, public drunkenness first became a criminal offence under an Act of 1606 – the penalty was a fine of five shillings or six hours in the stocks. In 1879 the Habitual Drunkards Act provided for retreats for voluntary treatment. The Inebriates Act 1898 authorized compulsory detention in reformatories, fifteen of which were set up; but by 1921 they had all closed, partly because they were underused by courts which did not believe in the effectiveness of compulsory treatment, and partly because financial responsibility was divided between local authorities and the Treasury, neither of whom was statutorily obliged to run them. In the Criminal Law Act of 1977 offences of simple drunkennness were made non-imprisonable, but since courts persist in the practice of fining penniless people, this has made no substantial difference: offenders are imprisoned for non-payment. In 1979 2,946 males and 128 females were sent to prison for drunkenness, and 221 males and 3 females for begging or sleeping out (Home Office, 1980 a). A working party of the Home Office (1971) recommended providing alternative accommodation, but only two detoxification centres have been set up, in Leeds and Manchester, and once again there is disagreement as to whether they should be paid for nationally or locally. The Home Secretary has announced plans for basic shelters for homeless alcoholics (but no second-tier facilities to which they might move on: this will continue to be left largely to voluntary organizations such as the Cyrenians). The implication is that drunkenness will remain within the scope of the criminal law.

The imprisonment of homeless drunken people is still sometimes justified as being in their interests, since they receive a few weeks' food, shelter and medical attention (see for example Home Office, 1974, p.15; 1976a). But this claim is belied in several ways. Entry into prison is not voluntary, nor could a person choose to stay there if he felt he was benefiting. The majority are not sentenced to immediate imprisonment but fined: they are thus given the chance to escape the supposed advantages of prison, but only if they have some money and are willing to part with the few pounds which represent their sole possibility of existing lawfully for the next day or two. Nor is this 'welfare' always provided when they might be assumed to need it most: it is just as likely to be during the summer, at the onset of the tourist season (a similar move was reported from Moscow to remove 'eyesores' before the Olympics: *Times,* 6 June 1980, and from Caracas, Venezuela, before the United Nations Crime Congress in 1980). A further danger of these laws is that they open the door to police harassment, of the kind described by Jeremy Sandford in *Smiling David* (1974). Sending such people to prison makes it harder for them to escape the 'revolving door'; it also puts pressure on the government to provide more prisons. In short, this law and its enforcement do not serve the purpose of forcing welfare on social casualties (which would be a questionable policy in any case), but provide a soft option for local communities, relieving them of their human responsibility to make proper provision.

Similar problems have been found in the United States: the Task Force on drunkenness of the U.S. President's Commission on Law Enforcement (1967) found that the criminal justice system appears ineffective to deter drunkenness or to meet the problems of the chronic alcoholic offender. One arrest in three is for public drunkenness (over two million a year): at $50 per arrest, excluding the cost of preventive measures or treatment, this involves a cost of $100 million a year and a serious misdirection of police resources (Morris and Hawkins, 1970). One solution, short of decriminalization, has been offered in Manhattan: a car patrols the skid row district of the Bowery, offering to take derelicts to the detoxification project to dry out. Once there, a man is free to leave: thus the workers know that they must meet the needs of the patient if they are to keep him. They claim that some alcoholics have been helped to recover, and others have longer periods between drinking bouts. Meanwhile pressure on the criminal justice system was reduced by a sharp drop in the number of arrests for drunkenness (New York City, 1970).

Prostitution, too, is high on reformers' list of offences to be removed from the criminal law – or rather, not prostitution itself, which is legal in this country, but publicly soliciting for that purpose. Again the numbers are small – 246 women were received into prison for prostitution offences in 1979 (Home Office, 1980a) – but the principle is important. The fact that a woman can be convicted without any complaint from a member of the public, on the word of a single policeman, leads to the risk of injustice. An unwanted proposition from a prostitute is something which a person should be able to shrug off; if it is persistent, it should be dealt with under the laws of nuisance. Even then, as the Howard League (1975) and others have argued, there should be no question of imprisonment. The Police Federation agrees that soliciting should be non-imprisonable. Welfare arguments are again used to justify keeping soliciting as a criminal offence: arresting a girl enables her to be put in touch with a probation officer. But there is no guarantee that it will: and the principle remains sound that the criminal law should not be used to impose welfare or to attempt to control certain forms of disapproved-of behaviour. The inappropriate use of prison for want of adequate social services is found elsewhere: in India, for example, Mary Tyler records that a starving beggar child aged about seven, too weak to stand, was brought into the jail (the prisoners persuaded the Superintendent to allow it), and saved from dying of starvation. There were also mentally sick prisoners, and a disturbed deaf and dumb girl, none of whom received any treatment apart from an occasional injection to quieten them down if they got too wild . . . The doctors could do little except urge their transfer to a mental home, but this was rarely granted, for there were very few facilities. There were, a jail doctor told her, over eighty lunatics in the male section at Hazaribagh prison (Tyler, 1977, p.132).

A debate continues similarly about cannabis: is it harmful, and if so is the criminal law the right means of controlling it? Some research suggests that long-term use may have harmful effects that are not yet appreciated: mental confusion, brain damage, reduced immunity to infection, and reproductive abnormalities; it may be more damaging than tobacco in causing cancer and diseases of the lungs. It also impairs driving skills (McNicoll, 1979). Even if it could be shown that it was less harmful than alcohol or tobacco, this would not be a strong argument, since it would frequently not replace either of them but be available in addition. Whether it is addictive or habit-forming or neither is still under debate, and so there does not seem to be an overwhelming case for dismantling all controls. Some people claim that because possession of cannabis is illegal, those who use it will be tempted into the criminal underworld where they may be exposed to the risk of hard drugs; others, that young people want the mild excitement of breaking the law, so that if cannabis were legalized they would have to use something more dangerous to show their defiance. It has certainly been assessed as less harmful than opiates, amphetamines and barbiturates (Advisory Council on Drug Dependence, 1968), and in the present state of knowledge it seems reasonable that to purchase or possess small quantities for personal use should not be criminal. For a first offence of possession for personal use, in small amounts (generally defined as under 10, 20 or 30 g), there is either no penalty, or a warning or small fine, in Austria, Denmark, Finland, Ireland, Italy, Norway, Sweden, Switzerland, West Germany, and Yugoslavia (Legalize Cannabis Campaign, 1979). At the same time whatever information is available about dangers should be publicized through health education organizations (using, perhaps, the money previously spent on this aspect of law enforcement).

There are other areas in which decriminalization could be adopted. For example, there are over 200,000 cases of shoplifting reported to the police each year, over half of them involving under £5; it has been suggested that these should be made non-criminal. This does not of course imply that this activity should be tolerated; it reflects an appreciation that the cost of arresting someone and processing him or her through the courts is disproportionate to the value of the goods stolen. The Home Office (1973) was surprised to find managers who seemed to work on the principle that if a self-service display doesn't tempt enough shoplifters, it won't attract enough customers; the supermarkets then use the courts at the public expense to prosecute. If instead they had to bear the cost of a civil action for small thefts, they would have an incentive to provide more staff to supervise goods (and incidentally provide a better service to customers); at the same time they should introduce better procedures, such as always providing receipts, to prevent inadvertent shoplifting and enable a person wrongly accused to clear his or her name (Adley and others, n.d.). The Scottish Council on Crime (1975, paras. 59 ff.) did not wish to put the onus unduly on the victim rather than the criminal and recognised the extent of professional shoplifting and thefts by employees, yet it referred to 'a continuing and increasing irresponsibility' on the part of retailers who, to maximize personal gain, have 'refused to exercise even a modicum of care' in the protection of their property, and warned that the resulting burden on the law enforcement services might lead to the decriminalization of shoplifting as in some European countries.

West Germany has gone some way towards decriminalizing shoplifting. A prosecution can be started only if the victim applies, or if there is a 'special public interest' for doing so. The prosecutor may also, where the suspect admits guilt, refrain from prosecution on certain conditions: these are reparation, payment of a sum to a charity or the exchequer, performance of some other act of public usefulness or the payment of maintenance in cases where the offender had neglected his financial duties towards his family. There is also a procedure for a civil claim against the offender. But there are objections to placing so much discretion in the hands of prosecuting officials, and dangers that this discretion may be exercised in favour of affluent offenders. There is a proposal to avoid these problems by punishing the offender only if he has committed his third shoplifting offence within two years, or if the value of the goods exceeds DM 500. On the first two occasions there is restitution of the goods plus an amount up to their price, or double the price if the goods were not returned, with a minimum of DM 50 (Huber, 1980a).

One example of the way in which some minor offences could be defined out of existence concerns tenants who are charged with thefts from prepayment gas of electricity meters in their own homes: if the cash in the meter remained the property of the consumer until collected, those who 'borrow' from their own meters would be committing no crime (Hotson, 1970). This has in effect been put into practice by London Electricity Board, which is prepared to install unlocked prepayment meters to which the customer can affix his own lock. He can thus also reduce the risk of theft by outsiders if he empties the meter regularly and pays the money into a savings account (O'Gara, 1981).

Another question, which is too complex to be discussed here, but should be kept under review, is the balance between the advantages and disadvantages of using the criminal law as a means of attempting to regulate sexual behaviour, including (at different times and in different countries) adultery, bigamy, incest, prostitution and homosexual acts.

One way of checking the overreach of the criminal law without 'decriminalization' has recently been proposed by Justice, the British

Section of the International Commission of Jurists. This is to distinguish crimes, in which there is an intent of dishonesty, deliberate physical injury or sexual gratification, from those breaches of administrative regulations which involve no criminal intent, such as using unauthorized abbreviations on packaged foods or sticking a road fund tax disc in the upper (instead of the lower) nearside corner of a car windscreen. Another class of offences requires only carelessness or omission not involving moral turpitude. There are only about 750 offences in the first category; it is proposed that many of the 6,500 in the other two groups could be designated 'contraventions', as is done in most other European countries, and dealt with (where the offence is not disputed) by administratively imposed penalties (Justice, 1980).

Fewer Prosecutions

When an offence comes to light it is not always necessary to prosecute, just as in private life it is not good policy to have a row over every misdemeanour of one's children, spouse or colleagues. Especially for minor offences, policemen can (and do) use their discretion to admonish the culprit without taking further action.

In other cases the offender may, if he admits his guilt and the victim consents, be brought to the police station, where a senior police officer (usually the superintendent) may decide not to prosecute but to give a stern and formal caution. In England and Wales this is done extensively with juveniles (to 44% of boys aged 10 to 16 who admitted to indictable offences in 1978, and 69% of girls); but only to 3% of males and 9% of females aged 17 and over (Home Office, 1979, p.96). These figures conceal wide regional variations in the level of cautioning, and there is no reason why areas with lower rates should not raise them. It is surprising that the cautioning rate is lower for non-indictable offences than for indictable ones.

In the United States the police decision to prosecute has been identified as a point at which the offender can be 'diverted' out of the criminal justice system, but it is common to make the waiver conditional upon the offender's participation in a local project designed to help disadvantaged young people. This can work well, although an offender who rejects the offer because the project is inefficiently run, or irrelevant to his needs, will lose out.

In the Netherlands there is, after the police, another screening of a number of cases: the Public Prosecutor has the power to dismiss a case, and the current policy is *not* to prosecute unless the public interest demands it. When prosecution is waived no sentence is passed, although there may be conditions, and the offender does not acquire a criminal record. In 1975 no less than 44% of cases were thus disposed (Tulkens, 1979). In the Netherlands and to some extent Sweden, family matters and violence within the family are often not prosecuted but referred to a social work agency. Prosecution is often waived where the offender appears to be mentally disordered (this applies in Denmark also); in England and Wales courts have power to send such offenders to hospital without proceeding to conviction, but for some reason seldom use it. In Denmark the police may impose traffic fines and may give cautions on the spot in minor cases of shoplifting. In some minor cases there, and in Sweden and the Netherlands, the prosecutor can impose a fine instead of bringing a case to court (Leigh and Hall Williams, 1980).

In the Scottish system for juveniles, power to sift out a substantial proportion of cases is entrusted to the Reporter. He may ask the youngsters or their parents to consent to do something to improve the situation (for instance to pay compensation, join a youth project, or seek social work help or psychiatric care) but they are under no compulsion to comply (Morris, 1978). A system of this kind can keep many petty offenders out of prison and the courts, which would enable courts to reduce their backlog and hence shorten the average period of remand in custody. There is of course a risk that a larger number of innocent people will be tempted to admit guilt in order to avoid the uncertainty of a long period awaiting trial, or to obtain the benefits of the 'diversion' scheme. But the risks are less serious if the caution does not carry the stigma of a court appearance and conviction. It is also important to note that all these executive decisions, not made in open court, need careful safeguards to preserve confidence in the integrity of the police or officials who make them.

Diversion after Conviction

In this country it is generally considered preferable not to 'divert' people until they have been found guilty by a court, which may then defer its sentence to give the offender a chance to sort himself out, for example by finding a job, resolving marital problems, acquiring a skill, or making restitution. One such scheme, which encouraged courts to defer sentence and then offered help to the offender, operated until recently in East London. The Newham Alternatives

Project (NAP) was a voluntary organization started by members of Radical Alternatives to Prison who wanted to demonstrate that many people are sent to prison unnecessarily. In order to do so they accepted (with some misgivings) the need to work within the system. When a defendant was in danger of being sent to prison NAP workers, where possible with the co-operation of the probation service, offered the court a 'package' of proposals which would enable him to resolve personal problems and improve his chances of not re-offending. Since it was central to NAP's philosophy that people can and should direct their own lives, these proposals were worked out by the defendant; although the project's workers stressed to participants the advantages of living within the law, NAP's role was to enable, perhaps mildly to persuade, but certainly not to control. After a period of not more than six months the court would pass sentence in the light of a report jointly drawn up by NAP workers and the participant, describing the latter's behaviour during the period. The importance of the community's behaviour was also recognized, however; NAP workers tried to persuade individuals, firms and the local authority to offer more employment, housing and general social services (Dronfield, 1980). For a time NAP showed how with non-authoritarian encouragement some offenders who are hostile to authority can change their attitudes and discover new strengths. Unfortunately it was not possible (because of faults on both sides, in my judgement) to maintain a working relationship with the courts and the probation service, and the project was wound up at the end of 1980.

The suspended sentence can be regarded as a form of diversion from prison, but its position is anomalous. It is supposed to be a prison sentence, indicating condemnation of the offence in the usual way; but recognising that to make the offender spend time in prison would serve no useful purpose, the court suspends the sentence, which makes it in practice less demanding than probation. To make up for this it appears (though there can be no evidence) that some courts make the sentence longer than if they had ordered immediate imprisonment; this leads to a further anomaly if the person is reconvicted during the period of suspension, in that he spends a longer time in prison for the original offence, in addition to a further period for the new offence. The measure is generally assumed to have resulted in more and longer prison sentences than would otherwise have been the case, and its drawbacks appear to outweigh its advantages. This is also the conclusion of the thorough study by Bottoms (1980). The partially suspended sentence, provided in Section 47 of the

Criminal Law Act of 1977 but not yet implemented, seems likely to suffer from similar disadvantages (*Howard Journal,* 1978).

Fewer Imprisonable Offences

Until the offences discussed at the beginning of this chapter are removed from the criminal law altogether, they should clearly be made non-imprisonable; and there are other petty offences for which the penalty of imprisonment should not be available. The case does not rest on the pros and cons of imprisonment for particular offences, but on a basic principle of justice: total deprivation of liberty is the most serious penalty in this country, and should be reserved for the gravest offences. Any other policy is not only unjust, but leads to a pointless escalation of penalties for the serious crimes. There will obviously be different views as to what constitutes a trivial offence. One ready-made definition would be non-indictable offences, i.e. those not serious enough to merit trial by jury; in 1978, 4,146 people were sentenced to immediate imprisonment for such offences (other than motoring offences). Alternatively, crimes involving less than a certain sum of money, and no violence or distress to victims, could be excluded. The creation of new imprisonable offences should also be closely scrutinized; it should require evidence that this would be in the public interest and, in view of the cost of imprisonment, Treasury permission. The power of the courts to use such a drastic (and expensive) penalty should also be carefully circumscribed; Lord Justice Scarman suggested, in his address to the Howard League in 1974, that the power to imprison ought not to be available to magistrates, provided that an adequate range of non-custodial penalties was at their disposal (Scarman, 1978). The ultimate ideal should be to restrict imprisonment to those who can be restrained from serious crime in no other way, and possibly those who refused to comply with non-custodial measures—although the arguments below relating to fine defaulters may apply also to them.

In 1979, 17,044 persons were sent to prison in England and Wales for not paying fines (Home Office, 1980a). In principle if an offence is only serious enough to merit a fine, not imprisonment, a person should not be sent to prison for it. The Wootton Committee (ACPS 1970, para. 26) stated: 'We think first that non-custodial penalties should be truly non-custodial, and second that offenders upon whom a fine has been imposed should not be committed to prison if they have failed to pay that fine solely for want of means to do so.'

Against this are counter-arguments of principle – that whatever the original offence, not paying a fine is a serious matter in itself, because law enforcement depends on it – and of practicality, since it is claimed that the threat of imprisonment is effective in inducing a high proportion of slow payers to pay, often after they have previously pleaded poverty (see for example Latham, 1973). A Home Office study of over 2,500 cases found that eighteen months after sentence, 9% had paid nothing, and almost a quarter had not completed their payments. On the other hand, 12% of the defaulters said that they reduced expenditure on food and housekeeping, and deferred payment of rent, rates, hire purchase commitments or other debts in order to pay off part of their fines: 'This finding is disturbing as it suggests that, in a small proportion of cases, pressure to pay fines caused serious financial difficulties' (Softley, 1978, pp 15, 27, 29). For those who are poor managers, or have low incomes, or both, the pressure to pay a fine can cause hardship to their families or push them further into the morass of debt; and of course the lower a person's income, the more skilled he or she must be in managing it in order to survive. Although only a small percentage end up in prison, many of them are those who are unable to pay rather than the wilful refusers. The system does not sort them accurately; a recent study found that in Birmingham they were seldom even legally defended (Wilkins, 1979). Of fine defaulters imprisoned in 1975, 54% served all or almost all of their sentences without paying their fines (Home Office, 1976b, p.34). Nothing is known of how the others found the money. Inevitably there is a risk that without the threat of imprisonment some who were able to pay would not do so. The fear seems exaggerated, however, for the abolition of imprisonment for most civil debts in 1971 has not been followed by noticeable evidence that businesses which give credit are foundering as a result. How is it possible to exact fines from those who have ample means, without inflicting disproportionate penalties on those who have not? The first essential must surely be to relate the fine to the offender's means – a commonsense principle recognised by such primitive people as the Ifugao of the Philippine Islands (Mead, 1937). The Swedish day-fine system, now adopted also in Austria, Bolivia, Costa Rica, Cuba, Denmark, Finland, the Federal Republic of Germany, Peru and other countries, also relates the fine to the offender's income (United Nations, 1980a). It has the further advantage of providing a consistent indication of the seriousness of the offence: if, as in the United Kingdom, the fine is expressed simply as a sum of money, a penalty which is high in relation to the income of a low-paid person may sound low in relation to his offence. Under the day-fine system this is avoided by fining both rich and poor a certain number of days' pay. More precisely, the seriousness of the offence is assessed (in the Swedish system) on a scale from 1 to 120 (or 180 for multiple offences): this gives the *number* of day-fines. The *amount* of each day-fine is estimated at 1/1000th of a person's annual gross income (with reductions for family liabilities and for expenses directly related to employment and an increase for capital exceeding a specific amount). The day-fine is between 2 kr. and 500 kr. (approximately 20p to £50); fines totalling under 500 kr. are not included in the system. The Advisory Council on the Penal System (1970), from which this information is taken, did not feel that day-fines would be practicable in the United Kingdom because in this country there is much less openness about how much people earn; but the House of Commons Expenditure Committee recommended in 1979 that the question should be looked at again. It is time this was done: it is hard to think of any creditable reasons why people should be secretive about their income, and it need not be mentioned in open court. There would be practical problems in ascertaining true incomes in some cases where precise information is not available; in West Germany this has been solved by giving judges power to make estimates, and despite some discrepancies it appears to be felt that the system is fairer than before, and the proportion of fines over 1,500 DM (£475) has risen from 8% in 1972 to 16% in 1975 (Huber, 1980b). Thus lawbreakers who can afford to pay more are being made to do so.

While imprisonment for non-payment of fines should be much reduced, it should be eliminated for those who have committed no offence. It is incongruous that imprisonment has been abolished for other forms of civil debt, but retained for non-payment of maintenance of a wife or children, or arrears under an affiliation order, for which a total of 2,477 men and 1 woman were sent to prison in 1979. Imprisonment often makes a family temporarily fatherless, and makes payment even less likely: in 1975, 76% of men spent virtually the full period in prison without paying. The Finer Committee on One-Parent Families, which would have supported methods of enforcement that were considered useful, was strongly against imprisonment (Department of Health and Social Security, 1974, paras. 4.162 ff).

People Who Should Not Go to Prison

Examples of categories for whom the use of imprisonment should be drastically reduced, and where possible avoided altogether, include those who have not been convicted of any crime, first offenders, those with no legal representation, juveniles, women and girls, and the mentally disordered.

The Unconvicted

Under the Bail Act 1976 there is a presumption that accused persons will be released on bail unless a court considers them likely to abscond, commit further serious offences, or pervert the course of justice. In practice, however, some are refused bail because they have no fixed address; the provision of more supervised lodgings or hostel places could help to overcome this. Others could be granted bail if the court knew more about them and could impose appropriate conditions; one English survey suggested that up to 4% fell into this category (Simpson, 1977). In the United States it was found that defendants with good community ties could safely be released on their own recognizances: in the Vera Institute's pioneer scheme in Manhattan only 1% of these failed to appear for trial, compared with 3% of those required to find a sum of money for bail according to the American system. During the 1960s similar programmes were introduced in over 100 jurisdictions (Vera Foundation, 1971?). In England some are granted bail subject to sureties, but are kept in prison until sureties are found; improved telephone facilities at courts and prisons could help here. Others are allowed bail until they have been tried and convicted, then kept in prison for medical and social reports, but are finally given a non-custodial sentence. In 1979 one third of the men and half the women received into prison before trial or conviction were subsequently given non-custodial sentences. Bail is still being withheld in too many cases. It is difficult to see why bail should not also be granted pending appeal, subject to the same criteria, as recommended by the Advisory Council on the Penal System (1974) for young adults.

First Offenders

In 1958 the Howard League promoted the First Offenders Act which required magistrates to state in writing their reasons for sending a

89

person to prison for the first time. Similarly, for those aged 17 or more, courts are now recommended, though not required, to consider a social enquiry report before passing a detention centre order or a first prison or borstal sentence on a male, or any prison sentence on a female. These provisions are a recognition of the problem, though there is no clear evidence that they have been successful.

The Unrepresented

People who have no legal representation should not be sent to prison: in 1963 the United States Supreme Court held, in the case of *Gideon* v. *Wainwright,* that everyone accused of a felony is entitled to be represented by a lawyer, and in 1972, in *Argersinger* v. *Hamlin,* that a judge may not imprison an indigent person for any length of time unless the person has been offered a court-appointed counsel. But lawyers should be better informed about sentencing options than some of them are at present: if defending lawyers were trained to make themselves familiar with non-custodial resources in their areas, they might, as the Howard League has proposed (1977a), be able to persuade courts not to be merely lenient, but to make a positive choice in favour of a local scheme which might be more constructive than prison.

Juveniles

As to juveniles, it is widely taken as axiomatic that the least coercive disposition appropriate to a particular case should be used, and that juveniles should not be placed in adult institutions. This implies that a juvenile should not be removed from home unless it is in his best interests, and should if possible be placed with a foster family rather than in an institution; the period of *compulsory* detention in an institution should be kept to a minimum; and the criteria for placement in a secure institution should be particularly stringent (Howard League, 1977b). Some evidence suggests that the earlier a child is placed in an institution, the greater the risk of his becoming delinquent. Recent research has shown that youngsters with previous institutional experience are more likely to be reconvicted (Millham and others, 1975, pp. 223–4), at least with the younger boys (pp.224–5). But these researchers did find that some schools were significantly more successful as regards reconviction rates (pp.228–229). They suggest that 'It is difficult to imagine a hostel providing the range of activity and the variety of care situations that seem to us essential for helping deprived children', and that therefore there are benefits which accrue from residential life, provided the institutions are well run, and do not take children who do not need to be there, nor keep for too long those who do. Bottoms and McClintock (1973, p.431) found that great institutional experience was correlated with reconviction rates. But generalizations should, as always, be treated with care: a good institution, well staffed and with proper safeguards, is better than a bad foster home.

Two examples show how a determined policy of keeping youngsters out of institutions can be made to work. In Kent, England, the principle of fostering has been extended from small children to adolescents in trouble. Foster-parents are paid a salary, sufficient to make it unnecessary for the foster-mother to go out to work – yet considerably less than the average cost of institutional care. Social workers provide support and guidance. The teenagers' right to share decisions is recognised; they are either looked after temporarily while their own parents get through a difficult period, or indefinitely, in which case the scheme provides, in effect, after-care for as long as it is needed. The great majority of placements have worked out successfully. Between May 1975 and July 1979, 85 boys and 71 girls were placed, two thirds of the boys and a quarter of the girls having been found to be delinquent. Of the total, 71% made good progress, although about half of these still had problem areas. Thirty-two were cautioned or convicted during the placement, of whom 14 were sent to an institution or borstal or prison. This is a small proportion, considering the backgrounds of these young people; and in several cases contact with the fostering family was maintained, so that their prospects after release were better than they would otherwise have been. (Kent Social Services Department, 1980). The project has now been integrated into the Social Services Department, and there are about thirty such schemes in the United Kingdom.

The second initiative was American. After abuses were uncovered in the Massachusetts Division for Youth Services, a new state governor appointed Dr Jerome Miller as commissioner. He tried first to reform the century-old reformatories but soon concluded that traditions and attitudes were too ingrained for him to make more than small changes. He decided that drastic action was necessary, and transferred the young inmates *en masse* out of the training schools. At first many were placed in university accommodation, with the help of students who had been prepared in advance. Then services were rapidly developed, because they had to be, to provide group homes, foster homes, and varied non-residential programmes, on a 'purchase of services' basis. There remain a small number of secure places for the most disturbed young people. There is no evidence that recidivism has either increased or decreased. It was a dramatic and somewhat untidy operation, but almost certainly no gradual policy could have achieved as much (Flackett, 1974; Serrill, 1975; Rutherford, 1978) and the main point has been vindicated: that putting children in institutions is to a large extent a habit, which can be broken.

Women

It has also been suggested that there should be positive discrimination in favour of women, especially those who are mothers or potential mothers, for the sake of their children who will form the next generation. It has been found for example by Millham and others (1975, p.226), that separation from the mother before the age of three was correlated with failure after release from approved school; thus if the criminal justice system inflicts such separation, it is potentially storing up trouble for the community which ostensibly it is trying to protect. In Norway, pregnant women and those nursing their children are not sent to prison (United Nations, 1980b, para. 24). The Howard League has proposed, in its evidence to the House of Commons Expenditure Committee, a new sentencing principle: that in sentencing a mother a major consideration of the court should be the welfare of the child or children and that therefore the sentence should be non-custodial unless there are compelling reasons to the contrary (Howard League, 1979). The League also points out that in some areas women and girls are more likely than men to be remanded in custody between conviction and sentence, despite having been granted bail before trial; and those who finally receive non-custodial sentences are more likely to have been remanded in custody. With mothers, the League pointed out, there can be no right solution: either the child is brought up in prison or it is separated from its mother. In certain circumstances the law permits the local authority to take the child into care, especially if the mother was not able to arrange, before being put in prison, for a relative to care for the child; when this happens, it can be very difficult for the mother to regain care of her child. The Prison Department itself has said (Home Office 1977a, para. 185): 'To send a woman to prison . . . is to take her away from her family; her children in particular, may suffer from this deprivation, which can lead to the break-up of the home even where there is a stable marriage . . .' It is worth pointing out that the same is often true of sending a man to prison.

The Mentally Disordered

Everyone regrets the imprisonment of mentally abnormal offenders, yet it continues. The Prison Department itself has several times referred to 'some hundreds' of offenders who are in need of, and capable of gaining benefit from, psychiatric hospital care (for example Home Office, 1977b, para. 257). In addition the Home Office Research Unit survey (1978) of adult male prisoners in south-east England found about one in eight assessed as mentally disordered in a wider sense, including personality disorder, sexual deviation and addiction; of these about a third were not considered to need imprisonment for the protection of the public, on the basis of their current offence, and past record.

Why are they sent to prison? The reasons include both public attitudes and failure to allocate sufficient resources (and the latter largely results from the former). When a person suffers from psychological disturbance, immaturity, or another personality disorder, the handicap, though just as real as a physical one, is not visible, and is therefore not always taken into account by courts. Even if it is, there is a shortage of organizations and individuals willing and able to provide appropriate care, support or supervision. As a result, some courts take the illogical step of 'doing something even if it is the wrong thing': instead of placing on probation a person who is mentally disordered without being dangerous, thus giving the probation service the responsibility of providing care, they send him to prison, from where he will emerge more damaged than before, and in most cases with no after-care unless he asks for it. There is also, as always, a need for more preventive work; some disordered people would not commit offences, or not so many, if they were cared for. Until the 'open door' policy introduced into psychiatric hospitals in the 1950s and '60s many people were kept in locked wards; but the Mental Health Act 1959 was not followed by the development of adequate community care, or even of a clear concept of what such care should comprise, and many patients drifted out into homelessness, often committing petty crimes in order to survive.

With those who are clearly mentally ill, the courts are in a still more difficult position. They cannot make a hospital order unless a hospital is willing to accept the patient; and hospitals and their staffs became increasingly reluctant to do so (Bluglass, 1978). After the emptying of the locked wards the traditional skills in dealing with these sometimes difficult patients began to fade. There has been an increasing tendency either for psychiatrists not to accept them, or for nursing staff to refuse to admit them on the grounds of 'the inadequate facilities for nursing a particular proposed admission' (COHSE, 1979). The court's choice is then between sending them to one of the special (secure) hospitals, sometimes exaggerating their 'dangerousness' in order to obtain admission (Bluglass, *op, cit.*), or sending them to prison.

The solution usually offered runs roughly as follows: 'Special hospitals are overcrowded, it is no use trying to compel general hospitals against their will, prisons are agreed to be inappropriate, therefore regional secure units should be built.' Accordingly, it was proposed that 1,000 secure places should be provided, and funds allocated to Regional Health Authorities (RHAs) for the purpose; but so low is the priority given to these patients that most of the money was unspent or was even diverted into the RHAs' general revenue. However, simply to provide a new type of secure institution is not necessarily the answer. It may be best to adapt the range of resources already available, creating new ones only where a clear gap exists. According to Dr Bluglass, 'Planning should concentrate more upon developing services and improving their interdependence, and move away from a pre-occupation with bricks and mortar. *Regional Secure Units alone will simply create new problems unless their relationship to other services is more clearly defined and understood.* Indeed, the need for Secure Units must be questioned if psychiatric hospitals were to return to their traditional role' (Bluglass, 1978, emphasis in original). Discussion continues as to whether the reintroduction of one or two locked wards in an otherwise open hospital might be preferable to sending the patient to a separate and totally locked institution. Many of the patients need care and intensive support rather than security: it could be more economical, when both money and qualified staff are scarce, to raise the staffing level in some wards of ordinary psychiatric hospitals, and to train and pay the staff in such a way that they were willing to work with offender patients. An integrated plan has been announced by the South-East Thames Regional Health Authority (SETRHA, 1979). It is based on out-patient and community services including sheltered work and social service support, four purpose-built in-patient clinics in existing psychiatric hospitals, a regional assessment centre, with the maximum security hospitals such as Broadmoor reserved for cases in which they were really necessary. Lastly and most importantly, many mentally disturbed offenders are not dangerous and need neither hospital treatment nor secure containment: they could be dealt with in hostels, day centres, specialist clinics or groups (for example for simple guidance on social relationships with the opposite sex, which some of them because of their disturbed upbringing have never received). When in addition they are socially isolated, the support and friendship of understanding members of the public could be valuable.

5. Constructive Penalties

If fewer people are to be sent to prison the inevitable question is, what should be done instead? The first answer is: As little as possible, on grounds not only of cost, although economy is as important in law enforcement as elsewhere, but of justice. When a person has broken the law the State's reaction should be kept to the minimum necessary, and should not be excessive in proportion to the offence; this is true whether the emphasis is more on punishing the offender or on helping him to do better in future.

Nominal Penalties

Penal measures which simply mark a finding of guilt but impose no substantive penalty are recommended in Resolution (76) 10 of the Ministers of Justice of the Council of Europe. English examples are the absolute discharge, in which the court considers that no further action is necessary beyond the finding of guilt; the conditional discharge, in which the offender is released without supervision on condition that he does not commit another offence (but if he does, he will be sentenced for the original offence as well); and binding over, where the offender is required to pledge a sum of money, with or without sureties, that he will be of good behaviour and keep any specified conditions; this may be done in any case except murder. Other deprivations, more substantial but still avoiding imprisonment, include the withdrawal of a driving licence and confiscation of a vehicle. In recent years about 50% of those convicted of indictable offences in England and Wales have been fined, and this proportion could well be increased; more use could also be made of on-the-spot fines or penalty tickets, such as are used in various countries for minor traffic offences and evasion of fares on public transport. In the Netherlands the Public Prosecutor has the power to make a financial disposition instead of prosecuting minor contraventions, and a Bill proposes to extend this power to more serious offences, provided the maximum penalty is not more than six years' imprisonment. As a check on this exercise of executive discretion, a citizen may apply to a court of justice to complain if a criminal offence is not prosecuted. The court appearance itself can be regarded as sufficient penalty in many cases, combined with the knowledge that it will become known to a person's family and the public. In a survey of 800 young people, 75% gave first or second place to the deterrent effect of what their family would think (and 49% put it first); 47% to the danger of losing their jobs; 25% to the publicity or shame of having to appear in court; while the formal punishment which might be inflicted by the court came in fourth place with 22% (only 10% putting it first) (Willcock, 1974, table 23). A Dutch criminal lawyer has described how, for misconduct by employees of Dutch railways, the punishments consisted of verbal condemnation, carefully graded: (1) reprimand, (2) severe reprimand, (3) censure, consisting in a declaration of dissatisfaction, (4) serious censure, consisting in a declaration of serious dissatisfaction, and (5) the same as (4), with a reminder, which means that if the offender commits a further offence of the same grade the sixth and final sanction of dismissal may be imposed. These moral punishments replace the fines that were formerly imposed, and are taken very seriously by both the management and the employees, according to van Bemmelen (1968), who suggests introducing the same principle into criminal law for minor offences, with prison in the place of dismissal as the punishment of last resort.

Using Offenders' Good Qualities

The idea of using the abilities of the offender is as old as the idea of making him work. A new and more idealistic version of this principle has become an accepted part of English practice in the form of the Community Service Order, another innovation of the Criminal Justice Act 1972. The order requires offenders aged 17 or over, convicted of imprisonable offences, to do from 40 to 240 hours of work useful to the community. Ideally the work is done in the company of volunteers, or of the recipients of the service, such as old people, handicapped children, and so on. Many offenders feel genuine remorse and welcome the opportunity to make amends for their wrongdoing. For some it is an occasion to re-appraise their lives and their relationships to other people. To critics who feel that this is not punitive enough it is justified on the grounds that it deprives people of liberty at the weekend; it also deprives certain offenders of the chance to demonstrate their *machismo* by showing that they can 'take' their punishment. Indeed, since offenders often enjoy it and continue to work voluntarily when the order has expired, it quite turns the idea of punishment upside down.

CSOs were introduced in six experimental areas in 1973; by 1979 they were available throughout England and Wales, and some 15,000 a year are now made; 1980 saw a big increase, but this replaced fines more than prison. About four fifths are successfully completed. Among the community services performed by offenders has been work in youth clubs, hospitals and old people's homes, driving buses for outings for old people, helping to teach handicapped children to swim, constructing adventure playgrounds, restoring short-life property for the homeless, and many more (Harding, 1978).

Like any worthwhile scheme it is not without pitfalls. In some places the choice of work has not been imaginative (Pease and McWilliams, 1977), and there is rumoured to be a church hall in East London which has been painted four times because the local probation service has run out of ideas. Inevitably there have been cases where community service orders have been imposed on minor offenders who would otherwise have had a lesser penalty, and it appears that this has been the experience in the United States also (Beha and others, 1977); but there is no doubt, in England and Wales at least, that substantial numbers of prison sentences have been avoided. The courts, the probation service and the public should be on the lookout to prevent the blemishes which could spoil the community service scheme, which is one of the most constructive innovations ever made in penal theory and practice; but since its early days it has not been well publicized. As regards its effect on recidivism, it is unfortunate that the Home Office has undertaken only one follow-up study, based on less than 800 cases in the first six experimental areas, whereas the total of orders to date is well over 70,000.

An earlier idea for drawing on offenders' strengths was 'New Careers'. It was born in the 1960s, the era of the Office of Economic Opportunity in the United States, where it was not limited to offenders, but involved those who were part of a social problem, such as the poor or unemployed, in tackling the problem. For a time, large numbers were engaged in self-help and campaigning projects. People with few educational attainments were encouraged to acquire qualifications, in courses planned to avoid the obstacles with which the professions surround themselves, such as pre-admission educational requirements; residents in neglected areas found that they could combine to induce landlords and municipal authorities to provide adequate services. In one project, in Vacaville prison, California, 18 prisoners aged between 22 and 35, several with very violent records, took an intensive social work course and 12 of them secured responsible jobs in the anti-poverty program (Briggs and Hodgkin, 1972; Briggs, 1975). An English scheme concentrated only on offenders who would otherwise have been sent to borstal: they were therefore under 21, and probably rather young for the scheme. In addition, the organizers were too optimistic about the willingness of the social work profession to modify its insistence on formal entry qualifications, which made it difficult for them to obtain social work careers as intended. Nevertheless, individuals' self-esteem often benefited, and it is to be hoped that the difficulties will be overcome so that the concept can be adapted and applied elsewhere, both for offenders and for other deprived groups (Millham and others, 1978).

Taking and driving motor vehicles accounted for 4,253 (16%) of receptions of males under 21 sentenced to detention centre, borstal or prison in 1979. Schemes like the Ilderton Motor Project in Lewisham, South London, and the Society of Roadcraft, Hailsham, East Sussex have developed to find a constructive use for these driving and related mechanical skills. The Ilderton project shows young motoring offenders how to repair and tune up old 'bangers', which they are then allowed to race on a private racetrack. The rehabilitative principle is the controversial one of giving the offender legitimately what he was trying to obtain by committing these offences (Ilderton Motor Project, 1978). This is reminiscent of A. S. Neill's famous suggestion for dealing with a boy who had stolen a bicycle: give him one of his own. The Society of Roadcraft (1977) operates on similar principles to those of the Ilderton project with motor-cycles, but differs in that it is also intended as a preventive measure.

Using the Community's Good Qualities

Writings on social problems often criticize 'the community' for not doing more to help, to set an example, and generally to concern itself – and this book is no exception. But 'the community' consists of individuals, among whom there is great potential goodwill. The more it is used, the better, not only because of the direct benefit to particular offenders, but because the more people are involved first hand, the more their attitudes will be realistic instead of being based on stereotypes of 'offenders', 'hooligans' and the like. In Kent, and by degrees in other areas, foster parents are recruited for adolescents with severe problems who might otherwise have been sent to institutions. The Kent Family Placement Project described in Chapter Four departs from the voluntary tradition, however, by paying a salary to foster-parents.

Members of the community can for example help with accommodation problems. Many offenders have no home, or not one to which it is advisable to return, and homelessness has long been known to be associated with a high risk of re-offending (Hood, 1966; *Home Office Research Bulletin*, 1978). Numerous schemes have therefore been started to try to alleviate the position, but they are like buckets in the ocean: there is a general shortage of low-cost housing, and the position is getting worse. Until recently the emphasis was on establishing hostels, but there are often difficulties in securing planning permission in the face of local residents' objections: the unaccepting face of the community (Wright, 1980). Other problems have included problems in finding suitable staff, and the fact that offenders (like many other people) are not always willing to live communally. Probation officers are therefore looking more to private landladies who are willing, given financial and other reassurances, to let rooms to people who have been in trouble.

Members of the community are recruited by the probation service to form a panel of volunteers, on call to help when needed, and are also enlisted for specific tasks, such as a bail verification scheme. One area probation office in Sheffield has a volunteer who is a musician and is teaching a probationer to play the piano, and another who runs a group for those who share his enthusiasm for angling. Community resources can also be used if, for example, a sports club or a branch of Alcoholics Anonymous accepts a probationer as a member. Finally, the skills of voluntary workers may be used in management, either of voluntary projects or through the statutory Probation and After-Care Committees of the probation service itself.

Until not long ago preventive work in the community by the police was not always regarded as relevant: in the 1950s a policeman who in his spare time ran a youth club in a rough area of London received sparse encouragement from his superiors in the Metropolitan Police (Richardson, 1965). Now, however, many schemes are starting to involve the police with the local community. In Cheshire, for example, the Juvenile Volunteer Scheme, nicknamed the 'Aunts and Uncles' scheme, has been running since 1976; juveniles who receive a caution after admitting relatively minor offences are referred to the scheme. They are put in touch with volunteers, with whom they may share such activities as football, tug-of-war or fishing; or the volunteer may teach them to read or to play an instrument, or just provide a 'shoulder to cry on'. Consent is required from parents but not from the young people themselves – a feature which will no doubt interest probation officers who have always laid great stress on the importance of consent in securing co-operation – and no specific time-period is laid down. So far the scheme has only taken a small proportion of those cautioned in the areas where it has been introduced, and it remains to be seen whether it will be extended to those whose needs may be just as great but whose offences are more serious (Cheshire Constabulary, 1980).

Enabling

Writing with the authority of an ex-prisoner (in a German concentration camp), Dr. Eugene Heimler (1967) states that 'when the satisfaction of a man's basic needs falls below a certain level he finds it increasingly difficult to struggle with his everyday life, with all the pressures and forces of social living.' When basic needs for food and shelter have been met a person can develop relationships with other people, and then he can (and needs to) find satisfaction in work and recreation, and will have the motivation to acquire the necessary skills. Using this approach, Heimler was able to help about half of a group of long-term unemployed back to work. Many petty offenders lack these basic necessities; until they are enabled to obtain them, no amount of punishment will make them into conforming members of society.

Illiteracy, as pointed out above, is a disadvantage commonly found among people convicted of crimes, and among the prison population, where a recent survey found 18% with a reading age of 10 or less (Home Office, 1980). It is possible that illiterate people commit more offences than others, because fewer legitimate opportunities are open to them; it is also possible that their crimes are more likely to be detected, and that for example they often come from areas where poverty and low educational standards exist side-by-side, and where police are more likely to look for suspects. If the illiterate come to notice through being convicted, the opportunity to learn to read is likely to extend their horizons. At least one probation officer, in London, has described her work teaching reading and writing, one-to-one and in groups, with the aid of trained volunteers. The chief magistrate at the local court has taken an interest in the scheme and when appropriate refers a defendant for assessment of his reading ability, after which, if the person consents, the court can incorporate the remedial reading classes in a probation order: attendance counts as reporting to the probation officer. In the first three years no one who attended the sessions regularly was re-convicted (Belville, 1978). It cannot of course be concluded that literacy training alone was responsible: other factors may have influenced the result, such as the care and support shown by the teacher and other participants and the fact that these individuals were motivated to seek self-improvement. A national educational advisory service for offenders has been set up by NACRO, and a local one in Manchester, where there is also a day centre, five days a week, on literacy, numeracy, employment seeking, health matters and welfare rights. Further schemes operate at Swindon, North London and a growing number of other places (Shore, 1980; Marks, 1979; NACRO [1981]).

Many offenders have poor work records; at a time of high unemployment, especially among school leavers, a substantial number have no experience of work at all. The Wildcat scheme in America and the Bulldog Employment project run by the Inner London Probation Service provide work experience, mainly in building and decorating, with a combination of close supervision and incentive: participants are paid more than they would receive as social security or unemployment benefits, but less than they could obtain outside the programme. They can leave with not only the habit of work but also an employer's reference.

These are of course offenders who are fully capable of work; but if what society wants to do to them is to make them work, why send them to prison for it? This makes it more difficult to arrange, because most prisons are either miles out in the country or desperately short of workshop space. Lord Justice Lawton and others have advocated 'hutted camps' – but that is exactly what a number of our existing institutions are, and several are on the point of falling down, so that an urgent decision is needed whether to rebuild them at considerable expense or replace them with more imaginative alternatives.

In some areas probation officers identify particular problems. In Gravesend, Kent, for example, there are a number of teenage girls rejected or estranged from their families, some with babies, lacking basic experience such as planning their expenditure. Through the Gravesend Budget Group, started in 1978, they meet weekly, share in the preparation of a meal, learn about budgeting and child-rearing;

in crises, instead of being dependent on an interview with a probation officer in an office, they can support each other. Another area has started a group for indecent exposers. Others help teenagers to prove themselves physically, with the interest and encouragement of adults, in five-a-side football, canoeing, rock climbing and camping. Many of these schemes are unique, or exist only in a few places; but there is a need for them in nearly every probation area. The range of skills needed is beyond the capabilities of the six or a dozen people who make up the average probation team. The probation service must draw more and more on resources in the community, either by paying for them or by recruiting volunteers; only where this cannot be done should they have to set up a special project under probation auspices. If a certain plan will enable and, it is hoped, motivate an offender to keep out of trouble, the court should know this before passing sentence.

A way of providing a framework for these services and encouraging continuity is day centres, which are developing in many areas, usually under probation service management to meet local needs. They use the skills of current members of the probation team, re-inforced by resources available in the community – courses, literacy schemes, libraries, and the talents and friendship of volunteers. Attendance is voluntary; but there are degrees of voluntariness from casual drop-in centres, to those where the participant makes a 'contract' with the probation officer to attend and those where the court makes attendance a condition of probation. The most structured are the day training centres, introduced under the Criminal Justice Act of 1972, but likely soon to lose their separate status. Using a range of activities they attempt to develop unsuspected abilities, build self-esteem, and progress to practical social skills such as job interviews, handling relationships at work, managing money, or relating to members of the opposite sex. Unfortunately the centres have not stated their aims very clearly, so that it has not been possible to eva-luate them satisfactorily; since some centres are intensively staffed and therefore expensive, this has put their future in doubt. But the standard period in a day training centre is three months: many offen-ders serve longer than this in prison, so that the total cost of a day training centre order can be less than that of a prison sentence. The centre improves the offender's prospect of finding a job, and hence paying taxes instead of drawing social security; and no cash value can be put on the fact that, if he has a home or family it does not forcibly separate him from them (Burney, 1980).

Too Little Punishment – Or Too Much Control?

These projects, which are only a random selection of those that exist, are based on the working assumption that the intervention of the criminal justice system should be kept to a minimum. But this philosophy is criticized from both liberal and conservative perspectives. Institutions 'in the community' can be not much less restrictive than prisons: in the early 1970s I visited a probation hostel where residents were not allowed to cook for themselves and misbehaviour could be punished, army-style, by 'confinement to barracks'. Intervention is also accused of perpetuating the attempt to control crime by applying sanctions to a small and mostly underprivileged sample of lawbreakers without reforming the social structure. The fact remains, however, that they have broken the law, and some of them have caused serious harm; society is entitled to make some demands on those who break the law, but it must also fulfil its part of the social contract with them.

One way in which non-custodial sanctions give rise to concern is that some such schemes may catch minor offenders who would otherwise have received lesser penalties or none. Apart from being an exessive invasion of their liberty, this overloads the whole system. 'Unless safeguards are built into the system, diversionary programs intended to narrow the domain of the juvenile justice system and promote less restrictive alternatives may result in the . . . processing of larger numbers of young people than ever before. It may prove necessary to close institutional facilities at the same time as opening new programs; otherwise we shall be left with both' (Bullington and others, 1978). Stan Cohen (1979) agrees, seeing 'not just a proliferation of agencies and services, finely calibrated in terms of their degree of coercion, intrusion or unpleasantness' but 'new programmes which supplement the existing system or else expand the system by attracting new populations – the net of social control is widened.' The wider intervention also spreads wider stigma: there is evidence that some unofficial police cautions have been replaced by official ones, which are recorded (Ditchfield, 1976); and that a youngster who takes part in an Intermediate Treatment project, if he later makes his first appearance in court and is found guilty, may have more chance of being 'sent away' (Draper, 1979). Proposals for limiting the controls to some extent have included replacing the imposition of treatment by the offer of help (see for example Bottoms and McWilliams, 1979); a chief constable has suggested that offenders might be allowed to choose between a range of sanctions over a fixed period (*Guardian*, 11 April 1979).

On the other side are those who see helping offenders as 'soft', and explaining their behaviour as 'making excuses'. They quote the stereotype of a young offender who has already been on a care order or probation more than once; even when the disadvantages of penal institutions are pointed out, they feel that further non-custodial measures appear neither deterrent nor controlling enough. Some offenders, they point out, repeatedly commit crimes which are by no means trivial. Any sentence other than imprisonment will therefore have to be restrictive if these critics are to regard it as adequate.

Supervision: A Constructive Penalty?

The previous section considered the risk that non-custodial measures might be applied to more and more minor offenders; but there are valid reasons for using them for the more serious ones who would otherwise have been placed in custody. In some cases existing schemes, including basic probation, would be adequate and should be used more, but in others the change from custody would not gain public support unless it was accompanied by closer supervision and control. This section will consider the degrees of supervision, their drawbacks and advantages, and an example of a possible scheme.

Supervision can vary considerably in intensity. It may consist merely of reporting every month or so; more frequent reporting; complying with conditions; or attendance at a day centre or residence at a hostel. With traditional probation supervision, however, there is a complication. It has come to be assumed by many probation officers that offenders have problems, often involving their adjustment to society and to life in general. This is often the case, but by no means always: some of those convicted in the courts have problems which result from their situation rather than their psychopathology, others have no more problems than most people. But probation has become linked with the technique of 'casework', making extensive use of interviews in which the probationer is asked to explore his attitudes and responses to people and situations. The Home Office Research Unit's IMPACT study showed that it is no use applying this approach indiscriminately: it found that although offenders with low criminal tendencies and many personal problems tended to respond slightly better to the extra attention and help they received, those who had moderate or high criminal tendencies were actually more likely to be reconvicted within a year than those who had the usual more-or-less nominal supervision (Folkard and others, 1976).

Although it is possible to be too sweeping about the ineffectiveness of attempts to help offenders, as will be seen in Chapter Eight, it is now generally accepted that many of those who come before the courts have no special need of 'casework', and the problems of many more lie in their situation, past and present, rather than in themselves: if the situation cannot be changed, what they need is help in coping with it. The number who are considered 'disturbed' is much smaller than it used to be; and the way in which these, too, are reacting to what has been done to them was pithily expressed by one teenager who had been in twenty different homes: 'Moved around from place to place – that's being disturbed, isn't it? ... They've always moved me, not them' (BBC television programme 'I'm not a bloody parcel', 1 July 1980). It is also increasingly felt that help or treatment should be offered and accepted voluntarily, rather than imposed, because of the rights of the individual and because compulsion is less likely to be effective.

At present an offender who needs more supervision also receives more social work, and *vice versa*, because orthodox probation practice combines both. Probation officers have been resistant to placing emphasis on surveillance, as they showed for example in their reaction to the Younger Report on *Young Adult Offenders* (ACPS, 1974); yet in practice they already often exert a considerable degree of control, for example in parole supervision, which almost invariably involves a strict insistence on weekly reporting, with prompt and severe action if there is any breach of conditions. It is beginning to be thought by probation officers (such as Bryant and others, 1978) and outside observers (such as Bottoms and McWilliams, 1979), that the two elements – control and the offer of help – should be separated: the former should be imposed by the court (though with consent as at present), the latter should be agreed between the offender and the probation officer. The gradient of control should be more systematic, and it should be recognised that supervision can be made quite severe without resorting to the extreme of imprisonment. The following proposal incorporates elements of existing practice, as well as extensions of it.

Frequency of reporting, as well as the duration of an order, would be decided by the court; they would depend on the seriousness of the offence or offences. Standard conditions would be imposed, as now, such as 'being of good behaviour', and not changing address or job without permission. Reporting would not involve the regular inter-view which is now usual, but merely the signing of a register at the reception desk of the probation office, and confirmation that the con-ditions were being observed (this could be checked from time to time, as far as possible). At the reception desk would be a person (not necessarily a probation officer) who would encourage any who needed help to ask for it. He or she would be assisted by a display letting callers know the kinds of help available: personal counselling, assistance with family problems, special education or vocational training, information about employment and accommodation, welfare rights advice, and so on. Those who wanted help with any of these would be referred to a probation officer, who would either 'advise, assist and befriend' in the usual way, or put the probationer in touch with the appropriate agency. The probation service could 'buy in' services which it could not provide itself. The help, as distinct from the reporting, would be on a voluntary basis. This would apply also to those who voluntarily make use of hostels or day centres; although some probation officers use informal 'contracts' as a means of keeping probationers (and themselves) up to the mark, these do not have legal force.

If the court considered that this degree of control was insufficient, for example where repeated attempts had been made to check the law-breaking with less severe sanctions, and there was a serious risk of recidivism, there would be a new penalty of intensive supervision. The aim would be that this should be seen by the offender and society as a more serious sanction than probation, by substantially interfer-ing with liberty, and at the same time making it more difficult to be involved with crime. There would be specific criteria to prevent an order being imposed on any except serious and persistent offenders, and it would consist in the imposition of conditions additional to the standard ones, the chief of which would be more frequent reporting – in serious cases this would be daily at first. But this should not be arranged so as to awaken attention, or to inconvenience the offender unreasonably, for example by requiring an undue amount of travel-ling. Probation officers could therefore arrange to be assisted by specially recruited voluntary supervisors such as the offender's employer or foreman, or some other person of standing in the com-munity living near the offender's home or place of work. This re-lationship need not remain purely formal: in many cases the voluntary supervisor would take a personal interest in the probation-er's progress and offer support where necessary. The probation officer would remain ultimately responsible, and should be accessible to both the probationer and the voluntary supervisor in case any problems arose.

Where further control was necessary, there could be a condition of residence in a hostel, with a requirement on the offender to notify the warden upon going out. Since these are considerable restrictions of liberty, intensive reporting should be limited to a maximum of six months, and residence in a hostel to three; both would be followed by a period of ordinary probation. Of course, when the hostel was proving beneficial, the probationer would be allowed to remain voluntarily, except where it was considered not to be in his best interests to become too dependent on its support, in which case he would be encouraged to move out, while retaining links with the people he had met there.

Enforcement would be strict in the event of non-compliance with court-imposed conditions. A court, or a specially constituted supervision board, could issue a warning, prolong the conditions of residence or reporting or the period of probation afterwards; but only a court could annul the intensive supervision order and replace it with a custodial sentence, which would not normally be done unless a fresh offence had been committed. All these decisions would be appealable.

These proposals are not in fact original. They are based on those of a group of probation officers in England (Bryant and others, 1978), and those of a Swedish committee set up expressly to consider the abolition of youth imprisonment (Sweden, 1977); the latter came into force in January 1980, and although, as in Massachusetts, abolition has not been achieved entirely, it is now much nearer.

There are some possible drawbacks to the use of supervision instead of custody. The offender is not under the temporary total control which prison affords, and is therefore not physically prevented for a period from committing further crimes in the community (but it should be remembered that a substantial minority of those sent to prison would almost certainly not re-offend in any case). In a country accustomed to widescale use of imprisonment it may seem to be insufficiently deterrent and an inadequate expression of social condemnation of crime. Supervision is seen as less unpleasant than imprisonment – though in some ways being free but subject to restrictions could be more irksome than adapting to the undemanding though uncomfortable régime of prison. It is free from some of the worst disadvantages of imprisonment, which removes the offender (often at some distance) from those who could offer him support, keeps him almost exclusively in the company of other offenders, and generally allows little opportunity for initiative, except perhaps in circumventing authority. Supervision, on the other hand, has few of the undesirable side-effects of imprisonment, and has potential advantages: it offers a difficult but genuine opportunity for self-determination and, ideally, an incentive to use it in legitimate directions. Instead of a rigid distinction between imprisonment and non-custodial penalties it offers flexibility of control: this can be used to make sure that no more restriction is imposed than necessary – indeed there must be safeguards to make sure of this, because a considerable degree of control is possible. It can extend the time for which a person's whereabouts are certainly known to someone in authority, which ranges from a few minutes a month to 8 hours a day – or 16 hours in the case of someone who is living in a hostel and attending a day centre; but in addition, the staff of a hostel, or of a day or evening centre where they undertake shared activities with him, will get to know him quite well, so that they are in a position to exert some influence over him, if for example they have reason to believe that he is breaking his conditions.

The word 'control' has been used uncomfortably often; but control, whether total or partial, is not necessarily the best way to secure a person's future co-operation. Against the possibility that the offender will refrain from lawbreaking because of fear of punishment must be weighed the possibility that in the long run just and generous treatment will lead him, and others like him, to respect, rather than reject, society and its laws. A lower level of control, and a greater measure of trust, may be more effective in winning people's allegiance. It is important to remember also that these proposals are weighing prison against less intensive control, not against abandonment of control. Harsh methods are not necessarily the most effective, and measures which respect proper standards of humanity need not lack firmness.

Half Way to Imprisonment

The conventional reformist case is based on erosion of imprisonment, seeing a commitment to abolition as premature. Some reformers accept the existence of prisons as 'dust-bins' without which progressive schemes would be impossible (Millham and others, 1978, pp.161–162). One way of trying to achieve at least part of the deterrent impact of prison without its most damaging side-effects would be to make it intermittent.

The least severe of these measures is probably the attendance centre order. Indeed it could be classed among non-custodial sentences, but it is placed in this section because its primary purpose is deprivation of leisure time as a punishment, and the stress is on strict discipline. There are now over 100 junior centres (including a few for girls or for both sexes) to which juveniles aged 10 to 16 can be sent for up to a total of 24 hours, spread over several weeks; but only four senior centres, for 17 to 20 year olds. The government is setting up more of them. Attendance is normally for two hours at a time on Saturday afternoons, and the stock example of an offence for which the centres can be used is football hooliganism (although it does not necessarily prevent this, since attendance is usually only on alternate Saturdays, and some matches are held mid-week; a determined hooligan can attend a centre and still get to the football ground in time to cause some end-of-match aggravation).

Surprisingly little was known about the centres, until at last the Home Office undertook some research (Dunlop, 1980). There is generally a period of strenuous physical exercise, followed by instruction in some handicraft. They are usually run by police officers in their spare time. The Home Office does not consider staff training to be necessary, nor does it publish annual reports; inspection is carried out by officials of the Department of Health and Social Security, but their findings are not published (*Hansard* [H.C.] 20 May, 1980, col. 99–100). In 1978, 7,610 orders were made. The Children and Young Persons Act 1969 intended their abolition; but although there is no obvious reason why they should be more beneficial than other penal measures, the youngsters are probably not there for long enough for much harm to be done; one advantage is that their existence may deflect courts from more inappropriate sentences. But before they are extended there should be some better method of ensuring general accountability and publishing information about their work and its results.

The next step towards deprivation of liberty is the periodic detention centre introduced in New Zealand in 1962. Offenders aged 15 or more, convicted of an imprisonable offence, and with little or no previous institutional background, may be sentenced to not more than a year; during the sentence they normally attend for 40 hours at the week-end and two to four hours on a weekday evening. The work performed at the eleven centres includes cleaning and cooking, community service, and educative activities, combined with fairly structured recreational periods. Different centres, as described by Gibson (1971), have different styles, according to the personality and ideas of the warden; discipline combined with an opportunity to criticise, with casework, with sharpening of cognitive processes, with individual counselling and weekly 15-minute question-and-answer sessions on religious and ethical topics, and so on. At some centres one Saturday every three months or so is devoted to recreational activities. The Order may be followed by up to one year's probation. In the first five years the two-year reconviction rate was 60%, of whom just under half were not given custodial sentences. Since 1967, non-residential centres have also been established.

Shorter Prison Sentences

Measures like the foregoing are needed urgently; where they are not yet available the courts have a responsibility to apply pressure for their introduction, by refusing to sentence people to imprisonment where a non-custodial disposition would be more appropriate. Insofar as they continue to impose imprisonment, however, it is important that sentences should be progressively reduced to the minimum necessary for the protection of the public, in the name of efficiency, justice and humanity. There is clearly no point in continuing to use an expensive resource more than necessary, and research studies comparing offenders serving shorter and longer sentences (Banks, 1964; Hammond and Chayen, 1963) point overwhelmingly to the conclusion that 'longer sentences offer no more guarantee of reducing criminal propensities than do shorter ones' (Brody, 1976, p. 16). In America no substantial association was found between length of time in prison and outcome after release for 1,546 federal prisoners (Beck and Hoffman, 1976). After the U.S. Supreme Court decision in *Gideon* v. *Wainwright* (372 U.S. 335 (1963)), over a thousand prisoners who had been imprisoned without legal representation were released prematurely in Florida alone. A research study found that after just over two years, only 13.6% had been reconvicted, compared with 25.4% in the control group (Eichman, 1966, pp.72–73). It makes no difference if sentences are shortened by administrative action, i.e. release on parole: those released earlier than normal had no higher failure rate than others paroled at the normal time, according to studies reviewed by Hood and Sparks (1970), whose conclusion is the same as Brody's in his 1976 research.

111

In the absence of clear evidence that the advantages of maintaining a large prison population outweigh the disadvantages, the number in prison should be reduced as much as is reasonably possible. The most rapid and effective way of doing so is to shorten sentences; since

$$\text{population} \quad = \quad \frac{\text{average}}{\text{time served}} \quad \times \quad \frac{\text{annual number}}{\text{of receptions}}$$

a reduction of one month in the average length of sentence served would, on current figures in England and Wales, reduce the prison population by about 3,000. The same result could of course be achieved by reducing the number of receptions, and it is to be hoped that courts will do this as well; this means that they will have to make more use of existing non-custodial measures where they are currently underused. Alternatively, new measures must be established, but this obviously takes time and money. However, if courts can be induced to shorten sentences, the population will begin to fall very soon. As the Home Secretary, Mr Whitelaw, recently pointed out to Leicestershire magistrates (13 February 1981):

> Let me suppose that, when considering sentences of imprisonment, each sentencer reduced the term imposed to the next most commonly used term for the particular offence. If that were done, excluding crimes of violence but for all other sentences including those over four years, then the reduction in the adult male sentenced population could be over 4,000 or about 15%. Thus, using lower sentences than imposed now would still leave abundant space for marking the relative seriousness of offences.

Mr Whitelaw said that if the growth in prison population were not checked he would consider legislation; instead of reducing maximum sentences, however, the Criminal Justice Bill 1981 proposes partly suspended sentences, whose efficacy is widely doubted.

The greater the average reduction in sentence length, the greater the saving in prison population (Pease and Sampson, 1977), although to be precise the calculation must be based on the time actually served, rather than the nominal length, because of the operation of the parole system. In 1973 the English courts sent about 135 people to prison for every 100 sent by the Dutch (after allowing for the relative sizes of the two countries' populations); but there were 350 people in English prisons for every 100 in Dutch ones. This was because in England and Wales only 56% of sentences were for 6 months or less, compared with 89% in the Netherlands (1975 figures, quoted by Tulkens, 1979). Pease calculated that by adopting the

Dutch tariff, English courts could cut the prison population by 40%. The picture is complicated by other differences: the Dutch imprison fewer petty offenders but more motoring offenders, especially drinking drivers, and it may be that in the Netherlands (and Scandinavia) there is more pressure to reform prisons because more middle-class people have experienced them at first hand.

Long sentences do not deter appreciably more than shorter ones because the deterrent effect of imprisonment is greatest in the early stages of a sentence. This view is supported by participant observation by Hammond (1977), who found that among first-time prisoners, those most likely to be deterred from re-offending were a small group who recognised that they had done wrong, and a larger group who were merely sobered at being sent to prison. The latter influence was greatest in the early stages of imprisonment. Hammond argues for a policy which makes full use of the initial shock of imprisonment without giving time for its effects to be blunted by acclimatization to prison life.

These and other findings support the conclusion of the Advisory Council on the Penal System (1977) in its Interim Report that 'there was no reason to suppose that longer sentences have a greater impact than shorter ones on the prisoner, and that whatever deterrent value imprisonment might possess it is not lessened in its impact by a reduction in sentence lengths,' and '. . . the general rule should now be . . . shorter sentences are much to be preferred.' Various devices have been proposed for shortening prison sentences. There can be an increase in remission for good conduct, from one third to one half; but this widens the gap between the declared and the actual sentence, and there is a risk that courts will compensate for this. The use of parole can be extended, either as a matter of Parole Board policy or by altering the rules; but this carries the same risk that courts will adjust their sentences so as to be sure of keeping offenders behind bars for a certain time, and the added risk that the Parole Board will not release them at the earliest moment, so that the position is made worse instead of better. (Parole will be further considered in Chapter Six.) Legislation to revise maximum penalties and remove anomalies was suggested by the Advisory Council in its final report (1978), but it conceded that this might make little difference. None of these solutions strike at the root of the problem, which is judicial misconceptions about what can be achieved through prison sentences. In the 1950s and 1960s reformers and enlightened administrators persuaded judges that training was provided in prison, and that sentences should be lengthened to allow adequate time for it. (In fact, little training took place, and its benefits were largely overlaid by the deleterious effects of imprisonment.) In the 1970s sentences were further lengthened in the hope of achieving deterrence, and of compensating for the effects of parole which was introduced in 1968. The best method in the short term is to ensure that judges are aware of the evidence as to the lack of constructive consequences of imprisonment, so that they can help in turn to lead public opinion by giving reasons for their modified sentencing policy. This, however, is an unsatisfactory compromise in the face of the overwhelming evidence of the effects of imprisonment. It it time to abandon altogether the idea that prison is the usual punishment, using a standard tariff, to which 'alternatives' may sometimes be considered if they can be justified. Instead there should be a range of measures, not involving total deprivation of liberty except as a last resort.

6. The Remaining Prisoners

At best, the reduction of the prison population will take time and there will always be a small number of offenders on whom society will refuse to impose anything less than a period of total deprivation of liberty. This prospect raises two issues. The first is, what is the maximum possible reduction of the prison population and the choice of policies for achieving it? The second is, what are the minimum acceptable prison standards for these remaining prisoners? To answer these questions entails defining the aims of imprisonment and of such central activities as work and education; it also calls for proposals to revise release procedures and aspects of prison discipline, in particular methods of resolving disputes and issues relating to prisoners' rights.

How Many Prisons?

Whilst there is no basis for selecting any particular figure as the ideal size to which the prison population could be reduced, two of the methods described in the last two chapters are widely recognized as those by which the reduction could principally be brought about. One is to send progressively fewer offenders to prison, the other is to shorten sentences. Similarly with those awaiting trial: the use of pre-trial detention should be limited to cases where it is essential, and there should be limits on its duration, which is too long in the United Kingdom, and in many countries worse still. The Home Office predicts that, despite falls in 1978 and 1979, the amount of recorded indictable crime will rise, so that the prison population is bound to rise correspondingly unless sentencing policy is changed. At best, they say, sentencing policy could be modified enough to hold the population steady in the face of increasing numbers entering the system; but as the prisons are already overcrowded, humanity demands that more prisons should be built to ease the conditions, while there is sufficient public concern to induce the Treasury to find

115

the money. If these forecasts turned out to be pessimistic after all, there would be some modern prisons, and some of the ancient ones could be pulled down. In one version of this argument, it has been suggested that the urban prisons should be demolished, and the land sold for large capital sums for office building or housing. (But Shaw (1980) estimates that several of the prisons with high site values are rural, such as Dartmoor, at £1 million, and Ford, at £5–6 million.) The suggestion of the Howard League (1974) and others that an increase in probation-based facilities could be financed through a major shift of resources from the prison service is dismissed as 'unrealistic' because 'it overlooks the need for new resources to be made available to the probation service' in order to set the process in motion (Home Office, 1977b, p.7), and because it is claimed that the marginal extra cost of each extra prisoner is negligible.

The general answer is that given the political will, the prison population could be reduced, using any or all of the methods described. As regards the cost, the additional cost of each new prison place is £20,000 to £40,000 for low and medium security respectively, plus the average annual cost per prisoner, currently about £6,000 to £12,000, depending on the security level in each case. But for many years the staff ratio has been maintained, as the prison population has grown, at about one prison officer to three prisoners; it seems therefore that the marginal extra cost per 100 extra prisoners, excluding new buildings, must at least include the salaries of about 30 prison officers. The average gross pay of basic grade prison officers was estimated by the May Committee as £6,344 (Committee of Inquiry, 1979, p.314), and in current job advertisements it is over £8,000 (e.g. *South London Press*, 12 September 1980). If the extra prisoners tipped the balance and made the building of a new prison necessary, their marginal cost would be huge – to say nothing of what would happen if they were the last straw (for prisoners, prison officers or administration) leading to a breakdown of discipline, destruction of buildings and even loss of life. Elsewhere the Home Office admits that 'an increase in the number or length of custodial sentences would require a substantial rise in capital and current expenditure on the prison service' (Home Office, 1977b, p.9). Moreover, the Home Office argument is circular, because its predictions assume constant sentencing policy, which is affected by the availability (or lack) of non-custodial facilities, whose provision is partly affected by sentencing policy . . . This is not of course a full summary of the influences on sentencing policy, which include other factors such as the recommendations made by probation officers in their social inquiry reports; but it is enough to suggest that the statisticians should produce more than one forecast, based on different assumptions (King and Morgan, 1980, p.62). Two major breaks in the vicious circle are possible. Firstly, the judges are not unresponsive to public opinion, though their reactions are slow; if they feel that the public wants shorter sentences, many of them will gradually conform; some, who have taken the time to inform themselves about prison realities, will go further and help to lead opinion. Secondly, governments do usually allocate some money for the development of the penal system, and it is a matter of simple arithmetic that each million pounds will do more to relieve overcrowding if spent on noncustodial resources than on prisons. (One or two types of community project, such as detoxification centres at £23,000 a place, can be as expensive as prisons; but assuming that a range of facilities is provided, the average cost is less than that of prisons.) Probation hostels and hostels for alcoholics cost only £7,000 and £4,000 per place, respectively, to establish (Committee of Inquiry 1979, p.48). As for running costs, the average cost of a Day Training Centre order, which is a relatively expensive non-custodial measure, has been estimated at £2,300, or less than half the average annual running cost of each new prison place (Burney, 1980, p.17). The average cost of a probation order in 1977/78 was about £337, a probation hostel placement £2,000, a community service order £345 (1978/79) and an attendance centre order £31 (1979/80) (Shaw, 1980, pp.41, 42, 44, 47).

Part of the available money should be allocated to repairing the worst of the old prisons and installing proper sanitation, but the rest should be used for community projects as long as any people for whom these would be suitable are still being sent to prison instead.

Another reason against a prison building policy is that experience both here and in the United States shows that if more prisons are built they tend to be used; and that even if this were not the case, new ones are usually at remote sites miles from anywhere, inconvenient for staff, for the provision of work for prisoners, and for visits by families, social workers, and lawyers. The old prisons, with all their faults, are at least often relatively accessible. There should therefore be a moratorium on extra prison construction as long as the prison population is by wide consent far larger than it need be. This is not to say that no money should be spent on buildings: the old ones could be brought up to standard, provided this did not increase the number of places available, and preferably reduced it. If the policy of reducing the prison population is successful, the simplest and most economical policy would be to close small prisons altogether, although it may be better to resist this: there are two other important criteria which should be applied. The first is the prison's proximity to the area in which the majority of its prisoners live, so as to facilitate visits. The other is the size of prisons. It is broadly true that the smaller a prison is, the fewer the difficulties in running a humane and constructive régime. Hugh Klare (1960, p.124), for example, said 'I also believe that if you really want to exercise social control over prisoners, you cannot do it adequately when there are 1,000 of them, or 500, or even 300', although he implied that division into small units within a prison might overcome the problems to some extent. One study, admittedly, found no higher rate of misconduct in large prisons, but this is not conclusive, as the authors did not take account of variations in types of prisoner or régime (Farrington and Nuttall, 1980). Some governors I have spoken to suggest that for short-sentence prisoners at least, the optimum size is probably between 50 and 150, but it is common for prisons to be ten times this size, and even larger in some countries. In Britain several have been locking up 1,000 or 1,500, and new ones for 400 and 800 are being built. If these two criteria conflict, as when a rural prison has few local inmates while a large urban one has too many, a balance will have to be struck, perhaps by dividing the large one into small units. As the population is reduced, it will be possible to convert every third cell in the old prisons to provide toilet facilities for those on either side of it. Many prisoners might well prefer to continue to share a cell, if this allowed them to have civilized sanitation; when this becomes possible, they should be offered the choice. Ultimately the aim should be to reduce the prison population to the point where whole blocks can be demolished or converted to other uses such as workshops or classrooms. There are several prisons where this could easily be done, since a new building has already been erected alongside: it is only necessary to pull down the old one.

The Aims of Imprisonment

It will be clear by now that this book is not advocating the immediate total abolition of prisons, nor is it suggesting, despite the very serious criticisms in earlier chapters, that all the damaging aspects of custodial institutions are inevitable. On the contrary, there have been a number of initiatives based on the general philosophy that if people must be sent to prison, their time should be spent as constructively as possible, with special emphasis on preparation for release. They have included, in Britain, officially inspired projects like Grendon and Coldingley prisons and the special unit at Barlinnie; schemes carried out in partnership with outside researchers such as the modified régime at Dover borstal and the pre-release schemes referred to at the end of this chapter. In several cases there has been a marked lack of official encouragement; often evaluation has remained unpublished or not been carried out at all. Yet it is on initiatives like these that the prison service must depend if it is to minimize the unavoidable drawbacks of imprisonment, and as far as possible to eliminate the avoidable ones.

The aims of imprisonment have changed over the years. Once it was used mainly to hold people until trial; in the nineteenth century it became also a standard punishment after conviction. In 1895 the Gladstone Committee suggested that reformation could be combined with punishment, and now it is frequently said that people are sent to prison as a punishment, not for punishment: apart from depriving people of their freedom, the régime should not be made deliberately unpleasant. What this amounts to is that the aims of the court in sending someone to prison do not coincide with those of the prison régime. For a time the tail wagged the dog: courts sometimes imposed prison sentences, or made them longer, in the belief that this would help offenders' rehabilitation, which was promoted to be Prison Rule no. 1:

> The purpose of the training and treatment of convicted prisoners shall be to encourage and assist them to lead a good and useful life. (*Prison Rules* 1964, S.I. 1964, no. 388)

Prison security was largely to ensure that prisoners received their rehabilitation: governors used to say, 'You can't train 'em unless you've got 'em'.

But by the end of the 1960s disillusionment began to spread, as criminological research seemed to show that 'treatment' was no more effective in rehabilitating people. This, combined with the security scare of 1966 and the publication of the Mountbatten Report (Home Office, 1966), led to a reversal: security was put in first place, with other aims subordinated to it. In 1971 an internal document began to circulate in the Prison Department, entitled 'Aims and Tasks of

Prison Department Establishments', with a new Rule 1:

> The role of the Prison Service is, *first*, under the law, to hold those com-
> mitted to custody . . . and to provide conditions for their detention which
> are currently acceptable to society. *Second*, in dealing with convicted
> offenders, . . . to do all that may be possible within the currency of the
> sentence to encourage and assist them to lead a law abiding life on dis-
> charge. [Emphasis mine]

It went on to list four main aims, including promoting inmates'
self-respect, and preparing them for discharge. These are humane
and reasonable, but, significantly, security is placed first. There are
several notable omissions. There is no specific mention of a grievance
procedure or means whereby a prisoner can claim his rights if they
are infringed. The need for decent visiting arrangements is not mentioned, nor the desirability of finding voluntary visitors for prisoners
who have no family or friends. Later some criminologists began to
suggest that not only was it wrong to lengthen sentences with the aim
of rehabilitating offenders, but that pressure should not be applied to
prisoners to undergo programmes which had not been shown to be
useful and could be demeaning. Some went so far as to say that work
should be optional. The phrase 'Secure and humane containment'
appeared (for example, in Home Office, 1977a, p.17). Some
members of the prison service disliked this idea, which they considered would make prisons ungovernable and reduce staff to demoralized turnkeys. The May Committee tried a new concept of
'positive custody':

> The purpose of the detention of convicted prisoners shall be to keep them
> in custody which is both secure and yet positive, and to that end the behav-
> iour of all the responsible authorities and staff towards them shall be such
> as to:
> (a) create an environment which can assist them to respond and con-
>   tribute to society as positively as possible;
> (b) preserve and promote their self-respect;
> (c) minimize, to the degree of security necessary in each particular case,
>   the harmful effects of their removal from normal life;
> (d) prepare them for and assist them on discharge. (Committee of
>   Inquiry, 1979, para. 4.26).

Once again, security is given precedence, and the essential question
of preparation for release is placed last.

In Italy, by contrast, Article 1 of a new Penitentiary Law (no. 354

of 26 July 1975) relegates containment to a subordinate clause:

> The treatment of prisoners subjected to deprivation of liberty consists in the offer of direct actions aimed at sustaining their human, cultural and occupational interests.

Similarly, the Swedish Act on Treatment in Correctional Institutions of 1974 states that all efforts should be made to promote social adjustment; the prisoner should be regarded as not being excluded from society but as still belonging to it, as far as possible. This reflects the fact that imprisonment is, in intention at least, not an end in itself but a means to several ends.

What then should be the principal aims of imprisonment for the prisoners who remain even when the use of custodial sentences is being progressively reduced? The first aim should not be the inward-looking one of holding people for the period ordered by the court, but forward-looking: to release them at the end of the sentence, having helped and encouraged them as much as possible to be able and willing to make a new start and lead a law abiding life. The statement of aims should go on to stress the principle of treating offenders fairly and humanely (which does not exclude treating them firmly) both because this is right and because it might encourage them to behave well. Failing this, at least it will not provide them with an excuse for continuing to behave badly. Another essential point is that these aims and tasks are not those of the prison service alone, but of the whole community. There is much to be said for making the prison service responsible for what happens to the offender after he leaves prison, as far as geographical considerations permit; at least the service should be given the duty of encouraging the community to accept its share of this responsibility. The process should begin as early as possible in a prisoner's sentence, by allowing members of the community to enter the prison to visit prisoners or take part in specific activities, and in suitable cases by allowing prisoners to leave the prison temporarily. This does of course happen already, but to a limited extent; it tends to be regarded as a concession by the authorities rather than an integral part of their work.

Much of the debate about the aims of imprisonment centres on the relative merits of 'treatment', 'humane containment' and the May Committee's 'positive custody'. King and Morgan (1980, p. 28) hope that this is not seen as a 'mere linguistic quibble'. Different concepts do underlie the phrases, but are not obvious from the terms themselves. 'Treatment', in this debate, is taken to imply:

121

(1) that the purpose of sending a person to prison includes bene-fiting him, with the danger that there is no other sufficient reason for sending him there, and that he is made to stay longer than he deserved.

(2) that the 'treatment' is compulsory, or under duress such as delaying parole if he does not co-operate.

(3) that the nature of the 'treatment' is described in a statement of good intentions, too vague to be enforceable.

(4) that the likelihood that the person will benefit from the 'treat-ment' is too small to justify imposing it on him.

The first three objections may be met by requiring:

(1) that the offender is sent to prison only for purposes such as deterrence, public protection or retribution.

(2) that any education or therapy is voluntary.

(3) that enforceable standards are laid down.

While the second and third of these could legitimately be described as 'treatment', it may be convenient to use a different word. As to the fourth point, however, it does seem to me that the penal system should remember its supposed purpose of reducing crime: although it should not impose 'treatment' on the offender, it should impose objectives on itself beyond merely keeping the prisons running. Of course the standards of imprisonment should be humane and enforce-able; but 'humane containment' and 'positive custody' sound as if they give priority to security, whereas 'preparation for release' is forward-looking, implying concern for the public and for the future of the offender himself. The question of 'treatment' will be further discussed in Chapter Eight.

The Régime in the Remaining Prisons

These liberal principles have however left out a vital dimension of imprisonment. Underlying them is the unspoken assumption that prison authorities are people of goodwill, trying to maintain high standards in a difficult job. So no doubt they are, with no more excep-tions than in any other profession; but it would be wrong to suggest, as I have heard governors do, that anyone proposing greater safe-guards for the prisoner is impugning their integrity. Administrators and governors, like other people, may be subject to superior orders, political constraints, trade union pressures, and errors of judgment, and they can never know, let alone control, everything that goes on in prisons. It is this structure, rather than the individuals working within it, which makes it possible for prisoners to be denied basic rights and justice. It is in systems theoretically committed to humane principles that prisoners can be reduced to rioting, can be beaten up and, as at Attica 'Correctional Facility', killed. It took Attica to prompt a serious official re-examination of the prison system in the United States. This Commission's first recommendation was that priority should be given not to security, not to the well-intentioned provision of constructive activities, but to the fundamental rights of prisoners as human beings: 'If prisoners are to learn to bear the responsibilities of citizens, they must have all the rights of other citizens except those that have been specifically taken away by court order' (New York State Special Commission, 1972, p. xvi–xvii).

The Commission went on to stress that prisoners must not be cut off from contact with the outside world, prisons must not be shrouded from public view, and members of the public should be involved in activities within the prisons both for the prisoners' own sake and to promote public understanding. To elevate and enhance the dignity and self-confidence of inmates, rather than debase and dehumanize them, they should have the maximum amount of freedom, consistent with the security of the institution and the well-being of all inmates, to conduct their own affairs. It is literally vital that it should not take any more Atticas to make sure that these principles are accepted wherever there are prisons. They should be the foundation of the specific reforms which will be considered in the remainder of this chapter.

Work

The next question is, what should life be like for the remaining occupants of prisons? On one point there is wide agreement. The prisoner should be allowed (many would say compelled) to work a full week, for a real wage, out of which he could pay taxes, and at least some of the cost of his keep in prison, maintenance of dependants, a sum to maintain himself after release until he finds work, and compensation to his victim. It is wrong to inflict extra punishments more or less by accident; but that is what society does in many ways, for example when it denies prisoners the chance to pay for National Insurance, so that unemployment benefits and pensions for them and their families are reduced (Corden, 1976). If that penalty is appropriate to a par-

123

ticular offence, it should be imposed by the court specifically; if not, prisoners should be able to earn enough to pay National Insurance, or contributions should be credited to them as to hospital patients. Much of this would be no more than a bookkeeping transaction between government departments, or between the prisoner and the Prison Department (such as paying him money much of which he has to return for his keep), and the worst that can be said of it is that its administration would require extra civil servants. But the advantages to the public's sense of fairness and the prisoner's self-respect could be considerable. One of the best known experiments on these lines is in Tillberga prison, Sweden. This began in 1973, and in 1975 was extended to another prison, Skogome. Taxes, and the cost of food on working days, are deducted; of the rest, 75% is allocated to the purposes listed above, and 25% is for the prisoner to use as he likes. A code has been agreed with the trade unions, stressing for example that the work should not be an end in itself, but an instrument for future employment after release. The scheme is less difficult to implement in Sweden where the prison population is small and the unemployment rate low (the availability of work is a problem, but the use of such schemes in countries with high unemployment needs more study than it has received) (Council of Europe, 1979). Ways of introducing this, on an experimental basis at first, should be studied by the Prison Department.

Work, when it is available, has its advantages, but thought should be given to what it is intended to achieve. The crank and treadwheel have long been rejected: there should be at least some job satisfaction, through knowledge that the work is useful. Work of the right kind can be a means of acquiring skills and the ability to handle personal relationships in the workshop. It can take the form of unpaid community service. American-style forestry camps have something to commend them; but there is little to be said for some of the work in English prisons, described in Chapter Two. If conditions are to be as near as possible to those of the outside world, work must be included. In Britain at present it is not an offence to be unemployed, but in order to claim social security a person must 'sign on' and be available for any suitable work. Logically, the same should apply to prisoners, who would then be required to pay for food and accommodation from their earnings or unemployment pay. Some prison governors would argue that this would be unworkable in prisons, because of the situation and the people involved; a variant has, however, been used at Coldingley prison for some years, although admittedly the sanction of transfer to a more unpleasant prison is available for those who abuse the privilege.

Education

The need for education in prisons has been obvious since at least the time of Elizabeth Fry's classes in Newgate. The amount has increased considerably over the years, in Great Britain at least: the grant for library funding has been increased, and in some prisons, some long-sentence prisoners can study up to degree level, through the Open University. But there is a long way to go. Despite the desperate shortage of work in prisons, day-time study receives little encouragement, and most education has to be in evening classes. This should be changed: greater use should be made of teachers, literacy tutors and so on from outside, and wherever possible prisoners should be allowed to use the educational facilities in the community, so that these need not be duplicated expensively and not always adequately inside. The goodwill of the public should be enlisted in obtaining text books, and that of the staff in not raising obstacles to allowing them in. An extension of this educational policy is followed in the United States, where in some prisons inmates are encouraged to spend their time studying law and assisting other prisoners, under the supervision of outside law firms. Formerly the authorities resisted prisoners' access to the law, as in Britain they still do, but they were spurred on by Supreme Court decisions such as *Johnson* v. *Avery* in 1969, in which it was held that inmates could not be barred from furnishing assistance to each other. It was also felt that 'jailhouse lawyers' are inevitable, but are likely to be less of a nuisance if they are correctly informed. This is, of course, no substitute for an adequate legal aid scheme with access to an outside lawyer.

Letters

Isolation is one of the most severe disabilities resultant from prison life which, as far as possible, must be combated in the remaining prisons. A loss of social contacts cannot be avoided, but by reforming certain current practices at least the difficulty would not be aggravated by imprisonment. For example, prisoners should be allowed to send as many letters as they can afford, to whomsoever they wish. Neither their outgoing nor incoming mail should normally be subject to censorship, beyond inspection in the prisoner's presence for contraband. The authorities should have power to order censorship of particular prisoners' mail for reasons of genuine security only, but such decisions should be subject to independent review at the prisoner's request. Similar considerations apply to telephoning. The reasons for censorship have to be considered when its relaxation is proposed. A major one is prison officers' fear of defamation, and they should be adequately protected by the law of the land, aided by their trade union if necessary. If it is possible, in the remaining prisons of the future, to reduce the feeling of antagonism between staff and inmates, as will be suggested below, the need for such protection will be reduced. Allied to this are bureaucratic reasons for censorship: if prisoners can write freely to lawyers and newspapers, they will sometimes make complaints, and complaints are always time-consuming. Prisoners should be able to write prison autobiographies or conduct businesses. Both of these are at present forbidden in the United Kingdom lest this create problems within the prison, but these reasons are not adequate to justify restricting free speech; and if some prisoners made money, ways should be found of requiring them to make restitution from the proceeds.

Visits

Restrictions on visits to a prisoner should be kept to a minimum. To begin with, he should be imprisoned as near to his home as possible (without artificial distinctions, as in England and Wales, between 'local' prisons for prisoners serving up to four years and the often remote 'training' prisons for long-term prisoners (King and Morgan, 1980). Sweden has taken a step in this direction: about half its places for convicted prisoners (2,000 out of 4,100) are in local prisons with administration decentralized into prison and probation regions with one or two counties in each; only the longer-sentence prisoners are in the other prisons, which are nationally administered (Marnell, 1981). The population of convicted prisoners in 1978 was only 3,000; it will be interesting to see whether the Swedes are able to reduce it still further, and if so, whether they are able to place more of the long-sentence prisoners nearer their homes. From the point of view of contact with the outside world, however, this logical arrangement is the wrong way round: it is not so serious for a short-term prisoner to be at a distance from his home for a few weeks or months, but in the course of a long sentence relatives and friends find the continual travelling a heavy burden which many of them cannot bear. Any long-term restructuring of the prison system should take account of this factor; if it becomes possible to close any prisons, the remote ones should be the first to go, even if they are the newest.

Even better than visits as a way of preserving contact is to allow home leave as a regular feature of prison sentences. These are a part of penal policy in some American states, and in Scandinavia; the Howard League (1979a, pp.30–31) shows that failure rates are low, and lower still (from 9% to below 1%) if minor problems such as lateness or returning drunk are excluded. The League's report suggested a modest start in which all prisoners would be entitled to twelve days' leave per year: almost from the beginning of short sentences, after one-third of longer ones. Leave would not be automatic, but those who were refused on grounds of risk of absconding or committing serious offences would be allowed to leave prison a corresponding number of days early at the end of their sentences.

For those who cannot be allowed home leave, the commonly suggested alternative is that the prisoner's wife should be allowed unsupervised, so-called 'conjugal' visits to him (see for example Short, 1979). This is allowed in over twenty countries, but has been strongly opposed in Great Britain by Home Office officials and ministers. The reasons for the strength of this opposition are not clear; apart from the problems of security and contraband, it may be that officials see the scheme as a potential administrative headache, or that they are bowing to resistance from hard-line elements in the Prison Officers' Association. There are admittedly potential difficulties with such a scheme. In Sweden, for example, since visits can last only up to six hours, some wives feel embarrassed because 'everyone knows what they are there for.' A decision has to be made as to who should be admitted to unsupervised visits: either they are restricted to wives and common-law wives, which would require an administrative system for verifying marriage or co-habitation, and would expose the authorities to the charge that they were acting as arbiters of morals; or girl-friends and even prostitutes are admitted, which could entail security problems and could be accused of condoning promiscuity. Fears are sometimes expressed that other inmates might be resentful, though in practice this has not been found a serious problem. Of course, security *is* also a real difficulty, but precautions must not be carried to excess. As the Howard League has put it, 'It should always be remembered that the ultimate purpose of prison is to preserve a civilized society, and that purpose is negated if the means of trying to achieve it fall below civilized standards'. Searches can be carried out tactfully, for example by requiring the prisoner to change into his own clothes for the visit: they can be searched when handed back. Visitors could be required to pass a metal detector.

The Howard League (1979a) has suggested that when there are children they should be allowed to visit, so as to help to preserve family bonds; the visits should last at least 24 hours, and take place in attractively furnished cottages or caravans away from other prison buildings, or in a separate prison establishment used for the purpose. The scheme could be introduced on a small scale at first, for long-sentence prisoners with stable marriages; in the light of this experience, and that of other countries, it could be extended. There are of course, sadly, many people in prison who have neither family nor friends to write or visit them, and others whose contacts wither away during their sentences. For them voluntary prison visitors and letter-writers could be found: if prison officers were encouraged to help to recruit these helpers, it could constitute an extension of a welfare role within their work.

When the prison population is reduced it should be possible to improve the physical conditions, using architectural design to create buildings in which security was not oppressive, and life could be lived as normally as possible in the circumstances, with facilities for work, meetings, education, recreation, and other activities which should make easier the eventual transition back to the community. One prison where architecture is claimed to have had a beneficial influence is Leesburg, New Jersey, which has a large amount of glass, and the dining room – often the focus for trouble in prisons – has a high ceiling that seems to dissipate heat and noise. Officers also thought the design and the glass promoted good behaviour by inmates (Nagel, 1973, pp.90–91). Not that modern architecture is in all ways an improvement: Victorian prisons with all their faults have a certain spaciousness, and new buildings are no guarantee of a progressive régime.

A Modern Role of Prison Management

With or without new architecture, how should the residual prisons be managed? Their task will be an inherently difficult one if the remaining prisoners are serving long sentences. As the length of sentence is increased, so is the likelihood of troublesome behaviour; courts can legitimately be asked to take this factor into account. For example, in Hull prison, men serving over seven years comprised 36% of the population, but 57% of the group considered 'troublesome' (Pope, 1976; Pope & Gibbens, 1979). No doubt in some cases this is partly because of the sort of person they are, but to some extent their response in prison (and probably after release) is the product of the length of their sentences. Judges should not make the task of the prisons more difficult by imposing long sentences without strong evidence that there is benefit to the public sufficient to outweigh the extra problems and possibly danger that could result. At the same time, prison management should not add to its problems by the strict regimentation which persists in some prisons, combined with considerable use of punishments and control measures such as segregation, or sudden transfer to other institutions. Not only do these techniques unsettle prisoners and risk making them *more* resentful and difficult (as Pope notes and visitors to the Howard League corroborate), but as long as they are permitted, prison management has less incentive to evolve new methods.

One simple improvement would be the payment of special merit awards to staff, for example to a prison governor who had pioneered a new scheme for grievance resolution or involvement of the local community; this would enable him to stay in the post for long enough to see it through without sacrificing the increase in salary which he could have obtained through promotion. Awards of this kind are, I understand, normally paid to government scientists who have made a discovery. Another aid to stability would be what is known in the jargon as 'fluid complementing' in middle grades, allowing promotion without transfer to another post. The prison service should make better use of its human resources: for example, a prison could encourage participation by forming an 'ideas committee' (*New Society*, 15 March 1979) drawn from staff at all levels – and, where security was not involved, from prisoners. Although admittedly an authoritarian structure needs to be retained because of the requirements of security, the service should adapt its style to the changing industrial climate in the outside world. One textbook on management, for example, recommends 'an acceptance by management of the need to extend joint decision-making within the enterprise. It will mean abandoning traditional employer beliefs about sacred subjects, or reserved areas of decision-making, that must always remain beyond union influence' (McCarthy and Ellis, 1973, p.184). This is certainly needed in the relations of prison management to staff, especially if the staff in turn are to be asked to adopt a similar approach to prisoners. 'What is proposed,' these authors say, 'is not a system of workers' control [or control by staff or inmates] but it is the most meaningful way of promoting the aims of workers' participation in management and the ideals of industrial democracy' (p. 185). An industrial democracy is what many prison officers and prisoners have worked in before, and some prisoners will return to; there is no reason why prisons should be more out of step with the rest of society than is inevitable from their nature, and indeed if they drag their feet they will be storing up trouble for themselves. The régime at Grendon, to be described below, although based on therapeutic ideas, approaches a democratic model and is one of the more trouble-free institutions.

The reorganization announced by the Home Secretary after the May Report could lead to improvements in prison management, although first signs are that it is being used to increase the centralized control over prison governors. However, it could be used to explore ways of reducing the preoccupation with security which has dominated Prison Department policy since the Mountbatten Report of 1966. It is to be hoped that he will establish a policy of consulting both staff and inmates. To this end, it is worth looking briefly at three examples, from Sweden, England and Scotland respectively, which already exist and may suggest useful frameworks from which new methods could be developed.

In Sweden, prisoners were given, in 1968, the right to form prisoners' councils (and incidentally the right to vote in ordinary elections). But in 1968 to 1970 there were strikes, protesting among other things at the refusal of a governor to participate in prisoners' council activities. The maximum security prison at Österåker became involved, and a hunger strike spread to half the prison population. The authorities made various concessions regarding visits, home leaves, censorship and the use of telephones, as well as for prisoners' councils themselves. Staff, however, not surprisingly objected particularly to the last of these developments, which meant that prisoners could negotiate direct with management over their heads; as a result, institution councils have now been set up in place of prisoners' councils (Marnell, 1981, p.134). Thus the authorities have built into the system a method for making decisions and resolving problems by discussion, involving both inmates and staff, and it now appears to be working relatively smoothly, at least for day-to-day matters. These events have been described by participants from an official point of view (Marnell, 1974) and a more radical one (Mathiesen, 1974).

The English example is Grendon Underwood prison. Visitors there find, as I did, an atmosphere different from that in most prisons, where visitors are usually escorted round by a member of staff, and introduced to the officer in charge of the kitchen, the workshop, or the wing. When I visited Grendon, by contrast, I was not escorted, and the assistant governor would not even direct me to the most interesting parts of the prison to visit: he suggested that I walk down the central corridor and consult any officers or prisoners I happened to meet. Later I was invited to attend an informal meeting of any prisoners, staff or visitors who wished to attend it, and one of the formal wing meetings which form a focal point of the régime. There are also small group therapy meetings, wing staff meetings at which prison officers and other staff can exchange information and support each other; and inter-wing staff meetings. In other words, very high value is set on communication on all relevant subjects, including prisoners' behaviour and the prison régime, and both prisoners and staff are closely involved. Whereas a prisoner at an ordinary prison who explodes with abuse towards an officer would find himself 'on report' next day, at Grendon, although it is open to staff to take such action, their usual way of handling such an incident was to try to bring into the open the emotions that had caused the outburst. This approach is reflected in inter-staff relationships. Decisions are made by vote or consensus, not by order; Gunn (1978, p.79) was told of a case where a doctor had been outvoted by officers regarding the desirability of keeping a man at Grendon, and accepted their decision. Grendon's population is selected because of psychiatric disturbance and other difficulties. Over half have committed acts of violence which are more than minimal, and a third have been involved in episodes of violence which have seriously endangered another person's life or health. It is true that Grendon inmates are considered to need treatment, and many of them desire it (but not by any means all); it is true also, as governors of other prisons are ready to point out, that prisoners who are too disruptive or too mad for Grendon are 'ghosted' out to ordinary prisons which do not have such a favourable staffing ratio but have to cope with them as best they can.

It seems in principle, however, that what is done in Grendon for therapeutic reasons could be done, without loss of control, in many if not all ordinary prisons as a style of management which develops responsibility in inmates and respects the dignity of both inmates and staff. It should also be in the interests of prison management, because the frequent communication should help to resolve the tensions and suspicions that can cause such trouble in prison life; Grendon has a very low level of violence and has been remarkably free of the major disturbances which have erupted in many other British prisons in recent years (Gunn, 1978, pp.57, 67, 80–81, 157–8). A committee system for ordinary prisons would have to be different from that at Grendon, which is focused on therapy and attitudes rather than on decision making. There would have to be safeguards, for example, to ensure that power was not monopolized by a small number of inmates; this might be done by providing for staff participation and frequent elections. The extent of democratic participation would be limited by the authorities' responsibility for security and for maintaining order within the institution, in addition to financial constraints and possibly apprehensions on the part of the staff union. There is nevertheless great scope for such developments, which could be encouraged by medical officers if they would use their considerable influence to secure modifications to the régime for the benefit of general mental health, and to take account of the disturbed inmates in particular.

The third example is another specialized institution, but very relevant to the remaining prisoners who may be in prison because they are considered difficult and dangerous, and may become still more difficult because they face long prison sentences. A number of such men were in the Scottish prisons in the early 1970s. The authorities saw that the traditional method of control by force, putting the prisoners in the infamous 'cages' of Peterhead prison, and other special security units, simply made things worse; on one occasion indeed the prisoners succeeded in smashing the partition walls in the new unit (Boyle, 1977). The proposal they came up with materialized as the special unit in Barlinnie prison. It is a small top-security unit in the middle of an old, grim prison. The unit, by contrast, is run on two basic principles: that life in prison should bear as close a relation to the outside world as is possible in the circumstances, and that people generally respond well if they are treated well. The story has become almost a legend, and is well told by the unit's most famous inmate Jimmy Boyle in his book, *A Sense of Freedom* (1977). At first the prisoners were suspicious that the authorities were playing some trick on them, which would lead to still further punishment and degradation. The staff, too, were wary, as well they might be when all the first batch of inmates had histories of serious violence both outside and inside prison. But regular meetings were held at which mutual distrust could be worked through; and it was on the issue of trust that the breakthrough came. A cell had been reserved for refractory prisoners; at one meeting prisoners challenged the staff, saying that if the staff trusted the inmates such a relic of control by physical force should not be necessary. The staff, persuaded in their heads though not yet in their hearts, agreed; the heavy door was taken off its hinges and the cell used to store weight-lifting equipment and other potentially lethal implements. Since then Jimmy Boyle has gone on to become a well-known sculptor, write a book, and marry, and the unit has held, with minimal violence, a number of less headline-catching inmates. It has not been without its critics, such as politicians who thought it was being 'soft' with serious criminals, and prison officers who felt that it undermined the traditional ways of running prisons – as indeed it does. The Scottish authorities have even talked of 'normalizing' it; by this they mean making life inside it approximate not, as might be supposed, more closely to the real world than it does already, but to 'normal' prisons. They have also said that the prison officer who has been associated with the unit from the start, Ken Murray, should return to the 'mainstream' of the prison service, and have transferred him to a small prison which can only be described as a backwater. Despite these inscrutable actions, the unit continues to attract attention and visitors from far and wide. It is possible that the legend has outgrown the reality, and that attempts to replicate the project may lack some essential trace element that was present in the chemistry of the prototype. Nevertheless, many people inside and outside the prison service intuitively feel that if anyone must be locked up for long periods, these or something like them are the conditions under which it should be done. The ordinary régime, then, should be so planned that many of the misunderstandings and disagreements that arise can be dealt with in a routine way, generally by raising them at regular meetings, or by the personal intervention of a member of staff. Staff should receive special training, if possible through exchange of experience with other services such as nursing staff in psychiatric hospitals, in preventing or 'de-fusing' violent situations; and there should be regular opportunities to discuss incidents and consider whether they might have been handled better. This is admittedly easier said than done, since the prisoners who remain are likely to include the most difficult, mentally disturbed, politically hostile, and those who try to dominate other prisoners; but progress must surely lead in the directions described above, rather than towards increasing reliance on force, drugs, or segregation in prisons within prisons.

Security

A separate though related problem is the prevention of escapes. Extreme security, like extreme deterrence, can be achieved only at the cost of humanly unacceptable measures. Prisoners in high security are by definition likely to be subjected to it for a long time; security should therefore not lose its human face. The $50 million Community Correctional Center at New Orleans, for example, is an electronically operated masterpiece where warders are separated from prisoners by glass panels and they have to speak to each other through intercommunication systems: a misuse of technology which widens the gap between captive and captor (Harding, 1980). The danger that control methods, such as searches, can become demeaning or harassing, has already been referred to: staff should be warned of this in their training, governors should control it, and prisoners should be enabled to make effective complaints if it happens. It has been suggested that it is wrong to attempt to achieve 100% security, because that would be destructive of the human spirit and, more pragmatically, because if prisoners can no longer contemplate escape, they are more likely to devote their energies to getting their own back on the system through its nearest representatives, the staff. As Lord Mountbatten pointed out, social and psychological factors are also important aids to security (Home Office, 1966, paras. 318 ff.). One experienced prison governor has echoed this to me recently, saying: 'I think that with increasing control and preoccupation with negative security the prison service may be laying down the foundations of troubles they could well do without. No one ever seems to think that good security is a by-product of sensible balanced treatment, something I learnt many years ago.' Another has written: 'As soon as security is the focus of interest, and when it mainly rests on mechanical arrangements that are developed beyond a certain limit, security no longer works and may prove to be counterproductive.' (Marnell, 1981, p.144). Moreover, as we have seen, the ultimate aim of prison is to preserve essential standards in society, and the means used must conform to those standards, or the whole exercise is in vain.

The problem is, then, how to hold those few prisoners for whom the greatest security is necessary, in conditions which are not oppressive to them or other prisoners. The Mountbatten report (Home Office 1966) concluded that those whose escape would be a danger to the public or an embarrassment to the government should be 'concentrated' in one or perhaps two prisons of maximum security.

To those who say that such a prison would become an 'Alcatraz', a fortress in which staff would have to maintain an intolerably tough régime in order to control the prisoners, it is replied that the prisoners whose escape must be prevented are not necessarily also the most difficult to manage, as is sometimes assumed. In current English policy less than 300 maximum security ('Category A') prisoners are dispersed among a much larger number of Category Bs and Cs in seven 'Dispersal' prisons with a total capacity of about 3,000; this breaches the principle that no one should be held under greater security restrictions than are warranted by his danger to the community if he escaped, as has been persuasively argued by King and Morgan (1980, Chapter 3). Some of the Category A prisoners have high status within the prison community and use it to tyrannize over others, which they would be less able to do in a prison where the other inmates were of their own kind. It is conceded that the 'concentration' policy could have serious disadvantages for the maximum security prisoners: they would have to spend their long sentences with almost no variation of surroundings or companions, and if they fell out with each other, or the staff, there would be nowhere else to go, unless to a prison within a prison such as the 'bunker' at Kumla, Sweden (Marnell, 1981). It is argued, however, that such a balance of disadvantage must surely be resolved in favour of the majority, who are also the less serious offenders. But if this conclusion is accepted, it must be *only on condition that safeguards for the long-term prisoners are rigorously upheld* as regards their conditions and complaints procedure. Their contacts with the outside world must also be preserved, for example by generous arrangements to facilitate travel by friends and relatives on visits.

The contrary case is that in such a prison safeguards would probably be eroded in the name of security, and it would be difficult to provide a sufficient range of activities, especially in countries with few prisoners of this type. Very small prisons with only a few high-risk prisoners may be unavoidable at some future date when these are the only offenders sent to prison at all; in the meantime, however, a more varied régime should be maintained. It has been shown that this can be done within a secure perimeter, without undue restrictions on prisoners of lower security ratings; extra security checks are imposed on selected prisoners only, as has long been done with prisoners on the 'escape list.' Insofar as the existing dispersal prisons are repressive, this is because some of them are remote, which would not be affected by a change in their security rating; and because some governors run an over-strict régime – but others have shown not only that this is unnecessary but that a less rigid policy can actually reduce the pressures towards riots and escapes. The maximum security prisoners tend to get better physical facilities, to help them to avoid becoming 'vegetables', and prisoners in lower security categories share the benefit of these. As for bullying, this is just as likely to be done by Category Bs, and can be countered by an open régime. But security should not, as at present, prevent low-security prisoners from leaving the prison for work or education.

There is another factor which weighs heavily with the authorities. Since the dispersal policy was invented, a considerable number of prisoners have been received whose offences were motivated by political hostility to the State. They are dedicated to fighting the authorities, and the more there are in any one prison, the more the authorities fear that they will cause major disorder and damage – as when three IRA men removed a roof in Parkhurst prison in March 1979. For them, the present dispersal policy is felt to be the only humane alternative to isolating them in small, claustrophobic segregation units. The small numbers involved and the seriousness of their crimes would not make this any less of an affront to human rights.

To summarize: a dispersal prison can be run in a way that does not impose excessive restrictions on prisoners of any security category; admittedly it could also be run repressively, but this is less likely to happen than in a 'concentration' prison. A policy of 'concentration', on the other hand, might spare Category B and C prisoners from some of the restrictions imposed in the name of security, but would not necessarily do so; and there would be a much greater risk that they would be imposed, to an intolerable degree, on the small number of top-security prisoners.

Looking further into an idealistic future, in which only those who pose a major threat to society are put in prison, what should their conditions be? If people are to be detained 'as a punishment and not for punishment,' and still more if protection of the public supersedes punishment as the primary aim, it follows that the place of detention should bear little relation to most present-day prisons, but should allow as nearly as possible normal life with a wall round it. There would be a secure perimeter to minimize escapes, but inside would be something approximating to a housing estate or a village. Normal economic activity of an industrial or agricultural kind would be encouraged, and family life for those whose families were willing to join them. There are precedents for correctional colonies of this kind in various countries (a Pakistani one is described by Hamiduzzafar, 1977, pp.125 ff.), but most are open: the difference would be the secure outer fence. Proposals of these lines have been made, but not worked out in detail, by for example Bowker (1980, pp.176–177) and Kane (1980).

Prison Rules – O.K.?

Even if prisons are run with maximum participation, inevitably some prisoners will claim that they have been improperly treated, that staff have broken the rules or interpreted them unfairly, or that the rules themselves are oppressive. It is on the procedures that are available to settle problems of this kind that prisoners and society will judge the fairness of the whole system. The rules which the prisoner must obey must be as precise as possible: he should not be in the position of not knowing what the rule is until he is on report for breaking it, and he should be made aware of the procedural safeguards available to him.

There must also be rules which the authorities have to obey. These too should be reasonably precise, embodying basic standards, not unrealistically higher than the present state of the prisons, and with a minimum of escape clauses (such as 'the governor may at his discretion', 'as far as possible'). A basis for such a set of rules is outlined by King and Morgan (1980, pp.38–39); several are suggested in this book.

Given a fair and practicable code of rules, the first requirement is that the prisoner should know them, as John Howard recognised. In Britain a copy of those prison rules that affect a prisoner is, or should be, placed in each cell; but a prisoner wishing to see the complete rules, including those which place requirements on staff, must ask permission. The Prison Standing Orders are not available to the public, let alone to prisoners. No doubt an equally unsatisfactory situation prevails in many other countries. Recently, however, the Prison Department has placed in each prison copies of its procedural rules for prison disciplinary hearings, and since 1978 the Standard Minimum Rules for the Treatment of Prisoners issued by the Council of Europe (adapted from the original United Nations rules) which surely is a step in the right direction, provided no one obstructs prisoners' access to them.

The second requirement is that the inmate should be able to seek redress if he claims that any rule is not being observed. The British system is an example of one which on paper provides considerable safeguards, but is inadequate in practice. A prisoner with a grievance can apply to the prison governor, and, if he is still dissatisfied, to the Board of Visitors (whose functions were described in Chapter Three). Prisoners, however, generally see them as an extension of authority, largely because they also have the task of adjudicating on serious disciplinary offences, and can impose substantial punishments: for this reason the Jellicoe Report proposed that the two functions be separated (Howard League and others, 1975).

The third requirement is that the prisoner should be able to inform someone outside the prison of his plight, so that it can be independently investigated. Prisoners are not allowed to complain to a Member of Parliament or a lawyer unless they have complained internally as described on p. 69; but if staff were illegally to prevent them from doing these things, they would have no means of informing anyone. At the very least the prisoner should be allowed to communicate without censorship to a member of his country's parliament or a lawyer (and there should be financial assistance for legal costs). But there is no satisfactory solution short of the virtual abolition of censorship, with only the exceptions described earlier in this chapter: the human need to reduce prisoners' isolation and the legal need to safeguard their basic rights both point to the same conclusion.

Would Prisoners Protest Too Much?

Prison administrators and governors sometimes defend restrictions on prisoners' access to external redress by conjuring up a nightmare in which they would spend half their time replying to sensational allegations in the press or dealing with court cases brought by litigious prisoners who have plenty of time to concoct them. It is true that in the United States many courts have required inmates to exhaust all administrative channels for redress before bringing an action (Bernstein, 1976, p.788). But the fact that the courts make this stipulation, rather than the prison authorities who are involved in the dispute, makes a crucial difference: it remains open to the court to decide that the inmate had good reason not to seek internal redress, such as suspicion that, given warning, members of staff might collude in preparing (or destroying) evidence; fear of harassment; or the fact that if he is challenging the rules themselves the authorities are unlikely to admit that the rules are at fault (Bernstein, p.789). In Britain another check on frivolous litigation is that prisoners would not be granted legal aid for trivial cases (Howard League, 1979b). A further reason for the restrictions, and probably a more potent one, is the fear that prison officers might be harassed by legal action by prisoners. Prison officers are concerned about this, as references in the *Prison Officers' Magazine* show (e.g., March 1979, p.50; September 1979, p.307; May 1980, p.173). The Prison Department has not shown itself anxious to force the issue, in view of the difficulties of industrial relations. When, for example, the European Court of Human Rights held that this country had breached the European Convention in the case of *Golder* v. *United Kingdom*, the occasion could have been used to introduce substantial improvements in the rules relating to prisoners' contacts with the outside world; instead, the rules were modified in a way which fell far short of giving prisoners unrestricted access to the law, and in the case of Silver and others the European Commission has again decisively condemned British practice as regards censorship of letters, access to courts, and provision of an effective remedy. The rules have now been reformed, but censorship has by no means been abolished.

It is not surprising if some staff are apprehensive when what they see as safeguards are removed, with nothing put in their place. It is the responsibility of the Prison Department, through training and leadership, to demonstrate that, in the words of John Howard, there is 'a way of managing some of the most desperate, with ease to yourself, and advantage to them' (Howard, 1792, p.39). The availability of adequate work and other activities for inmates is obviously a desirable basis for a good atmosphere in prisons. Beyond that, there should be a preventive policy in relation to staff-inmate friction: that is, to identify situations in which it can arise, and to develop formal and informal ways of preventing those concerned from taking up positions which it is difficult to modify without loss of face. At one establishment, for example, an argumentative inmate who was treated with scrupulous correctness grudgingly admitted to the governor: 'You have denied me the right to hate you' (*Prison Service Journal*, 1975 January, p.10) – which should surely be included among the aims of prisons. It should be possible to explore with staff the ways of abolishing unnecessary rules and handling situations so as not to engender resentment or use force where persuasion could have succeeded. Prison officers, in their brief (thirteen-week) training, learn to rely on the rule book, and at least until they acquire experience and maturity, may tend to regard breaches of the rules as challenges to authority, to which the standard response is punishment. If staff are imbued with this attitude but the governor is not, there is a danger that they will dismiss him as 'soft' and inflict unofficial punishments on prisoners. Training programmes should be revised accordingly, and steps taken wherever possible to prevent the traditional staff sub-culture from perpetuating itself and neutralizing the sound precepts of the training school. The best opportunity to do this is at the opening of a new or re-furbished institution: the first staff and inmates can be hand-picked and develop a new ethos.

Clearing the Air: How Prisoners Can Ventilate a Grievance

When, however, incidents and complaints do arise, the first need is for some method of 'troubleshooting'. At the simplest this can consist of one person, like the Institutional Complaint Investigator appointed to the staff of all state correctional institutions in Wisconsin under the three-tier grievance procedure initiated in 1972. He personally screens all complaints within 24 hours, attempts to mediate, and reports within five days to the warden (National Association of Attorneys General, 1974). A more elaborate first-level procedure is included in the system designed for Massachusetts Correctional Institution, Concord. If inmates cannot resolve grievances through appropriate staff members, which they are encouraged to do in the first instance, they can refer them to the Committee for Institutional Improvement. This consists of two inmates, selected from the elected inmate council for periods of two weeks; two staff members appointed by the superintendent; and a non-voting chairman from a panel of outside volunteers.

If this initial attempt at resolution does not satisfy the inmate, most of the schemes provide for further stages, involving the governor of the institution, the higher administration, and an independent element or recourse to the courts. The details vary – what matters is the principles (McGillis and others, 1976). Some of the most important are: that inmates and uniformed staff should be involved in the design of the scheme; that it should be relatively simple to understand and properly explained to staff and inmates; that decisions should be given in writing, with reasons; that all complaints should be answered; that there should be a time limit for each stage of the process, and the inmate should be entitled to proceed to the next stage if he received no reply in time; that there should be outside review; that the administration should be committed to the scheme;

and that a copy of the grievance should not be included in the prisoner's parole dossier. It is also desirable to conduct surveys among inmates from time to time to assess whether they still have confidence in the scheme (Keating, 1975; Hepburn and Laue, 1980; Denenberg, n.d.). Where prisoners are liable to substantial punishment they should be allowed to be represented – not necessarily by a lawyer. Ideally the proceedings should be open to press and public, but this might have to be reconsidered if too many prisoners made the system unworkable by 'playing to the gallery'.

Implicit in this approach towards government with the consent of the governed, as far as possible in the circumstances, is a reliance less on severe punishments and more on rewards, in order to uphold prison discipline. The state should discourage the use of force by its own example. The use of fetters and darkened cells is already condemned by the United Nations Standard Minimum Rules; solitary confinement should be progressively reduced until it, also, can be abolished. The longest permissible period of administrative segregation 'for the maintenance of good order and discipline' should also be progressively lowered to an absolute minimum, and the criteria for using it more closely defined; those who are segregated should not be deprived of any rights or privileges except that of associating with other prisoners. It is not to be denied that this approach requires skilful implementation. One danger is that, given an adequate degree of control over their own lives, the stronger prisoners may also dominate the weaker. Also to be avoided is the collusion whereby staff turn a blind eye to certain things if inmates enforce among themselves the unwritten rules, such as obeying the written ones when an officer is looking. Discipline should be based on the positive principle that inmates should have tolerable conditions which they are unwilling to forfeit; insofar as punishments are used, they should consist of fines and the loss of privileges, not deprivation of rights. As was seen in Chapter Two the distinction between rights and privileges is difficult to draw in practice, but it is not impossible; what is important is that even privileges should not be withdrawn arbitrarily, and that if they are, the prisoner should have effective means of redress.

A further concern is the procedure by which the alleged 'subversives' are segregated – the prison equivalent of detention without trial. A person identified as a 'subversive' should have adequate opportunity to state his case; one who has decided to change his ways should be given the chance to do so. Other methods of containing such people should be sought, such as democratic structures capable of enabling other prisoners to prevent one of their number from dominating others, or conversely to make it unnecessary for anyone to confront the authorities in order to resolve a grievance.

Access to Records

It is vital, too, that régimes should be much more open, both internally and in the contact they allow with the outside world. Internally, prisoners should, unless there are compelling reasons to the contrary, be allowed to see the files that are kept on them. It is too much to suggest that the captors should have no secrets from the captives, but these should normally be limited to what is directly necessary to prevent escape. If a prisoner is suspected of being a troublemaker, either the suspicion is correct, in which case his record will be a factual account of what is held against him and there is no reason why he should not see it; or he is wrongly suspected, in which case there is a possibility that rumours and hearsay have been included in his file and he should have the opportunity to refute them. As regards welfare reports, social workers are beginning to adopt the practice of agreeing with their clients the contents of reports about them. This must make those who write reports more careful. Some prisoners are strongly suspicious that misstatements on their files have prevented their being granted parole, and in the present system they cannot be proved wrong: we have seen in Chapter Three what some prisoners think of the files that are kept on them.

There are two main objections to this approach. Firstly, prisoners may challenge statements which are accurate but uncomplimentary, or staff will refrain from recording critical comments, and perhaps maintain unofficial files which might be concealed even from a public inquiry or ombudsman. This appears generally to have fewer dangers, in the view of those like myself who have confidence in the capacity of trained and experienced staff to recognize ethical dilemmas and by degrees to develop standards of practice to cope with them. If the inmate disagrees with their version he should be allowed to record his own in the same file. Secondly, it is possible that there can in a very few cases be information which it is not in the prisoner's interest that he should know. This argument must however be used very sparingly. If his wife has left him, or his mother had refused to have him at home, or his mental balance is in doubt, would it be damaging for him to know the truth? What if information has been given to the prison authorities in confidence? A safeguard suggested in relation to Mental Health Review Tribunals is that the patient should have a capable and experienced representative to whom such information would be given in confidence, so that he could, if necessary, challenge it on the patient's behalf (Committee on Mental Health Review Tribunal Procedure, 1978). A similar arrangement could be made in the case of prisoners. The difficulty with this is that unless the process were adopted for all prisoners wishing to see their files, which would be a major administrative exercise, it would be used only for those with sensitive statements in their files, in which case they would not just be left wondering, as at present, but would know for a fact that such statements had been made and were being withheld from them. Another model is followed by industrial tribunals, where the House of Lords has held that applicants should not have an automatic right to see confidential files, but only those which a county court judge or tribunal chairman considered necessary (*Daily Telegraph*, 2 November 1979). This would be satisfactory provided that all concerned have confidence in the discretion and impartiality exercised by the chairman or judge. On balance, full disclosure except for strictly security reasons seems to offer the fewest disadvantages.

The importance of external contacts has been stressed for humanitarian reasons; but it is also important as a safeguard. The ultimate protection of the prisoner is to be able to let someone outside know of his plight. The objections offered by administrators are not without substance, as we have seen; but injustices can occur even in humanely run prisons with elaborate grievance procedures – and all the more in the many prisons which still fall short of those standards. Secrecy inevitably makes people ask 'what have the authorities got to hide?'; and that is not good for justice.

A Prisoners' Union

One way to press for increased safeguards would be through the formation of a prisoners' union. This would, after all, be a reflexion of a well-established feature of the outside world. It should be remembered, however, that unions were born of conflict. In the nineteenth century employers resisted the very existence of unions; in the 1920s Ernest Bevin found it useless to appeal to employers' sense of justice, humanity or even long-term identity of interests with their workpeople, and could force them and the Government to pay attention only through 'counter-assertion of power' (Bullock, 1960). One of the most recent battles for the right to form a union was fought against the Home Office by the Prison Officers' Association (Cronin, 1967), which does not, however, believe that prisoners should have one. Today, belatedly, there is much interest in profit-sharing and other forms of industrial democracy which, if they had been introduced in the last century might have made it unnecessary to resort to the formation of unions in order to secure fair treatment. The inference from these historical parallels is this. Prisons, despite their isolation, are not immune from the influence of society; as more politically aware, better educated prisoners come into the system, they are going to demand an up-to-date style of prison management. The Home Office has a choice. It can move with the times by introducing a degree of participation through staff/inmate committees, grievance-resolving procedures, and similar measures designed to avert most kinds of problems before they fester. Or it can allow itself to be pushed into tolerating the formation of a prisoners' union, which – in my view – would be less satisfactory than a good participatory style of management, since it would confirm the polarization of 'us' and 'them' instead of seeking to show that even between prisoners and staff there can be a degree of legitimate community of interest. Or, lastly, it can risk staff/inmate friction, periodic riots and possible bloodshed by trying to prop up an anachronistic structure which is ill-suited both to trouble-free management and to preparing prisoners for their return to the modern world. As an American penologist has said, 'Men who can negotiate their own fates do not have to turn to violence as a method of achieving change' (Fogel, 1978).

The Process of Release

At the beginning of this chapter it was suggested that prison régimes should look forward to the prisoner's release; special attention needs to be given to the process of release itself. This includes the decision of when to release, as well as preparation for release.

Parole

The question whether sentences should be for a fixed period or able to be modified through release on parole is a complex one which cannot be studied in detail here. The idea that sentences should be for a fixed period is based on strict proportionality of punishment to offence; the idea that a person should be released earlier if he appears unlikely to re-offend is incompatible with that, for it is based on the principle that people can change their attitudes during their sentence and should then be released. But even if that be accepted, the proposition that it is possible to tell, in a reasonable majority of cases, when this change has taken place receives little support from research findings. Many of the factors which have been shown to be associated with future reconviction, such as the number of previous convictions or the age at first conviction, are already known at the time of sentence. They could therefore be used in determining the sentence, making all the labour of compiling and reading parole dossiers unnecessary (but of course they bear no necessary relation to the gravity of the current offence, which is the traditional basis for sentencing). A person's behaviour in prison by itself gives little indication of whether he is likely to re-offend (Tucker, in press). Good home circumstances and employment prospects, insofar as these can be forecast while the person is still in prison, may be assumed to be associated with a favourable prognosis; but if those who have them are released earlier than those who have not, it is tantamount to giving favourable treatment to those who are already the more fortunate. It is inescapable that in a parole system the length of time spent in prison is affected by other criteria besides the seriousness of the offence. Two people may have committed very similar offences, but one may spend longer in prison for some reason outside his control, for example, that he was brought up in institutions or has been disowned by his family, and is therefore a 'worse risk' than the other. This cannot be defended on grounds of justice; if it is to be justified on grounds of public interest, a convincing case must be made out.

These dilemmas are inherent in the concept of parole; but the English parole scheme is further criticized for its criteria and its procedure. Much misunderstanding is caused by the fact that there are three independent criteria for parole, and that a person may, for example, be apparently a good risk, and have behaved well in prison, but still not be granted parole, possibly because the Parole Board regards his offence as being of a serious kind. Another contradiction is that since ex-prisoners generally receive no compulsory supervision unless they are paroled, some worse risks are apparently paroled earlier in order to make sure that they are supervised. In other cases, those considered poor risks are given little or no parole, and hence little or no supervision; whereas good risks are released earlier and are therefore supervised for a longer period after release.

As for the procedure, it is hard to justify the Parole Board's refusal to give reasons for withholding parole. The explanations usually given are that reasons would be difficult to formulate, except in a stereotyped way, and that there might be cases where it was not in the prisoner's interest that certain facts should be revealed to him. There may also be a fear that reasons would be challenged. Some sort of review is necessary, as with any administrative system, to ensure that the relevant documents are all present and contain no inaccuracies; and a person should have a proper hearing before his parole is revoked. Both these complex problems, parole and the prolonged detention of the so-called 'dangerous' offender, have been studied in recent Howard League reports.

Preparation for Release

Preparation for release has been developed in Sweden, where prisons have committees including representatives of staff, prisoners, local employers and trade unions to consider prisoners' employment prospects. Whether or not they are effective in finding jobs, the committees do something to educate the public about the effects of imprisonment. The English Prison Department accepts in principle the idea of preparing for release, but has put it into practice only on a limited scale. Over twenty-five years ago the 'hostel scheme' was started in a Bristol prison, to help prisoners re-adjust to the world of work by going out to jobs outside the prison, and receiving normal wages. It is now called the Pre-Release Employment Scheme, because in some prisons the prisoners do not live in a hostel outside the prison walls, but in a separate part of the prison itself. When it was started, the scheme was limited to prisoners serving four years or more, and the threshold has never been reduced. One reason given for the failure to expand the scheme is the difficult employment situation in this country; but as far as I know no move was made to take advantage of the government's job creation schemes, nor has PRES been extended to allow prisoners to take part in further education outside prison which would help them on release. (The number participating in any year has generally been less than a thousand.)

A rather different project is running at two prisons in the Midlands, Ranby and Ashwell, where industrial psychologists have used the skills of prison officers to prepare men for the world outside. The courses last for six weeks, and include role-play situations, group therapy, and training in everyday techniques such as replying to a job advertisement by telephone (*Observer*, 23 July 1978; Priestley, 1978). Other initiatives have been started at Pentonville prison, where prison officers help short-term prisoners to find accommodation and jobs, and Recidivists Anonymous, started by prisoners themselves to help each other over the difficulties facing them on release: the last surviving group of R.A. was closed in 1980. In none of these schemes has the Prison Department taken any substantial steps to extend them, or even to raise the morale of both the prisoners and staff taking part by publicizing them. Because so little is known about them, it is difficult to say whether these particular schemes have been successful, though the Midlands project claims that reconviction rates are substantially lower for men who have taken part. But what is certain is that schemes like these, properly planned and evaluated, should be developed for those who are still sent to prison, to help them over the disorientating transition from the artificial world of prison to outside life.

7. Bringing Change About

Human institutions will never be perfect, and should therefore be designed not as static structures but as organisms which contain their own system for continuous review and improvement. In the case of the systems for social control, it is further assumed that they should be so designed as to encourage evolution towards the least possible intervention in the lives of individuals, consistent with protecting people from each other; if that also means pressure towards less costly methods, and towards prevention, so much the better. Three aspects of the system need particular scrutiny. The executive structure should eliminate division of responsibilty, especially where this means that human beings can be shunted by one government department into institutions administered by another department that are more restrictive to them and more expensive to the taxpayer. Secondly, the structure for making and enforcing policy should be both receptive to new ideas from researchers and practitioners, and well equipped to spread information. Thirdly, the system should make the greatest use of community resources, and the minimum of scarce and expensive professional ones.

The Executive Structure: Division of Responsibility

The problems which arise from the inter-departmental division of responsibility between sections of the criminal justice system may be illustrated by examples from other areas of government. Doctors are responsible for treating their patients, but not for the allocation of funds in the National Health Service; this makes it easier for some of them to interpret 'clinical freedom' as a licence to pay little attention to cost and resources which their prescriptions demand. Courts are in an analogous position: since they are not responsible for the penal budget, they claim immunity from accusations of overspending. To take another example, there would be many financial and social advantages in encouraging people to look after elderly relatives at home by offering financial incentives large enough to allow a wife to give up work or work part time, and meet the extra costs of heating, laundry and domestic help. Among the social advantages would be that active elderly people could look after children (giving them more attention and on occasion discipline), relieving the pressure on day nurseries; houses would not be empty during the day, which would reduce the risk of burglary. The automatic financial benefits would be that every time an allowance was claimed, either a house or flat would become available or a bed in a hospital or old people's home would be freed. But these advantages would accrue to health and housing authorities, while the cost would have to be borne by, presumably, social security funds: in the absence of inter-departmental arrangements, the number of old people reluctantly living alone or in hospital is higher than it need be.

Similar divisions are built into the criminal justice system. If a boy aged 14 to 16 is refused bail before trial, the (locally funded) social service department should provide accommodation for him; but if it fails to do so, and can claim that he is 'unruly', it can effect his transfer to a (centrally funded) prison department establishment. This loophole became so notorious that after persistent parliamentary and other pressure an attempt has been made to close it by tightening the definition of 'unruliness' for boys, and requiring girls of this age to be remanded to the care of the local authority, not a prison. When the youngsters are sentenced, the same division is repeated. The juvenile court may be willing to authorize an Intermediate Treatment order, providing supervised activity in the community or a residential course of limited duration. But if social services have not developed such resources in the area, the court is left with the choice between making a care order (which many courts consider to be inadequate because it does not necessarily result in the youngster's being closely supervised or sent away to a community home) or sending the young person to a penal institution. As Morris (1978) has pointed out, this system 'imposes a financial penalty upon local authorities for undertaking the care and treatment of difficult juveniles and creates a financial reward when they avoid such youngsters':

> to the degree a Social Services Director avoids undertaking the care of difficult adolescents ... that much more money is available for the mentally ill, the mentally handicapped, and the aged. On the other hand, if the local authorities actually should reduce institutional commitments, the resultant savings would accrue to the Prison Department.

The pattern is repeated with adults. When they come to court, the probation service often makes a social inquiry report; this may make recommendations, which are usually followed, or it may pointedly refrain from doing so, in which case the offender will often be sent to prison. Then he will not take up the probation service's time, unless he asks for voluntary after-care on release. Thus instead of having, say, ten difficult cases on probation, a probation officer might end up with about half of them on after-care; the price of this easing of his load is borne by the Prison Department. But if probation officers recommend a higher proportion for probation, the probation service does not receive extra resources for the purpose. This is not the only factor which influences probation officers, but it is admitted to be one of the factors: 'some officers are known to operate a self-rationing system to prevent their case-load rising beyond the level they consider manageable' (CCPACC, 1978). Hostels for homeless alcoholics could be developed by the probation service, or local authority social services, or the Department of Health and Social Security, but, once again, the financial advantage would go to the Prison Department of the Home Office. (Two detoxification centres have been set up by the DHSS, and there has been an argument about the transfer of financial responsibility to the local authority.) A final example is provided by mentally disturbed offenders: as was explained in Chapter Four, courts can make hospital orders only if a hospital can be found willing to accept the patient. Faced with refusal by the consultants or their staff, judges have the choice of putting someone on probation, discharging him (which they are sometimes willing to do if the offence was a minor one) or sending him inappropriately to prison. There he is unlikely to receive treatment, because it is apparently the policy of the Prison Department not to provide more than a token amount of psychotherapy – to do so would weaken the Department's case for insisting that the Department of Health should shoulder its responsibility for these unfortunate people.

Thus another agency can influence the court's decision and steer unwanted customers away from itself, by claiming that it is fully subscribed or under-staffed, or already has too high a proportion of disturbed individuals, or that the individual has failed to respond on a previous occasion; but prisons cannot. (Some idea of the effect of doing so was given when prison officers refused admissions during their dispute at the end of 1980.) They are filled up with a substantial proportion of people for whom they were not designed, and when conditions become revolting enough to turn the stomach of a not very sympathetic public, the Prison Department presses its case for money to build new ones.

All these are examples of disregard of Martin's Law, which states that:

> If it is desired that more people should be allocated to Department A (for example, probation or social services) rather than to Department B (borstal, remand centre, prison, hospital), and A has a say in the allocation, the system should not be arranged in such a way that a placement in B saves A's time, trouble and expense.

The results of ignoring this law were summarized in *The Economics of Penal Policy* (Howard League 1976):

–too few community resources
  (hostels, day centres, adolescent psychiatric units, intermediate treatment schemes, etc.):
–courts, feeling that they must do *something* , impose prison sentences or detention centre orders:
–gross overcrowding leads to pressure for more penal institutions:
–the more money is spent on penal institutions, which have to be purpose-built and intensively staffed, the less is available for community projects, although most of these can deal with more people at less cost:

> Hence ... the dismal fact ... that a substantial number of our prison population is made up of the mentally disordered or maladjusted, the homeless and the elderly. At the other end of the scale, teenagers are subjected to an institutional experience which is a highly questionable way of preparing them for citizenship.

The Home Office (1977b, p.7, and elsewhere) advances the conventional counter-argument that 'The possibility of financing an increase in probation based facilities through a major shift of resources from the prison service is unrealistic; it overlooks the need for new resources to be made available to the probation service until substantial enough inroads have been made into the prison population to allow compensatory savings to be made from the prison budget.' Reformers argue that this in turn overlooks the capital sums set aside for new prisons, and the accompanying running costs, which could and should be diverted to the non-custodial sector. But even more essential are changes in the structure.

The House of Commons Expenditure Committee (1978, para. 77) appreciated this when it suggested that the DHSS should pay for the accommodation in prisons for mentally disordered offenders until such time as they can be transferred to mental hospitals. Similarly, the Howard League (1979c) has suggested that local authorities should retain financial responsibility for young persons, whatever disposal the courts select (para. 29). The League has also (1979b) suggested a similar integration of financial management of resources by the setting up of a Joint Commission for the Penal System, with a combined budget for prison and probation expenditure. Another way of doing this would be to start at the bottom instead of the top, and to require the probation service to meet the cost of every disposal, whether custodial or not. Since probation is financed partly (20%) by local authority contributions, and is supervised by local committees, this could apply some pressure towards the choice of more economical penal sanctions. With prison sentences in England and Wales averaging 11.8 months (Home Office, 1980a) the average cost per sentence is in excess of £7,000 and the 56 probation areas send an average of more than 1,000 people to prison annually; thus there would be considerable savings to be made if the number and length of prison sentences in an area could be reduced.

A Financial Incentive to Change

This might be regarded as a somewhat blunt instrument with which to effect change. A more precise approach has been developed in California, under the name California Probation Subsidy. A number of those concerned with the correctional system in the state had become convinced of the advantages of non-institutional methods. Research projects had shown that probation was no less effective in protecting the public, and that at least 25% of those currently being incarcerated could just as well be supervised 'in the local communities where the problems are, where they must be resolved, and where both the offender and the correctional agency are subject to local influences and control' (Smith, 1972). It was found, however, that simply to spend more on probation did not improve the reconviction rate or lower the incarceration rate. The idea was conceived that the state legislature, cost-conscious and not notably liberal, might be persuaded to allocate money if there were a built-in method of ensuring that fewer people would be sent to prison so that extra probation expenditure would be matched by savings in the prison budget. Projections of the prison population showed that unless something was done to change drastically the current trends, the cost of building and running enough prisons would be astronomical within a few years.

But if even 25% could be kept out, the savings would soon run into millions of dollars.

Here was a method which was no less effective than prison, allowed offenders to remain in the community without the harmful side-effects of institutions, and yet promised to save money: it was an offer the legislature could not refuse. The question was how to re-route the offenders. The Youth Authority had prepared the ground with extensive research, and one of its findings was that courts more often than not followed the recommendations of probation officers. This has been supported by research in England (for example by Hine and others, 1978). The point of decision at which to aim, therefore, need not be the court, but could be the probation officer. The method proposed was to alter the arrangement which gave probation officers no extra resources if they successfully recommended more probation orders; now they would be given funds in proportion to the number of people they kept out of prison, and the cost would come out of the the prison budget, so that the Department of Finance could see that there would be savings to match the extra expenditure. The cost of an average 8-month prison sentence at that time was $4,000. If for example in a certain county it was forecast that the number of people sent to prison in a given year would be 110, and the actual figure was only 105, the county would be able to claim $20,000 or what had actually been spent on the programme, whichever was the less. Counties were free to choose whether to join the scheme.

Several conditions were attached to the subsidies. They were not to be used merely to increase existing probation funds, to allow a few more staff to be employed and probation officers' case-loads to be reduced from the very high levels then prevailing in California. Instead, ordinary probation was to continue as before; the subsidy could be claimed only for special projects. Each scheme must use a specific allocation method for selecting suitable participants, and not proceed by hunch or determination to fill the places somehow. Minimum staffing levels were prescribed. Considerable attention was given to explaining the scheme to probation staff, related services such as the police, and the public. There must be a clearly stated plan and goals for each project; its operation must be independently evaluated. Many schemes included counselling in small groups, and others were aimed at drug abusers, those who needed remedial education, and so on. Sports and recreation could be included where there was considered to be a need for them (as with the English Intermediate Treatment). Some used offenders as paid staff helping others in their

153

rehabilitation; one even employed probationers as professional consultants to the staff, offering criticism and advice about making contact with people brought up in a different sub-culture from that of most probation officers. There were schemes offering 24-hour crisis intervention, and community education in social skills such as going for job interviews, looking after children, household budgeting, family planning, cookery and so on (Briggs, 1975).

The result, as described by Smith (1972), was that probation officers were given an incentive to reassess their work and think of ways in which they could branch out from the traditional advice-giving and case-work. Instead of hesitating to recommend probation to the courts because it would involve adding a time-consuming client to their case-load who would leave them even less time for the others, they were on the look-out for candidates for their projects, to keep the numbers up and the grants coming in. The cash grants meant that they were no longer limited in the main to full-time probation-trained staff, but could employ educators, therapists, psychologists (or, as we have seen, ex-offender advisers), for anything from one session a week to full-time. Provided the prison receptions were kept down, there was no requirement that participants be limited to probationers: people at risk can be invited to use the services provided, giving probation officers a chance to develop a new field – preventive work which, if successful, would obviously reduce the institutional population still more.

Claims for the success of probation subsidy are based, not on changes in the crime rate or reconviction rate, but on whether it influenced the allocation of offenders to probation instead of prison, and whether it saved money. It was however claimed that the reconviction rate for the first 17,000 on special probation supervision was 19%, as compared with 27% to 31% for those receiving normal supervision in the same period. It is reported that in the first five years, from 1966, $96 million worth of prison construction was cancelled, and the saving of running costs on this, and of institutions closed (or never opened after being built) amounted to over $90 million, a total of $186 million. The total expenditure on probation subsidy was $60 million, and the net saving over five years was therefore $126 million.

What are the snags? Firstly there is the objection raised by the Home Office that the 'seed money' has to be found in addition to the existing budget before the savings can begin to be made. This was solved in California by arranging for the subsidy to be paid quarterly, so that counties would be reimbursed before the end of the financial year for expenditure incurred at the beginning. After the initial period each year's expenditure could be met out of the previous year's subsidy. Secondly, there have been criticisms of the way the scheme was implemented, such as Lerman's book *Community treatment and social control* (1975), from which some people appear to have concluded that the principle itself was unsound. 'It appears,' Lerman says in his introduction, ' . . . that probation subsidy *need not be* associated with economic savings or a reduction in total institutionalization' (p.15, emphasis added). The first flying machines weren't an unqualified success either; the Californian experience could show others the pitfalls to avoid. Another objection sometimes made is that the Californian system is so different from, for example, the English that it could not be transplanted; but the basic principle of tying government grants to performance is one which no financial administrator should lightly reject. The subsidy did reverse an upward trend in the number of initial committals to State institutions. The drawbacks were, firstly, that the indeterminate sentencing laws of the time made it possible for some institutions to keep their numbers up by increasing the average length of stay. This was probably partly due to a more restrictive climate of opinion at the time, and partly to 'institutional survival' – a feeling among staff that falling numbers would lead to staff redundancies. The second drawback was that although fewer young people were sent to State institutions, the number of county facilities such as camps, schools and homes and the number of young people admitted to them went on rising, though at a slower rate than before. This is an example of a 'law' which can be observed elsewhere (with the English Community Service Order, for example): if a new tier is introduced into the scale of penal measures, in the hope of attracting downwards some of the more severe penalties, it will probably also attract upwards some of the less severe. When this is recognised, it is possible to some extent to guard against it, for example by means of criteria which schemes, and offenders allocated to them, have to meet.

The scheme also encourages flexibility in the range of facilities provided; the probation service can not only employ specialist staff but can use subsidy money to pay for individual probationers to be enrolled in services already available in the community, rather than build its own empire of facilities for offenders alone. Fees paid to existing voluntary or statutory agencies would strengthen their often inadequate funds and enable them to extend their work, for example by taking on extra staff or buying better equipment. This would benefit not only offenders but the community generally, including preventive work which would offer help to the disadvantaged before they get into trouble.

Probation subsidy had its critics, however: police objected that counties were being paid to keep offenders *on* the streets – supporters of the scheme allege that the police felt they weren't getting their share of the money; supporters also claim that it was suffering because the amount of the subsidy had lagged far behind the rising cost of imprisonment, to which it should have been linked. Be that as it may, a new County Justice Subvention Program (AB 90) was introduced in 1978, with a different scheme for allocating money to counties which do not increase their imprisonment rate. But the new scheme followed the determinate sentencing law of 1976 (mentioned in Chapter 1); committals to state institutions have been going up, but it is too soon to say whether, but for AB 90, they would have risen even faster *(Community Corrections,* 1980).

The principle of financial incentives has been taken a step further in Minnesota, by the Community Corrections Act. The state pays a subsidy to counties that set up approved schemes to care for offenders at the community level; but then the county is charged for every offender sent to state-run prisons (except for serious offenders sentenced to five years or more). Judges serve on the local advisory boards and have co-operated in stepping up the use of the less expensive community alternatives. Five per cent of the subsidy must be used for research and evaluation. So far the scheme has only been able to claim that the state's prison population has been kept steady while it has been increasing elsewhere; but the administration is optimistic for the future (Blackmore, 1978).

Policy: Encouraging New Ideas

It is the nature of bureaucracies to aspire to a relatively stable order, in which changes are introduced infrequently and only when they have been advocated with a degree of persistence and persuasiveness that suggests that they will work. But as society changes, so do people's ideas about anti-social behaviour and ways of preventing or dealing with it that are effective and tolerable, and this suggests that we would be better served by a system which actively encourages new ideas, tries them out, seeks public acceptance for them, adopts them – and then is prepared to discard them if later they're found to be ineffective or objectionable. Going too far in the direction of constant change obviously brings problems; but civil servants and the general public sometimes fail to see the dangers of not going far enough.

Coordination

The reduction in the amount of crime is the concern not only of the Home Office but of the Department of Health and Social Security (with its responsibility for juveniles, alcoholics and the mentally ill), the Department of the Environment (because of the link between homelessness and reoffending), the Department of Employment, the Department of Education and Science, the Lord Chancellor (who appoints magistrates and often makes statements about sentencing) and the Director of Public Prosecutions. Even this list is not complete. Some departments, notably the Prison and Criminal Policy Departments of the Home Office, are centralized; others have devolved their powers to local authorities which they can influence only by persuasion or by providing central funds. In some cases the head of an agency, such as a community home or psychiatric hospital, can refuse to accept an individual; health service trade unions have recently also been responsible for turning mentally ill offenders away from hospitals.

It would seem obvious that there should be good coordination between these agencies in relation to the prevention of crime and re-acceptance of offenders. But there is not. A few years ago it was announced that there would be a Joint Approach to Social Policy, with ministerial meetings on this and other fields which included the territories of several departments; but since then little has been heard of it. Then, we have had two bodies concerned with an overview of penal policy. The Advisory Council on the Penal System was set up after the dissolution of the Royal Commission on the Penal System in 1966. Its purpose was 'To make recommendations about such matters relating to the prevention of crime and the treatment of offenders as the Home Secretary may from time to time refer to it, or as the Council itself, after consulation with the Home Secretary, may decide to consider.' Its members have included judges, barristers, chief constables, trade unionists, magistrates, and others, but it has not been inter-departmental in the sense suggested above. Reports from the Council were followed by, for example, the introduction of revised policies in detention centres, and several provisions of the Criminal Justice Act 1972: compensation, criminal bankruptcy, community service orders, deferment of sentence, forfeiture of property, and driving disqualification for non-motoring crimes. Since then it has produced a major report on *Young Adult Offenders* (ACPS 1974), and one on maximum prison sentences *(Sentences of Imprisonment: A Review of Maximum Penalties* (ACPS 1978), which is still the subject of discussion – but it has never been asked to review crime prevention. Home Secretaries (or the Home Office) do not seem to have regarded the Council as an indispensable adjunct to government.

A recent study of this Advisory Council recommended that its position should be confirmed by statute (Morgan, 1979); but the government has set its face against 'quangos' (quasi-autonomous non-governmental organizations) and in January 1980 the Home Secretary announced that it would be abolished, and *ad hoc* committees set up on specific issues on which he needed advice. It is to be hoped that their composition will be more representative than, for example, the Home Office Working Party on Vagrancy and Street Offences in 1974-76, which contained no one from a relevant voluntary organization, only one member of the Department of Health and Social Security, and was almost entirely composed of Home Office officials and senior police officers.

The Home Office has arranged its own coordination, but characteristically this has been almost entirely internal. The Crime Policy Planning Organization was set up in 1974 'To co-ordinate and develop policy in the prevention of crime, the administration of justice and the treatment of offenders' (Train, 1977; see also Morris, 1980). The senior steering committee was composed of the Permanent Under-Secretary (the head of the Home Office) and other top officials, meeting six-monthly, with the working committee, the Planning Committee, meeting monthly. It did bring in part-time consultants: a statistician, and economist, a prison governor, a probation inspector, a senior police officer or others on special issues. There was also formal and informal contact with other departments, but no provision for regular membership of these specialists and other departments, who should be contributing to a joint approach to this vital area of social policy. The Committees were serviced by the full-time Crime Policy Planning Unit, which defined its task as the identification of issues, the definition of objectives, and the analysis of ways of achieving them. This definition is noticeably more theoretical than American ones tend to be, with their emphasis on measurable goals and verified achievement; admittedly the CPPU was concerned not only with analysing what ought to happen, but with ensuring that it does happen. The Unit only published one report

(Hansard [H.C.] 6 December 1979, col. *304;* 22 January 1980, col. *105-6).*

The prospects for research as an independent influence on policy making are not good in Britain at present. The Home Secretary has merged the Home Office Research Unit with the CPPU and abolished the committees (Hansard [H.C.] 17 June 1981, col. *369).* This means a reduction of staff, and some of the remaining staff have been 'outposted' to other Home Office departments; this in effect isolates them and makes it more difficult for them to obtain permission for research projects which they believe to be desirable, but which may produce findings which are regarded as inconvenient politically or from the point of view of labour relations. Despite assurances that funding of extra-mural research will continue, there are fears that it may be subject to similar constraints (for example, research that is 'intramural', in the sense of being inside prisons, appears to be regarded as sensitive and therefore unwelcome). Surprisingly, the Home Secretary's statement made no mention of research in the Prison Psychologists' service. Perhaps this is because its research is not published. The reasons for its non-publication are not clear; it is possible that there are departmental fears that the findings may be controversial, or may not stand up to academic scrutiny.

Reforming should not, however, be left to committees; it is essential to provide a structure of management and funding which encourages people to develop good ideas. One example of this, adopted to overcome division of responsibility between departments, is the California probation subsidy (described on pp.152–6) which stimulated the initiative of probation officers. The process of introducing change encounters fewest obstacles when only one department is involved: this was the position in two of the schemes described in Chapter Four. In Kent, England, only the Social Services Committee needed to be convinced that 'it was legitimate to spend as much on a family placement as the placement of the same child/young person would have cost in a residential establishment' (Hazel and Cox, 1976). Thus the director of social services and his committee had the power to close a residential establishment and use the money to pay salaries to foster parents. The other ingredient which can make for easier policy change is that the agency providing the services is the same as the one deciding the allocation. This was also present in Kent: under the Children and Young Persons Act 1969, once a care order is made by the court, the social services department can decide the youngster's placement.

Similarly, Dr. Jerome Miller's well known revolution in Massachusetts, in which nearly all the young people were transferred out of the century-old training schools to community placements, was possible because the Department of Youth Services alone had authority to decide placements after a court had committed them to its care. There were, of course, other factors, such as Miller's ability to secure the state Governor's support and to explain his ideas to the media, and the availability of a block grant from the Law Enforcement Assistance Administration to meet the cost of starting the new program before the old institutions were closed (Flackett, 1974; Rutherford, 1978).

Setting the Example and Spreading the Word

Research and information are vital in bringing about change with a properly thought-out basis, although they too do not of themselves guarantee that it will result. This was recognised, for example, in Australia, where the Criminology Research Act 1971 established, firstly, the Australian Institute of Criminology, an independent statutory body, government-funded, to carry out research and training, and to maintain a library and newspaper cuttings collection. It emphasises the two-way exchange of information with other countries. An important element is the publicity section, which disseminates research findings through newsletters, information bulletins and occasional papers. Secondly, there is a Criminology Research Fund administered by a Council (with representatives of government and States) which assesses needs in criminological research and, again, stresses the dissemination of information.

Encouragement to innovation is carried out on a large scale in the United States. Information is made widely available by the massive National Criminal Justice Reference Service, which incidentally is generous in providing services to overseas organizations. In addition the Department of Justice, through the Law Enforcement Assistance Administration (LEAA), encourages new projects by the simple but effective device of providing substantial funds to agencies which want to develop them. This does not necessarily entail extra expense, since if it is successful it can save building prisons. The LEAA's Exemplary Projects Program is described as: 'a systematic method of identifying outstanding criminal justice programs throughout the country, verifying their achievements, and publicizing them widely.

The goal: to encourage widespread use of advanced criminal justice practices.' A unit within the LEAA's research centre, the National Institute of Law Enforcement and Criminal Justice (NILECJ), screens the projects to make sure they are suitable. They must have a clear definition of their goal, which has to include either the reduction of crime or an improvement in the operations and quality of the criminal justice system; the goal must be measurable, and the project must be cost/effective. It must be capable of being reproduced elsewhere, and its staff must be willing to supply information to enquirers from other communities. By August 1979 there were 32 exemplary projects which had made contributions to community involvement, law enforcement, prosecution, adjudication and defence, corrections, juvenile programs and alternative services (NILECJ, [1979]). Well selected schemes like these should have good potential for improving the quality of law enforcement.

Even this is no guarantee of success. A critical review of the LEAA's activity since its formation under the Omnibus Crime Control and Safe Streets Act of 1968 shows that it has spent over $5 billion but its impact on the criminal justice system, let alone on crime, has not been overwhelming. The exemplary projects have been successful in arousing interest among other agencies; information is not yet available as to how many of these went on to replicate the projects, nor their results when they did so (Allinson, 1979). No doubt it takes even longer to reform a criminal justice system than an individual offender, but it is worth attempting, and much can be learnt in the process.

There is, of course, criminological research in Britain, and demonstration projects, and their results are published; but the policy for research is not clear (nor the process by which it is decided), criteria for projects are often not spelt out, and the system for spreading information is underdeveloped. The Home Office Research Unit (HORU) publishes a Research Bulletin, but it is in the main confined to the Unit's own research. Experimental projects funded by the Home Office do not necessarily include any allocation in their budgets for independent evaluation; if they do, the reports have to take their chance competing for a mention in social work periodicals, the *Prison Service Journal*, the *Howard Journal*, and others. No one has the specific job of seeing that information from all sources reaches the people whose work would benefit by it. At a conference organized by the Howard League and other organizations, one speaker after another said that an improved information service would help his work (NELP, 1978). Barbara Wootton (1978) has stressed the same point:

> I hope that the results of every new move [in penal policy] will be strictly monitored by research ... But I must renew my appeal for improvement in communication between research workers and practitioners. Skilled interpreters, able to translate the abracadabra of research findings into the vernacular, should be employed to redirect the present flow of HORU reports away from their resting places on the shelves of academic libraries, towards quarters in which their contents would be more influential in practical decisions.

Meanwhile there have been attempts to set up specialist bodies for prison governors and probation officers, judges are to have their own information bulletin from the Judicial Studies Board (if the recommendation of the Bridge Committee is followed), and local probation and social services run their own information departments. The May Committee was surprised to find no house journal that circulates throughout the prison service, and recommended that one should be started (Committee of Inquiry, 1979, para. 5.89). It is a picture of uncoordinated duplication of effort, not calculated to disseminate new ideas so that they can be adopted or exposed to criticism.

Crime Prevention

One section of the law enforcement system in England operates as an integrated national and local structure: crime prevention. It is worth looking at its activity, and then at two foreign examples; in the light of these a proposal will be made for a broader approach, at both national and local level, to bring together those whose work should in various ways help to reduce crime. In 1960 the then Home Secretary appointed a committee of chief constables to study police procedures for crime prevention, following which a Standing Committee on Crime Prevention was set up, including representatives of (among others) the Confederation of British Industry, the British Insurance Association, the Trades Union Congress, the Association of British Chambers of Commerce, the British Security Industry Association, the police service and the Home Office. Its functions are wide – 'to enable representatives of commerce and industry to discuss problems of crime prevention, and to make recommendations' – but its composition ensured that its focus has been largely towards the prevention of property crime by means of security measures: an important aspect of crime prevention, obviously, but far from the whole story. Its initiatives have included negotiating with the Society of Motor Manufacturers and Traders to secure that all motor cars and light vans made from 1971 onwards are fitted with anti-theft devices. It has two sub-committees, one on mobile property, the other on immovable property, enjoying the title of 'the Static Sub-Committee', which have respectively studied such matters as the payment of wages by means of other than cash, false alarms from intruder alarm installations, and shoplifting and thefts by staff. There are signs, however, that interest is being broadened to include social aspects of crime prevention. In 1978, for example, a second national conference on vandalism reviewed such measures as the National Youth Bureau's project in Manchester, sending youth leaders on to the streets to find youngsters who would not be attracted to clubs, and the Save the Children Fund's coordination of activities to counter the alienation which breeds vandalism; and a seminar in Droitwich considered the question 'Is punishment crime prevention?' The Home Office issues an attractively presented *Crime Prevention News*, and posters and other publicity material. A Crime Prevention Centre has been set up, in Stafford.

Activity is also promoted at local level. Police forces appoint crime prevention officers, about 500 in all, to advise the public on crime matters and especially target hardening. Crime Prevention Panels were set up in Bristol and Nottingham in 1966, and the following year in Sheffield after a six-week 'Crime-cut campaign'. By 1981 there were over 200. They are usually initiated by the police, and although little information is available about their membership, a Home Office Circular in 1968 suggested that they should include senior CID officers and local representatives of the commercial and industrial organizations which send members to the Standing Committee. They see their job mainly as supporting the police in public education on reducing opportunities for crime (information from Home Office). In one or two areas there have been independent initiatives. Mr. John Alderson, the Chief Constable of Devon and Cornwall, tries to counter the common view that if only the courts would find the right methods of punishment, crime would drop; his community policing scheme is described in Chapter Nine. The new town of Milton Keynes set up an Offenders Project to collect information from its own area and other new towns, and to try to discover whether a community can be planned from the outset so as to avoid crime and the multiple social deprivation which is so often associated with it.

There is nothing wrong with scattered local initiatives except that they tend to remain scattered and local. The national picture is hardly one of purposeful collaboration towards a common goal. One method of national coordination has been tried in Sweden, where since 1974 the National Council for Crime Prevention has operated as a government agency under the Ministry of Justice, with the task of 'promoting efforts to prevent crime in different walks of life' – trying to coordinate various efforts towards preventing criminal activity, with particular emphasis on research and development work and evaluating and disseminating the results. It is headed by a 19-member Board including politicians of all parties, the permanent heads of the ministries of Justice, Health and Social Affairs, and Education, and members of the associations of county councils and local authorities. The chairmen of the Confederation of Trade Unions and the Central Organization of Salaried Employees are members, and so is the managing director of the Employers' Confederation. There are also representatives of insurance companies and criminological research. Attached to the Council is a group of heads of central administrative agencies who can be consulted on different issues: the Chief Public Prosecutor and the directors of the national boards for Police, Prison and Probation, Courts, Social Welfare Board and Education. There is a further reference group of research specialists in criminology, sociology, penal law, and other fields. The composition has been set out in some detail to show the determination to coordinate different areas of public life, at the highest level, in the interests of arriving at an informed crime policy and securing acceptance of it. Nor is that all. The Council has working groups on such subjects as crime prevention, trends in crime, information, drugs, co-operation between social and child welfare authorities, schools and police, rehabilitation of offenders, teaching schoolchildren about legislation, juveniles, and criminal policy. Each is chaired by one of the members of parliament, senior officials or other members of the Council and its advisory groups; they include between five and seventeen members each, almost 100 in all, with representatives of a further range of associations and statutory bodies. There is a staff of about 15, with some 13 others full- or part-time on various projects and working groups. Altogether this represents a considerable investment of high-powered effort in the attempt to reduce crime. It is not of course an infallible recipe, and the Swedish government has taken a critical look at the Council to make sure that it does not become mere decoration; but bringing together such a representative range of people to discuss crime prevention should at least extend knowledge and change attitudes (Sweden, 1979).

A national structure on these lines could be complemented by local initiatives on the lines described by an American judge at the United Nations Crime Congress in Geneva in 1975. She illustrated the process as follows:

> The governor of a state or mayor of a city convenes a committee on standards and goals. It is composed of criminal justice professionals and laymen who represent all segments of the community. The committee looks at the entire criminal justice process in its locality and identifies the problem areas. It then reviews potential problem solutions ... Thereafter, using its local expertise, it divides responsibility for solving the problems...

Particular stress was placed on asking members of the community to set their own standards and goals, because these would then be realistic proposals with a good chance of being implemented.

> Specific standards and goals, in contrast to generalizations and statements of principle, enable professionals and the public to know where the system is heading, what it is trying to achieve, and what, in fact, it is achieving. ... Standards do not speak in terms such as "crime should be reduced" or "diversion programs should be developed." Standards speak in terms of the amount by which crime should be reduced. They speak in terms of the precise responsibilities for community organizations...

particularly those whose work is not primarily focused on criminal justice and work with offenders (Bacon, 1975).

The present British government is looking for ways of reducing the number of 'quangos,' but rather than dispense completely with the former Advisory Council on the Penal System it might consider the advantages of grafting its functions on to those of the Standing Committee on Crime Prevention. The Council on Crime Prevention (as it might be called, since crime prevention is ostensibly the main aim of the penal system) would, like its Swedish counterpart, include representatives of the police, prison and probation services, the heads of the relevant government departments, MPs from the corresponding Select Committees, the chairman of the Judicial Studies Board, and the director or general secretary of the Confederation of British Industry and the Trades Union Congress. National voluntary organizations such as the National Association for Care and Resettlement of Offenders (NACRO) and the National Association of Victim

Support Schemes would also be represented, as well as academic criminologists. The Council, with its sub-committees which could co-opt relevant specialists, would advise the Home Secretary on all aspects of crime prevention from truancy and foster care to employment policy and security, including of course probation, prisons and the police. It might hold some of its meetings in public, as parliamentary select committees do. An important sub-division would be responsible for research and development (a concept from the world of industry which could be usefully applied to social policy) and information. At the level of counties (or groups of two or three counties) there could be councils similarly composed, combining functions such as those at present performed by the Probation and After-Care Committee, the Crime Prevention Panel and prison Boards of Visitors. Each prison would have its Board as at present, and towns could have Crime Prevention Panels; this structure would link them with the rest of the system.

The system would make the fullest use of voluntary organizations and individuals; their contribution will be considered in the next section. Examples of community crime prevention in action will be given in Chapter Nine.

Involving the Public

A healthy system is well constructed so as to tend toward developments which are less costly and involve the least possible amount of intervention, as well as encouraging new ideas. But it should also include a third element, which is valuable in its own right and is conducive to the other two: involvement of the public. This is of two kinds, which overlap with each other: participation in the system, and observing it and suggesting reforms.

Participation in turn can be divided into personal help and service on various kinds of committee. One of the oldest traditions of voluntary help is visiting people in prison. The prison visitor, although he or she must be approved by the authorities, is completely independent, and receives no fee or expenses. He simply talks, and especially listens, to prisoners to provide one contact with the outside world to whom the inmate can speak freely knowing that by doing so he is not risking official displeasure or spoiling his chances of parole. No one has proved that it 'does any good', but it helps the time to pass, it is an expression of society's concern, and it may be instructive for the visitor. Unfortunately there are only just under 600 in England and

Wales (Home Office, 1980b, para. 185), so that only a fraction of the prison population has the chance to see one; the Home Office and its ministers do little to encourage visitors, and some prison governors even discourage them, thereby depriving the prison of one of its safety valves.

Prison visitors do not necessarily keep in touch with prisoners after release. Another group of volunteers, known by the rather bureaucratic name of voluntary associates, make contact with prisoners expressly in order to offer them friendship and moral support as they re-settle themselves into the community. There are about 8,000 of them, but many work only with the probation service, and in any case the number is still nowhere near the 60,000 released from prison sentences each year. In Sweden the number of voluntary associates is roughly equal to the number of prisoners released annually, and they are paid expenses and a small fee. In very approximate figures, about one person per thousand of the Swedish population is involved in work with ex-prisoners, as against about one in 25,000 in England and Wales; this may have contributed to the liberal attitude to penal policy there, especially the recognition of the need to keep sentences to a minimum. The effect of voluntary associates has also not been evaluated, but there is reason to believe that they could make a useful contribution if there were more (Dickson, 1976). They are available outside normal working hours, they do not have a score or more of other cases to deal with, and they can interpose a human buffer between the offender and the law enforcement bureaucracy. The Howard League (1979a) has suggested that prison officers might be encouraged to help to interest more people in this work.

Among some members of the probation service there has also been a tendency to regard social work as requiring strictly professional skills; much of it does, of course, but there is beginning to be a wider recognition of those aspects of the work which do not require training, or at least only a short induction course. Probation officers also organize self-help groups of prisoners' wives; other groups, such as the Prisoners' Wives and Families Society, are formed by spontaneous initiative. Ex-prisoners have sometimes tried to help each other in a similar way, for example through Recidivists Anonymous; but, as we saw in Chapter Six, this has received little support from prisoners and less from the authorities, despite the work of a few prison officers, and no longer exists. Some ex-prisoners, keenly aware of the need for accommodation, have started hostels (see for example Sugden and Skinner, 1978).

167

A second level of public participation has been through serving on committees. There are the Boards of Visitors attached to all penal establishments, whose function was described in Chapter Six. Probation and After-Care Committees operate at the local level, and have a little more of a policy-making role than the Boards. In addition there are any number of management committees of projects run by voluntary organizations. Service on committees of these kinds does not necessarily open the eyes of those concerned, of course, nor do they always speak out when they should; but at least the opportunity is provided for the more open-minded of them to learn a little about the system's operation, and perhaps to influence it for the better.

Bureaucracies should always be subject to public scrutiny, especially when they have such total power over the lives of individuals behind high walls. The authorities should recognise that this is a healthy arrangement, even though it can sometimes be a nuisance for them. The British democratic system is organized to allow the harrying of officialdom, and the chairman of the then Prison Commission once said that the Howard League was to the Commission what the official Opposition in Parliament was to the Government (Rose, 1961). One difficulty faced by penal reformers is that many of those with first-hand experience on the receiving end of the penal system are reluctant to become involved in a public campaign and few possess the confidence, skills and time required to make a sustained protest. Reformers need support from people within the criminal justice system (such as magistrates, probation and prison officers, as well as ex-offenders) to be well informed, and from outside the system to express objections publicly when necessary. (There are also of course people who criticize the system from within; when their views are rejected by the senior hierarchy, it is useful to have an independent organization which can take up their proposals or criticisms.)

Reform organizations are concerned with policy. They are as well informed as their resources allow, collecting information from official data, research reports, and personal communications from concerned people working within the system; they also encourage those on the receiving end, offenders and their relatives and friends, to give their point of view. They develop international contacts, so as to learn of new ideas in other countries. The next stage is making the information known, in the form of reports to the public drawing attention to relevant facts. Thirdly, they make proposals: sometimes these are radical and try to make people think differently, sometimes there

is wide agreement about aims (such as reducing the prison population) but the reformers may offer a new approach to achieving it.
This is done by compiling reports, or presenting evidence to official
inquiries, and may be called the 'think-tank' function, which has been
the primary activity of the Howard League. It may be supplemented
by the demonstration project, of which NACRO is a leading expon-
ent: the organization tries out a new method of operation, evaluates
it, and then seeks to persuade the authorities to adopt it as normal
practice. Bail reform, anti-vandalism projects, and schemes for education of offenders on probation are among the many examples of this
method of introducing reform. Fourthly, then, the reformers try to
bring about the proposed changes. The method may be through discussion with the relevant government ministry, such as the Prison
Department, for changes that can be effected through administrative
action; others may require legislation, and hence the support of
Members of Parliament – although senior civil servants are not
without influence.

In addition, however, reformers need to act as watch-dogs, to
make sure that the system is obeying its own rules and that the rules
themselves are compatible with prevailing beliefs about human
rights. This may be called the 'conscience' function: it is more difficult than being a 'think-tank', because those who work within the
system may see it as presumptuous for outsiders to judge their
conduct – and indeed it may be so. Critics on the outside do not know
what it is like to do the job; but the answer is of course that they do
not know how to run a railway or a hotel either, but that does not
mean that they have not the right to insist on punctual and courteous
service.

What is done to prisoners is, in a democratic country, done in the
name of all of us: we have not only a right but a duty to see that the
standards of humanity and fairness are maintained. This may involve
investigation (see for example the descriptions of incidents compiled
by Amnesty International and others (1977), National Prisoners'
Movement – PROP (1976), and PROP (1979)) which will not make
the reformist organization popular. Or, it may involve litigation, if
the authorities or their servants appear to have broken the law or contravened the European Declaration of Human Rights, or a similar
Bill of Rights incorporated into the legislation of the country concerned, as in the Constitution of the United States.

The courts are a potential bulwark for prisoners against inhu-
manity and injustice (and for prison staff against defamation by pris-

169

oners). But they do not help prisoners unless prisoners have access to them, and unless either the courts are seized of the importance of justice and legality within prisons, or the law unambiguously prescribes the standards to be upheld. Litigation as a means of reform has been pursued with some success by the National Prison Project of the American Civil Liberties Union which has, for example, won $518,000 damages from the State of Virginia in 1979 for a prisoner who lost the use of both legs through neglect by hospital and prison doctors. The Project has also secured rulings that several prisons, and the entire prison systems of the States of Rhode Island and Alabama, were unconstitutional, because conditions constituted 'cruel and unusual punishment' (in the cases of *Palmigiano* v. *Garrahy* and *Pugh and James* v. *Britton*, respectively); similar action is being taken against Arkansas and Florida. In the United Kingdom litigation has been less successful, and the courts less robust in their defence of human rights. There was a step forward in the *St Germain* case, in which the Court of Appeal held that the procedure at prison disciplinary adjudications must be subject to supervision by the courts; but a year later came a disappointing decision that detention of a prisoner in intensified segregation in a 'control unit' was legally justified, even though Prison Rules had been broken (in *Williams* v. *Home Office*, 9 May 1980, one of several cases conducted on behalf of prisoners by the National Council for Civil Liberties). Applications to the European Commission of Human Rights have in some cases induced the Home Office to relax its restrictions, for example on prisoners' right to marry; but in the recent case of *Guilfoyle* the court surprisingly held that a prisoner's correspondence with his solicitor about an application to the Commission may be opened and read. In England there is clearly a need for reform of the law, and particularly the Prison Rules, as well as of prison management.

8. The Sentence of the Court: What Can It Achieve?

The Role of Punishment in Criminal Justice

A discussion of prisons and non-custodial measures, like that in the early chapters of this book, tends to be seen in terms of the conventional antithesis between punishment and rehabilitation. But prisons aim to do other things besides punishing people, such as containing them; and rehabilitation also involves some deprivation of liberty. Similarly, the man in the street, if he stops to think about it, recognises that punishment has more than one aim. It can deter – and a distinction should be made between general deterrence (frightening the population at large into good behaviour) and individual deterrence (in which punishment is imposed on offenders who have been caught to discourage them from re-offending). It can be intended to protect the public, by keeping a person under close supervision or in prison. It can express public condemnation of the act, and allegiance to the law, by showing that offenders, if caught, are made to suffer. So it would appear that there is no one underlying purpose which justifies punishment. Rather, as Hart (1959) has pointed out, any justification involves several different principles. Moreover, as will be seen, there can be advantages to limiting penalties, and disadvantages to increasing them.

The first part of this chapter will consider ethical and practical aspects of three principal aspects of punishment – deterrence, denunciation and, when the punishment involves deprivation of liberty, protection of the public. If punishment is justified, it will be suggested, certain conditions must be fulfilled. The second part will review the attempt to introduce a different principle, rehabilitation, into the criminal justice system, disillusion currently felt about this ideal, and the attempt to reinstate the principle of punishment. Finally, it will ask whether there could be other possible ways of meeting the criticisms of rehabilitation.

First, it is necessary to be clear about the definition of punishment.

The word will be taken to mean the deliberate infliction of some unpleasant measure, such as deprivation of money or liberty, *because it is unpleasant*. There is a sense in which any compulsory measure is a punishment; for example, requiring a person to undergo rehabilitation or to make restitution means that he must forgo some time or money, respectively. Indeed, he *may* find it unpleasant. In this sense the authorities can impose punishment without intending to. For present purposes, however, the intention will be taken as the criterion; it will be assumed that even if unintentional punishment cannot be avoided, safeguards could be introduced so that it is reduced to a minimum. This point will be considered further in Chapter Ten.

What Is a Deterrent?

Suppose the assumption that the threat of punishment is the most effective way of inducing people to be law-abiding were carried to its logical conclusion, and a Minister for Deterrence were appointed. He threatens his senior civil servants with instant dismissal if they do not produce a briefing on his new duties by the following morning: what should it contain?

To begin with, some basic distinctions have to be emphasised. The effectiveness of punishment as a deterrent depends on the degree of *probability* that the offender will be brought to justice, as well as on the *severity* of the punishment if and when it comes. Next, it must be considered whether the intention is primarily to deter the individual from re-offending, or whether the threat of punishment is aimed at the population in general, for which it needs to be widely known and even exaggerated. Finally, the Minister should recognise that his colleagues will insist on considering the costs, the question of which deterrents overstep the limits of humanity or justice, and whether there are any side-effects.

DETERRENCE BY INCREASING THE PROBABILITY OF DETECTION

Probability of detection has long been acknowledged as a more effective deterrent than severity of punishment, and an extensive review of research bears this out (Beyleveld, 1978, 1979). The shock of appearing in court and worrying about the effect on family and friends can be enough, particularly for first offenders. Readers of *The Wind in the Willows* will remember that Toad of Toad Hall, imprisoned for furious driving and other offences, found prison a miserable experience; but no sooner had he escaped than, undeterred, he committed the same offence again; and it was only after firm peer-group pressure from his friends that he became 'an altered Toad' and compensated the engine-driver and the barge-woman for what he had done (Grahame, 1908).

Probability of conviction is linked to several factors. One is the allocation of police resources: if the police service devoted more of its time, public statements and enlistment of public support to, say, company fraud or the sale of alcohol and tobacco to under-age children, the number of such offences known and cleared up would presumably increase. The effects of police action alone, however, are limited. The great majority of crimes known to the police are not discovered by them but reported by members of the public (Steer, 1980). Of these, only a minority are cleared up, and then often because the identity of the offender was known from the start (for example, when a person was assaulted by someone he knew) or because an offender accused of one crime asks for others to be 'taken into consideration'. It does not follow, therefore, that increases in policing will make much impact on detection rates and hence on deterrence. There are limits to the amount of regulation we want in our society, and particularly to intervention in people's daily lives in the shape of, for example, telephone tapping or searching people or their homes. Nor is the presence of more police in itself a guarantee that trouble will be reduced. The use of Special Patrol Groups, without special training in community relations, has attracted considerable hostility from black members of the community, who feel that they are picked on, and there has been such criticism of police use of their powers to arrest people on suspicion ('sus') that the Government has introduced new legislation. In Kansas City a scheme was introduced with the characteristically American name of LOP and POP (Location-oriented Patrol and Perpetrator-oriented Patrol), with the aim of supervising high-crime areas and suspected individuals, respectively. Neither was found to be a great improvement on the usual methods, but there was a substantial increase in the citizen complaint rate (Newton, 1978).

For purposes of deterrence, what people *believe* to be the probability of conviction is more important than the actual probability. This is clearly shown by the history of the British Road Safety Act of 1967, which made it an offence to drive with a blood/alcohol concentration of 0.08% or more, and introduced the 'breathalyser' and blood or urine tests. The penalty is normally a fine and disqualification from driving for a year on the first offence. From the day the new legislation went into effect there was a considerable drop in road casualties as compared with previous years: in the first three months casualties were 16% lower and deaths 23% lower. The reduction was most marked at times when drinking and driving is most usual, between 8 p.m. and 4 a.m. But by the end of 1970 the figures had regained their former level. At the time of its introduction the Act received considerable publicity, giving the public exaggerated ideas of the probability of conviction; but police enforcement could not match those expectations, and the public realized this. One constraint on the police was that they were forbidden, in the name of liberty of the individual and police/community relations, to give breath tests randomly; in addition, some motorists and their lawyers discovered loopholes (Ross, 1973).

People's susceptibility to deterrence can be affected by different factors. As part of a controlled experiment, a police campaign against driving cars with worn tyres was widely publicized in one town in the Netherlands, but not in another. Twice as many motorists in the first town who had worn tyres replaced them; but it was found that those who did not comply tended to be younger, less well educated, and barely able to afford a car. The inference is that the same amount of deterrence will affect people differently, depending on factors such as their financial position (Beyleveld, 1979).

Measures against hijacking of aircraft in the United States show that the effect of severity is outweighed by probability of detection, and still more by proper preventive measures. In 1961, after the first hijacking of an American airliner flying to Cuba, the punishment for this offence was increased to a maximum of life imprisonment or death, but security measures were unchanged. There was a slight drop in 'skyjacking', but in 1968 the number of incidents rose sharply. In 1969 Cuba began returning skyjackers to the U.S.A. (a change in probability but not in severity) and soon afterwards the U.S.A. skyjacking rate began to fall, though it remained at a high level. In 1970 sky marshals authorized to shoot and kill were planted on airlines (an increase in both probability and severity) and in 1972 a 45-year sentence for skyjacking received enormous publicity; neither of these seems to have had a significant effect. But early in 1973 screening of passengers for metal was introduced, and the levels of skyjacking dropped (Chauncey (1975), quoted in Beyleveld (1978)).

DETERRENCE BY INCREASING THE SEVERITY OF PUNISHMENT

As for severity, folk wisdom asserts that an *increase* in the severity of punishment will be *more* effective in keeping us close to the straight and narrow path. This proposition can be tested, for example, comparing the position before and after a change in the level of punishment and, in general, the evidence does not support it. Since the belief in severity is so persistent, it is worth taking several examples. An early instance relates to capital punishment. Roy Calvert (1936, p.10) shows that, for several offences for which the death penalty was abolished or discontinued between 1820 and 1841, the number of persons committed in the three years after repeal was generally less than in the three years before. For cattle stealing, for example, there were 113 committals before, 67 after; for robbery, 1,053 before, 889 after. Some offences increased, including sheep stealing and attempts to murder; but the total number went down, and the pattern, or rather absence of pattern, suggests that the death penalty had little effect either way.

Advocates of corporal punishment have often cited the Security from Violence Act of 1862 (the 'Garotters Act'), which made robbery with violence punishable by flogging, after a sharp rise in the number of street robberies in London known to the police. At the November 1862 sessions at the Central Criminal Court 24 men, apparently members of the gang chiefly responsible, were sentenced under the old legislation. The number of offences was lower for the first three months of the next year, before the new Act had come into force; by 1864 the rate had risen again, despite the new penalty (Pike, 1876, vol. 2, p.575; Rose, 1961, pp.11–12; ACPS, 1978, p.61). Similarly it was widely believed that a wave of attacks on black people in Notting Hill, London, in 1958 was stamped out by exemplary sentences subsequently imposed on nine youths at the Old Bailey; but other factors such as increased police activity are at least as likely to have been responsible (ACPS, 1978, p.91). Another recent instance is reminiscent of the concern about street robbery in the 1860s: a century later, in the early 1970s, it is called 'mugging', and judges have been repeatedly reported as giving severe sentences that were intended to be exemplary. In one particularly serious case, classed as attempted murder as well as robbery, a 16-year old boy was sentenced in 1973 to 20 years' detention; this was presented to the public as a general deterrent, and probably received as much publicity as any sentence in recent years. If any severe sentence could act as a general deterrent,

175

this one should. A comparison was made of the rates of robbery or assault with intent to rob in six urban police areas. The level remained constant before and after the sentence; later it did drop, however, and this appeared to be associated with increased police activity (Baxter & Nuttall, 1975).

In another case which has been studied in detail, increased severity was not found to have a deterrent effect. Sometimes a single crime or group of crimes arouses particular horror and leads to demands for heavier punishment, and this happened in Pennsylvania after three men broke into a house on Palm Sunday 1966 and raped and maltreated an 80-year old widow, her daughter and granddaughter. Within a few weeks new legislation drastically raised the penalties: for rape with injury, a minimum of 15 years and a maximum of life imprisonment. A careful analysis of the number of rapes found no decreases that could be attributed to the new law or the publicity surrounding it (Schwartz, 1968).

If increased severity were as effective as is commonly supposed, it would be expected that decreases would be followed by higher crime rates. But the evidence points the other way. In 1892 Charles Hopwood, Q.C., Recorder of Liverpool showed that in six years he had reduced the average sentence there from over 13 months to under 3. At the old rate he would have imposed 2,967 years of imprisonment, whereas in fact he imposed 618 years. Apart from the saving in human misery, inflicted mainly on poor people, which he compassionately describes, he quotes the crime statistics of the Head Constable of Liverpool, which were the lowest since figures were first published in 1857. In the last three years recorded indictable offences fell by 23%, burglary etc., by 39% and serious crimes of violence by 38%. Hopwood does not claim credit for the decrease (though as he says he would doubtless have had the discredit of the increase, had there been one) but merely that moderate sentences are as effective as excessive ones; and he gives an example which shows how radically different his policy was:

> A poor woman pleaded guilty before me, charged with stealing a duck. I looked at her record. She had already endured, for stealing meat, 12 months'; again, for stealing butter, seven years' penal servitude; again, for stealing meat, seven years'; again, for stealing meat, seven years'; or 22 years of sentences for stealing a few shillings' worth of food! My sentence for the duck was one month, and I regret it now as too much. I have never since seen her.   (Quoted in ACPS, 1978, pp.187–189).

When judges and magistrates look back on the prison sentences they have imposed, they might reflect on the third of the 'gifts reserved for age' in T. S. Eliot's *Little Gidding:*

> And last, the rending pain of re-enactment
>> Of all that you have done, and been; the shame
>> Of motives late revealed, and the awareness
> Of things ill done and done to others' harm
>> Which once you took for exercise of virtue,
>> Then fools' approval stings, and honour stains.

WHEN DETERRENCE WON'T WORK OR BACKFIRES

A case can be made for a policy based on deterrence if it can be shown to work; but can it be fair? The amount of punishment required for deterrence is unrelated to the seriousness of the offence. Although the probability of being caught is the main deterrent, suppose it were accepted that severity does also have some effect. What would a policy based on deterrent punishment involve? The difficulty is that it may lead to rough justice, because the severity required to deter different people may vary, out of proportion to the offence itself. If A would 'get the message' from a conditional discharge, while B who has committed a similar offence would be influenced by nothing less than prison, then any sentences on both of them must be either unequal, or unfair to A, or inadequate for B. It is a mistake to ask the general question whether sanctions deter crime, as Beyleveld (1978) points out: 'Instead, it should be asked which sanctions deter which persons, from which crimes, under which circumstances. It is also necessary to ask not only how a deterrent effect can be achieved, but how it can be maintained.... In no instance has research been adequately formulated for reasonable policy directives to be inferred.' Morris and Zimring (1969) agree: 'Only field experiments provide sufficient opportunity for the independent variation of a single component in the deterrence strategy.' They comment that such experiments are expensive, politically unpopular, and raise legal problems; these difficulties might be overcome, but there would also be ethical ones which might prove more intractable.

General deterrence consists of a threat towards the general population; but when it fails to deter a particular individual, the threatened punishment has to be carried out against him or her, although for many people it is the opposite of the most suitable measures to keep them from offending again. Moreover, they can only be deterred to the extent that they have something to lose. Martin and Webster (1971, p.215), studying the social consequences of conviction, comment that '"He that is down need fear no fall": if a man's ordinary life contains little that he values . . . then a deterrent sentence is not going to mean very much. It is the people who have a stake in life who can be deterred, not men living the disorganized lives of some of our criminals.' They do not necessarily stop to weigh up the risks. Indeed, Robert Allerton, having spent 12½ of his 33 years' life in jail, concluded that deterrent theory depended upon the doubtful assumption that criminals premeditate their actions and make rational calculations about the probability of being caught and the pay-off in various eventualities (Parker and Allerton, 1962, p.187). Prisons are of course full of people who have not been deterred. To be more exact, the prisoner is often afraid of the consequences of re-offending, but his fear is overwhelmed by the still more powerful pressures which he is unable to control such as being homeless or jobless or having no friends except other ex-offenders; and the very fact of having been in prison makes him less able to withstand them. As Bernard Shaw (1922) pointed out, 'If you are to punish a man retributively, you must injure him. If you are to reform him, you must improve him. And men are not improved by injuries.' It is useless, as well as unfair, to try to bludgeon people into what they are incapable of. The punishment is intended to deter, but it has other consequences which must be weighed against this: the deterrent system, Shaw goes on,

> necessarily leaves the interests of the victim [i.e., the person punished] wholly out of account. It injures and degrades him; destroys the reputation without which he cannot get employment; and when the punishment is prison under our system, atrophies his powers of fending for himself in the world. . . . He is, at the expiration of his sentence, flung out of the prison into the streets to earn his living in a labour market where nobody will employ an ex-prisoner . . . There is only one lucrative occupation available for him; and that is crime. He has no compunction as to society: why should he have any? Society, for its own selfish protection, having done its worst to him, he has no feeling about it except a desire to get a bit of his own back.

The case should not be overstated: of course deterrence has certain advantages. But it must be remembered that it has disadvantages too. It may inspire not fear but bravado. Jimmy Boyle, whose book *A Sense of Freedom* should be required reading for anyone concerned about penal policy, sentenced to two years imprisonment at the age of 18, considered this sentence 'quite big for a guy of my age with no prison sentence before but I wasn't really horrified at it. There was a sort of pride in it as I felt really good to be in beside lots of hard men as I was on the way to being one myself' (Boyle, 1977, p.107). Another ex-prisoner, Victor Carasov (1971), confirms this. In addition, deterrent policies can lead to counter-productive prison régimes, and are sometimes interpreted by staff as a licence for unauthorized violence. Boyle describes his reaction: 'While sitting there in this totally defenceless position a group of screws came in and attacked me. I knew that if I did anything back there would be more charges so I more or less took what they gave . . . The fact that I had heavy bruising on one side of my face didn't raise the Governor's curiosity. I returned to the punishment cell and decided that I hated all bastard screws. What I couldn't accept was their rendering me absolutely helpless before coming in and attacking me'.

The attempt to reduce crime by means of deterrence often leads to excessive punishments; but these probably make offenders go to great lengths to escape them. At one end of the scale they clog up the machinery of justice with hopeless not-guilty pleas and appeals and have a greater incentive to offering bribes or absconding from bail. More seriously, they may deter people under stress, such as some of the parents who ill-treat or neglect their children, from seeking help. They may induce offenders to go to greater lengths to escape detection and resist arrest, sometimes violently. Less then two centuries ago, the remark that 'you might as well be hanged for a sheep as a lamb' was no metaphor but literally true, and it is quite probable that a number of victims of rape and other serious offences would be alive today if their attackers, panicking at the consequences if they should be caught, had not tried to escape by killing the only witness. Lastly, excessive punishments make offenders even less likely to feel contrition and more likely to feel resentment (which creates difficulties for the prison authorities, as well as for the public after their release); and may make the public feel sympathy for the offender. The way in which would-be deterrent punishments can be counter-productive has been noted by two great educators a century apart. Mary Carpenter wrote that

> A vindictive element in chastisement excites in the mind of him who receives it, especially of the child, a rebellious and vindictive feeling in return. Such punishment defeats its object (Manton, 1976, p.164).

Similarly, William Temple (1934, p.38):

> I should certainly expect to find that a State-inflicted flogging tends to turn juvenile delinquents into definite criminals, because it makes the State appear as stern and hostile so that its inevitable consequence is to range the will of the offender in determined opposition to the State.

Experimental psychology also offers some insights, although allowance must be made for the artificiality of laboratory research. A famous experiment by the psychologist Skinner not only shows the long-term ineffectiveness of punishment, by itself, as a means of influencing behaviour, but also suggests why popular belief in punishment nevertheless persists. When rats were punished for pulling the food-supply lever, at first they pulled it very much less; but by the end of a few hours they were doing it as much as unpunished rats. Thus, punishment may appear to be an effective deterrent in the short term; but its effects wear off.

Punishment can deter unwanted behaviour if it is prompt, predictable, mild, and informative rather than retaliatory, for example, when a child is sternly spoken to when playing with an electric plug. Severe punishments can produce lasting effects, but some of these are undesirable, including anxiety, neurosis and an inability to respond. Very severe punishments can produce the pathological response of fixating the behaviour punished instead of eliminating it. They are also likely to lead people to reject, rather than respect, those responsible for the punishment, such as the school or the law enforcement authorities. There is a better chance that punishment will extinguish the unwanted behaviour where the person punished has enough adequately rewarded legitimate options open to him, such as vocational skills, job opportunities, and social acceptance. In other words he must know how to behave in such a way as to avoid being punished, and many recidivists simply do not know how to behave otherwise than they do. Punishment is less likely to be effective where the behaviour has become a deeply ingrained habit and carries its own reward, as when a person has become an experienced burglar or con-man and makes a lucrative living. Some of the effects may however be unwanted: a person may, for example, not refrain from his behaviour, but devise ways of escaping punishment – and prison affords ample opportunities for thinking up illegitimate activities which seem to give better prospects of avoiding discovery. More effective reinforcement is achieved by rewards for the desired behaviour, especially when they are given intermittently: that is, people will be encouraged to choose a law-abiding course of action if from time to time they are rewarded, for example financially or by the approval of someone they respect. In this, psychological research is in accord with everyday experience, and offers support to those who question the utility of punishment as a prime instrument of social control.

The above discussion shows that it is, at the very least, far from self-evident that it is justifiable to use deterrent punishment as an instrument of law enforcement policy. There are thus three main questions that have to be asked, one practical and two ethical. The practical one is whether it works better than other methods which do not have such harmful side-effects. Next, as regards the effects on individuals, is it justifiable, as Walker (1979) suggests, to inflict harm within certain limits, and can we be sure that the limits will not be exceeded? Are deterrents tolerable provided they stop short of, for example, death, mutilation, corporal punishment, permanent stigma, prolonged imprisonment, or the penalization of innocent dependants? Thirdly, as regards the effects on society, is it right or necessary that the basis of law enforcement should be fear? Shaw says that the proper name of deterrence is terrorism; similarly, Radzinowicz and King (1977) quote Dr. Johnson's definition of 'to deter' as 'to discourage by terror, to fright from anything.' But they add: 'We may utterly reject the concept of a society ruled by terror. That does not mean we must go to the other extreme and deny the usefulness of an element of deterrence, even of fear, in the balance of human relations.' Shaw concedes this: 'there is all the difference in the world between deterrence as an incident in the operation of criminal law, and deterrence as its sole object and justification.' Fear is an undesirable principle on which to base society – unless it is the fear of losing one's self-respect.

Why should good behaviour be conditioned only by fear? Anyone who has been fortunate enough to have a respected and considerate parent or employer knows that people's motives often have nothing to do with fear, except in the sense of fear of letting down someone who has put trust in them. Some speakers, such as James Anderton, Chief Constable of Greater Manchester, have recommended humiliating 'young thugs'; others want to chain petty offenders to lamp posts (*Daily Telegraph,* 12 July 1979) and the like. Apart from ethical considerations, it is dubious whether this is good psychology. Many such offenders already have a poor opinion of themselves, and this will only be confirmed by further rejection; those who do have some self-confidence will pride themselves in showing that they can take the punishment, and emerge with their anti-authority attitudes confirmed. This has been the effect of detention centres (Norris, 1979) and corporal punishment. A borstal governor, Martin Burnett (1978) reports that time and again ex-inmates who decided to 'go straight' told him they did so because someone had put trust in them. There are two key words here. Firstly 'trust': a person in authority was earning respect by demonstrating one of the virtues on which society is built, not instilling fear by his ability to inflict pain. Secondly 'someone': an individual can trust and inspire respect, but a system cannot – it can only create conditions in which trust, respect, loyalty and other virtues are more, or less, likely to grow.

Protecting the Public

Imprisonment is often imposed with several concurrent purposes, including to punish the offender, to deter, and to protect the public by restraining him for a period. The latter purpose, however, can be pursued without being deliberately punitive, as was suggested in Chapter Six, and in some cases without total deprivation of liberty, by means of the close supervision described in Chapter Five. Nevertheless, it tends to be regarded as being usually achieved by imprisonment and with punishment, and it is therefore appropriate to consider it here.

Before considering the primary object, which is to incapacitate a person so that he cannot commit any more offences for a time, it is worth looking at two other effects which tend to counteract it. Firstly, offences are committed daily inside prison, among inmates and between inmates and staff. In 1979, for example, there were 2,762 assaults and 33 cases of gross personal violence to an officer in prisons in England and Wales, among an average of 42,220 inmates (Home Office 1980, Chapter Nine); this is about 66 cases per 1,000 prisoners. In addition there are offences such as homosexual rapes, intimidation and bribery, though little is known about their prevalence. Thus although the total, including unreported cases, can never be known, there must be a considerable number of offences which would not have occurred but for the existence of prisons; this fact must be among those taken into account when deciding whether to use custodial or non-custodial sentences. Secondly, one of the harmful effects prison can have is to 'incapacitate' people in the other sense of the word: to render them incapable of getting or holding down a job, and hence more prone to relapse into crime.

As regards the main object, however, attempts to estimate the number of crimes which could be prevented by the use of longer sentences are little more than informed guesswork, since they depend on the assumptions made. For example, we have no means of knowing how many of the unsolved crimes were committed by people who had no previous convictions, and who therefore could not have been prevented however tough the incarceration policy (Pease & Wolfson, 1979; Tarling, 1979). The highest estimate of crimes preventable by heavy prison sentences was made by R. and S. Shinnar (1975). They estimated that there is a class of criminal committing about 6 to 14 crimes per year each, who account for most of the 70% of reported crimes which are not cleared up. On this basis they calculated that if every convicted 'mugger' were sent to prison for five years, the volume of 'mugging' would be reduced by 80%. Other researchers have criticized their formula, and have shown that they were much too optimistic about the rise in prison population that would result. Another study considered the effects of an even tougher policy: if it were conceivable that a five-year sentence could be imposed on everyone convicted of *any* felony (which corresponds approximately to an imprisonable offence), including first-time and non-violent offenders, this research indicated that up to 34% of the recorded violent crimes might have been prevented. But the cost would be astronomical: the prison population would increase three- to five-fold. Even a less stringent policy (five years for any *violent* felony) would mean keeping 90 people locked up who would not in fact have committed a further violent crime for every 10 who would have done so. This would be unjust, inefficient and impossibly expensive (Van Dine and others, 1979).

So far we have been considering the effectiveness of incapacitation; but there is also a question as to whether it can be applied fairly. Who should be detained, and for how long? Human behaviour cannot (fortunately) be reliably predicted: even if it is known that statistically 60% of a given group is likely to commit further serious crimes, there is no way of identifying the other 40% so as to release them. The latter, technically known as 'false positives', are therefore kept in prison because of the offences which the others might otherwise commit. A similar dilemma arises in deciding how long any individual is to be detained. As Sommer (1976, p.30) asks in *The End of Imprisonment*, 'If a person poses a threat to society in 1975, is there any justification for turning him loose in 1978 or 1984, particularly since his anti-social attitudes are likely to worsen during confinement?' Sommer concludes: 'The incapacitation model provides no basis for deciding when the inmate is to be released.' Incapacitation must therefore be either forever, or its duration must be determined by another criterion, such as the seriousness of the offence.

But does this protect the public? Its effect is to provide a maximum, after which all offenders except the most serious are freed. In some cases they will commit further crimes. The answer to this is that in criminal justice, as in other spheres of human life, complete absence of risk is unattainable: dangers must be weighed against benefits. Usually we trade risk for convenience. The benefits of travel and the employment provided by the aircraft and motor industries are allowed to outweigh the wrecking of the quality of life for people who live near airports or motorways, and the statistical certainty that many hundreds of people will be killed each year in crashes. Similarly with nuclear power and the risk of accidents or military abuse. In the case of law enforcement the risk is balanced against a higher ideal than convenience: justice. This is accepted in principle in regard to policing: whilst the number of arrests might be increased by giving police greater rights to detain people, this needs to be balanced against citizens' liberty. The principle in releasing people from custody is no different.

Perhaps the principle can be explained with a diagram (see facing page). The public impression, fostered by the disproportionate attention given by the media to a small number of exceptional events, appears to be that there are many criminals in prison who are liable to commit further serious offences when they are released. The reality is that citizens are exposed to a large variety of risks, of which becoming the victim of a violent crime is a very rare one. Of these the only harmful acts that could have been prevented by longer prison sentences are those of the recidivists; and the majority of their crimes are non-violent. This is not, of course, what some sections of the press might caricature as a 'plea for leniency,' but a plea for balance. Indeed, there may be cases where the risk outweighs the requirements of justice, if a person has a history of committing extremely serious offences, and the probability that he will do so again is assessed as being very high. In some cases he may actually have indicated his determination to do so. One reprieved murderer had talked of killing both himself and his wife, who had left him, and was actually convicted of prowling round her house with an air pistol; but the warning signal was not recognised, he was not recalled to prison, and

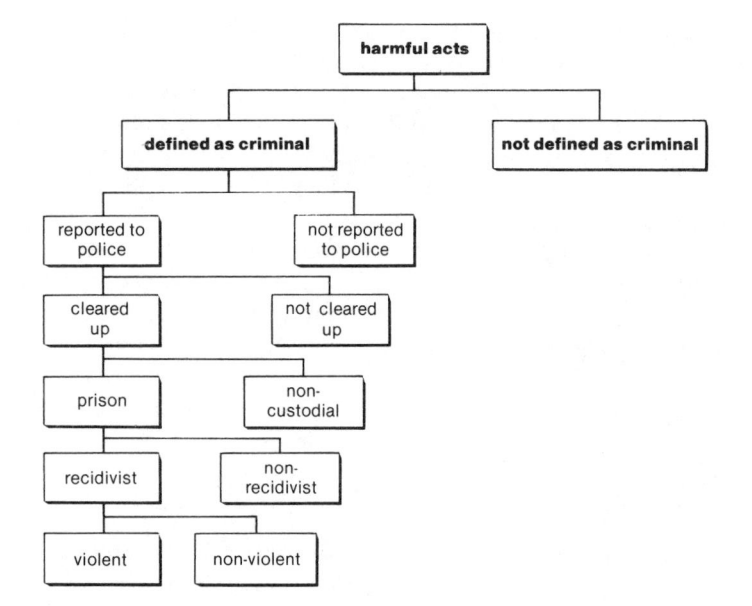

eleven days later he went on the rampage with a rifle, killing his sister-in-law before shooting himself in the stomach (Blom-Cooper, 1965). But any such exceptions must be carefully circumscribed if they are not to degenerate into an over-simplified assumption that the intention of protecting the public is sufficient to justify labelling certain offenders as 'dangerous' and locking them up for extended periods.

Symbolic Denunciation

If punishment were employed only as a means to an end, the problem would be less complex: its effects could be measured, and its use decided accordingly. But it has also a symbolic function: there are certain things people traditionally, or instinctively, do to show their condemnation, just as there are others to show their pleasure. Punishments are felt to express respect for the law and sympathy for the victim. If these actions are relatively harmless, there is no need to suggest change; but if they are harmful, counter-productive or ethically objectionable, they should be modified.

Walker (1969, pp.19–21) questions the legitimacy of denunciation as an aim. He asks, 'Who is supposed to be impressed?' He has not found, in discussion with prisoners, that they are impressed; on the other hand, he says, there is no point in merely 'providing a frisson for the law-abiding.' So long as the advocates of denunciation insist that it take the form of actual suffering inflicted on the offender, he says, either they are asking us to treat the criminal as a human sacrifice, a mere instrument in a ritual, or they are just 'retributivists in fancy dress.'

The question of punishment as the expression of moral indignation has also been considered by Bedau. He quotes lawyers, philosophers and even divines who regarded it as right to express moral attitudes by punishing and hating the 'wicked', overcoming any 'natural reluctance' to do so (which, one may remark in passing, has not been a very dominant feature of the history of punishment). Bedau concludes that if punishment is to be used for purposes of denunciation, as opposed to the utilitarian aims mentioned earlier, it must fulfil three criteria:

1. The rules must be fair, necessary, reasonable and not arbitrary;
2. The offender must have had an opportunity to comply, and must have known of the punishment; and
3. There must be no non-punitive alternative (Bedau, 1980).

As to the first, there is an inherent difficulty, because there is no way of matching quantum of punishment to heinousness of offence that is anything but arbitrary. It is impossible to show why a particular burglary or assault was 'worth' a certain punishment, except by comparison with other punishments. The second aim is met in many cases, but the pressures and temptations not to comply bear very unequally on some sections of the population. And with regard to the third, an attempt to propose a non-punitive alternative will be made at the end of this book, where it will be suggested that there are other ways of marking condemnation of crimes no less forcefully, but more constructively.

Retribution

The justifications of punishment so far considered are utilitarian: that something is achieved by it, such as deterring offenders or expressing disgust. There is also, however, a moral argument, that punishment is somehow *right*. No matter if it fails to achieve these results, or even *de*habilitates people, besides causing undeserved suffering to their families: they should have thought of that before, for crime without punishment is felt to be as incomplete as a play without applause or a seedtime without a harvest. In support of this view Patricia Morgan, author of *Delinquent Fantasies* (1978), argues in an article entitled 'Crime and *punishment*' (*Daily Telegraph,* 28 December 1978, italics in original) that punishment is not in itself directly concerned with altering the future. In contradiction of Bernard Shaw (1922) she maintains that there is a distinction between punishment and revenge (Shaw calls it vindictiveness): punishment's point is 'to reassert the seriousness of certain moral rules of a community. Punishment makes a drastic and public distinction between those who have broken the rules and those who have not,' through shaming, ostracism, injury or even death. It restores the balance of just deserts; the virtuous shall prosper and the wicked shall not. The balance should not, according to Morgan, be supposed to be some sort of attempt to optimize happiness or benefit. 'Punishment in its pure sense is not *in order* to get people in future to obey a moral rule; it is an expression of that rule itself. It is therefore mistaken to ask "What is punishment *for?*" unless one is prepared to ask the same question about morality. And once we ask "Why morality?" we are asking "Why human society?"' This symbolic function of punishment is of course associated particularly with imprisonment: Mr. Justice Melford Stevenson, for example, sentenced a young man who had violently attacked an old woman to ten years' imprisonment 'to cleanse society of the sort of person you are' (*Daily Telegraph,* 12 July 1978). The idea of retributive punishment is of course very old, but that does not necessarily justify it; if I may quote what I have written elsewhere (Wright, 1977), '"Crime and punishment" is used as an everyday cliché, as if the two necessarily belong together. People assume that there is a certain rightness about punishment; but for many years they accepted the rightness of the feudal system, the divine right of kings and the inequality of the sexes.'

The Old Testament is often invoked in support of retribution. But the Chief Rabbi has pointed out (*Daily Telegraph,* 24 July 1979) that the idea of retaliation is alien to the Judaic heritage. The much-quoted phrase from Exodus should literally be rendered: 'For (the loss of) an eye substitute an eye,' i.e. by monetary compensation. Capital punishment was theoretically permitted, but only on almost impossible conditions (the testimony of two eye-witnesses who must have given a prior warning to the criminal); in practice the penalty was abolished in Jewish law at the beginning of the current era. Israel has imposed no death sentence, with the sole exception of the Nazi mass killer Eichmann. Biblical doctrine requires human beings to be inviolate – eye, tooth and all.

Keeping Punishment in Check

If punishment is not to be rejected completely, its application should be subject to certain conditions. The United Nations Standard Minimum Rules, as has been noted earlier, lay down that neither punishment nor treatment shall be cruel, inhuman or degrading; they thus recognise that 'treatment', too, can be misapplied. The following seven principles are offered as the basis of a code for punishers; some apply particularly where the punishment is intended as a deterrent, and some apply also to measures intended to be rehabilitative.

The first is that the threat or use of punishment can be ethically defensible only if it is effective. (In this context 'effective' should be taken as meaning 'effective in limiting the amount of crime'.) To inflict pain on fellow human beings to no purpose is intolerable. Moreover, the threatened penalties must be demonstrably *more* effective than less severe or non-punitive methods of controlling crime (unless these are objectionable on other grounds, for example that they involve control through subliminal television messages, or drugs, or Big Brother surveillance). This has always been one of the decisive arguments against capital punishment. It is not enough to show that it is a deterrent; the evidence for this is to say the least ambiguous, since many murderers commit suicide, or are mentally disordered, or believe that they can escape detection. Even if it is not accepted that judicial killing is always wrong in principle, advocates of the death penalty must accept the burden of proving that it is a *greater* deterrent than life imprisonment. This they have never done; indeed, although the number who *are* deterred can of course never be known, there is some evidence of a 'brutalizing effect', as a result of which executions are followed by an increase in the number of homicides (Bowers and Pierce, 1980).

The second condition is necessary to satisfy the first: that there should be research to assess the results. No new measure, particularly if it is a harsher one, should be introduced unless a reasoned case can be made for it based on previous findings, and research planned to evaluate it. (The need for evaluation is beginning to be understood by British politicians, but not always the need for a reasoned case. Consider the following exchange in a debate on law and order initiated by

Mr. William Whitelaw, then opposition spokesman on home affairs (*Hansard* [H.C.] 27 February 1978, cols. 44–45):

> **Mr. Whitelaw:** ... I want to go further and have one [detention] centre with severer discipline... Those who criticize me must answer this question – if we do not try an experiment on these lines, what is the alternative? My critics have no alternative.... I do not say that this scheme will necessarily succeed.
>
> **The Minister of State, Home Office** (Mr. Brynmor John): It will not.
>
> **Mr. Whitelaw:** By what right does the Minister of State say that? He has no more idea than I whether it will work.

The research requirement entails a moral obligation to act on research findings. If a harsh sanction cannot be shown to work better than a less severe one, it should be abandoned. At present, for example, it is generally accepted that prison is pointless for homeless alcoholics, and that detoxification centres, with after-care, are comparable in cost and offer more hope for the future. It is therefore clear that as long as people are being sent to prison who could benefit in a centre, more centres are needed, rather than more prisons, in order to relieve overcrowding. With other, less expensive alternatives to imprisonment the case is even more clear-cut. Research should also monitor cost/effectiveness. The law of diminishing returns applies. Just as after a certain point larger amounts of chemicals spread on the land do not give significantly greater yields of crops, but are washed away by the rain to pollute the rivers, so unnecessarily increased punishments produce no further return on their cost, measured not only in money but in human suffering and resentment.

Paradoxically, the converse may also be true: for some people, and for some offences, deterrence might be effective, but only when inflicted on a scale that is intolerable on moral grounds. It could be compared to a drug which does not suppress the symptoms unless it is administered in such large doses as to cause intolerable side-effects. In other words, there may be deterrent potential in punishments that are, in the words of the Universal Declaration of Human Rights, 'cruel, inhuman or degrading', and the third ethical principle for the use of punishment is that we should refuse to employ such methods. Lord Gardiner made this point firmly in relation to interrogation techniques, in his minority report on the interrogation of suspected terrorists in Northern Ireland:

> I do not believe that, whether in peace time for the purpose of obtaining

information relating to men like the Richardson gang or the Kray gang, or in emergency terrorist conditions, or even in the war against a ruthless enemy, such procedures are morally justifiable ... even in the light of any marginal advantages which may thereby be obtained.

If it is to be made legal to employ methods not now legal ... I, like many of our witnesses have searched for, but been unable to find, either in logic or in morals, any limit to the degree of ill-treatment to be legalized.

He then quotes a statement from the World Conference on Religion and Peace, 1970:

The torture and ill-treatment of prisoners which is carried out with the authority of some governments constitute not only a crime against humanity, but also a crime against the moral law.

(Committee ... to consider ... interrogation, 1972)

It is sad to find the Bennett Report admitting several years later that 'Our own examination of medical evidence reveals cases in which injuries, whatever their precise cause, were not self-inflicted and were sustained in police custody' (quoted in *Police,* April 1979, p.8). But it is difficult, if not impossible, to draw a satisfactory line between acceptable and intolerable infliction of pain. Perhaps the answer is that it is right, and even in the long run more effective, for the State to concentrate less on instilling fear into its citizens, and more on gaining their respect. As Lord Wigoder said in a debate on 'the decline in respect for authority, and the need to assert the primacy of the law': 'In a civilized society, however uncivilized some of its members may be, we do not deal with them in an uncivilized way' (*Hansard* [H.L.] 1 March 1978, col. 488). Similarly, no irrevocable punishments should be used, such as capital punishment or mutilation, since they cannot be put right if an error of justice is found to have occurred. In a sense this applies also to imprisonment, since it is 'time out of life' which can never be restored.

The fourth condition is that the punishment should be proportionate to an individual's crime only. A penalty that is excessive or degrading cannot be defended on the grounds that it is never, or seldom used, rather as some school teachers keep a cane but claim that they do not use it. If it is never imposed (like the death penalty in the Channel Islands, which is invariably commuted), it becomes an empty threat; and it is no justification to say that it is not used very often (as the Saudi Arabians say that they do not actually cut off many hands), because one barbarity is one too many. History is full of the most sadistic tortures – yet the fact that they have frequently had to be used shows that they have not been very effective deterrents. But even within the range of moderate punishments, it is not fair that an offender should have his punishment increased beyond what he deserves in the uncertain hope of deterring other people. As Lord Justice Asquith (1950) said, 'an exemplary sentence is unjust; and unjust to the precise extent that it is exemplary.' Yet this happens all the time: it is justified by the fiction that what the courts are doing is only to impose a sentence at the upper end of the permissible range for the offence in question.

Fifthly, any punishment must be inflicted fairly. If it is a fine, there should be reasonable time to pay – taken for granted now, but only since the Criminal Justice Act 1914 introduced this reform, for which the Howard Association had campaigned (Rose, 1961, pp.68–69). If it involves imprisonment, there should be adequate physical conditions and safeguards against arbitrary treatment or violence. If it allows release on licence, the conditions must be clear and attainable, and a person on parole should not be recalled to prison for an alleged breach of licence conditions without a proper procedure for defending himself.

Sixthly, if individuals (and often their families) are to be made to suffer as a deliberate act of State policy, the State, including fellow members of the community, should make it possible for them to get back on their feet afterwards, by the provision of adequate aftercare. This may be compared to the provision of a doctor to dress the wounds after a flogging; to say that, it had better be stressed once more, is not to denigrate the prison service, but refers again to the effects inseparable from imprisonment. The State should set an example by making it possible for them to obtain employment; but at present government departments and nationalized industries do not have a good record for employing ex-offenders. Until they find work, people leaving prison should have enough to live on (not necessarily as a hand-out – it would be better if they were paid proper wages in prison). Above all, for the large number who are isolated from any family and friends they once had, there must be people – individual volunteers, sports clubs, and so on – who will offer them friendship, support and ideas for non-criminal occupations.

Lastly, the use of deterrence may be ethically justified (if at all) only when all possible efforts are being made to prevent people from incurring the punishments. Many people might well be dissuaded from drifting into crime by preventive measures such as those described elsewhere in this book: security precautions, the reduction of temptations, social incentives to be law-abiding, and so on. Obviously people cannot be shielded from every temptation. But when a new man-made physical hazard is created, it is accepted that safety precautions should be introduced, such as promoting road safety and putting fences round quarries; in the same way, many features of society are man-made, and potentially dangerous, and people should be afforded reasonable protection from pressures to which some of them are bound to succumb. As Barbara Wootton has written, in the concluding words of her book *Crime and Penal Policy* (1978, emphasis in original):

> The upshot of these reflections on my long experience is the hope that if we were less obsessed with the attempt to punish . . . criminals as we think they deserve, and more eager to make the path of virtue both more accessible to them and more glamorous – then perhaps in their turn *they* might take a kindlier view of *our* deserts.

The Search for an Alternative

Rehabilitation: The Ideal That Went Out of Fashion

Already in the last century, as we have seen, there were doubts about the efficacy, let alone the humanity, of prolonged, harsh punishment, and since the Gladstone report (Prisons Committee, 1895) it has been accepted in principle that it should be combined with treatment and training. The word 'treatment', however, causes confusion, because it can mean in a neutral sense 'the way someone is dealt with, fairly, unsympathetically, and so on,' or in a medical sense 'therapy applied to try to change the person treated.' I shall put the word in inverted commas except when using it in its neutral sense; for the other methods I shall use specific words, or the general term 'rehabilitation', though it is also not entirely satisfactory. Rehabilitation has been cynically defined as 'finding a man a bedsitter and a job as a kitchen porter,' but with a little more optimism I will define it as 'offering, to a person who has broken the law, help which is intended to encourage and enable him to overcome any problems that beset him, in the hope that it will be easier for him to avoid breaking the law again.' This definition avoids the 'treatment' approach, in which the client is seen as suffering from some malfunction of personality or attitude, and the probation officer diagnoses and 'treats' it. Instead, the client shares in assessing his problems, and is offered help. This 'non-treatment paradigm' has been set forth in detail by Bottoms and McWilliams (1979). It can be extended to include advocacy on behalf of a client who is, for example, having difficulty in claiming welfare or housing entitlements and may know no other articulate person except the probation officer (or a volunteer working with him) who can tackle the bureaucracy on his behalf. The problems are at least as likely to lie in his surroundings as in himself; or if they are within him, they may reflect deficiencies in his education and upbringing rather than his personality. Other offenders have no such problems in their personality or upbringing, and need rehabilitation only to overcome the effects of the punishment itself.

The 'continual failure of a mainly punitive system to diminish the volume of crime' was pointed out by Barbara Wootton (1963, p.40) in the Hamlyn Lectures; indeed she quoted Sir Thomas More as recognising the same neglected truth: 'If you do not remedy the conditions which produced thieves, the vigorous execution of justice in punishing them will be in vain.' In any case, Wootton felt that punishing the wicked and trying to prevent the recurrence of forbidden acts are not compatible objectives, as many people would like to believe. A further difficulty with punishment is that it leads to injustice unless the complex question of guilty intent, or *mens rea,* is taken into consideration. Her solution was to bypass this legal and psychological jungle, by leaving aside the concept of guilt followed by punishment: instead she proposed a wider concept of responsibility followed by action to make repetition less likely. The question would not be 'Did he mean to do it? If so how much punishment does he deserve?' nor 'How much punishment must we inflict on him in order to frighten others?' but simply 'Did he do it? If so, what is the minimum action which offers an adequate prospect of preventing future offences by the offender himself?' (pp.56, 95, 101).

The implication was that action ordered by the court could make a contribution to preventing offenders from re-offending. This was a general assumption of reformers until recently. Today there is less optimism: the rehabilitative ideal is criticized, rightly but perhaps excessively. This section will consider the criticisms; Chapters Nine and Ten will suggest another way of responding.

Five main objections are raised against the 'treatment' principle as a basis for the criminal justice system: that it is punishment in disguise, is wrongly conceived, often deprives people of liberty for longer than if they had been punished, can be degrading, and does not work. These arguments paradoxically lead hard-liners and *avant-garde* criminologists to join in calling for a return to punishment; they are therefore worth examining in more detail.

The first objection was alluded to in the definition of punishment at the beginning of this chapter: that despite intentions to the contrary, rehabilitative measures are often tantamount to punishment from the offender's point of view. (Such measures have the worst of both worlds, for from the public's point of view they fail to deter offenders or denounce offences adquately.) Indeed, those who want to intervene are sometimes so confident that they wish to do so before an offence has been committed. In his textbook, *Crime and Its Treatment*, Mays (1970) defended the idea of spotting the delinquency-prone child, and adopting preventive measures. He admitted that 'All we can say with any degree of confidence is that, given the information available, Mr. X looks very probably as though he will turn out to be a success when exposed to a particular treatment' (p.115); yet he believed, a couple of pages later, that 'when the idea of prevention gets firmer hold and after the new legislation [the Children and Young Persons Act 1969] is securely established, it may become more acceptable, and be considered no more damaging to be regarded as delinquency-prone than it is at present to have a below-average IQ or a tendency to asthma or epileptic fits.' This is humanely intended, but contains the danger that it will be a self-fulfilling prophecy. Once a child is labelled as 'pre-delinquent', or still worse as delinquent, he acquires a status by which he will be treated differently and he may come to think of himself as being what he is told he is. One danger, then, is that the prediction will prove itself right; a second is that it will be wrong. Not only in that some of those who offend will escape notice; but also some who would not have offended are subjected to treatment that they neither need nor want. Social reforms should be provided because they are desirable in themselves, not imposed as a means of checking deviant behaviour (Bottomley, 1979, pp.150–162).

These scruples about excessive intervention should not, however, justify doing nothing. It is the common experience of teachers and social workers to know of a handful of young people who seem to be clearly heading for trouble. It may be a boy who throws tantrums, or suffers from compulsions or fears, or is unnaturally violent or uncontrollable; if he truants, or is suspended or expelled he is likely to drift into the company of others who have refused school for various reasons and follow them into delinquent behaviour, besides being unable to form a relationship with any teachers who might be able to help him, simply because he does not meet them. Children like this need help because they are disturbed, not because they are delinquent; but they should be persuaded, not coerced, into accepting it.

The second objection follows from the first: it suggests that the rehabilitative ideal is conceptually mistaken. The eighteenth-century lawyer Beccaria had considered that punishment should be strictly graded according to the crime committed; and that the harm that it caused just out-weighed the good that the criminal derived from the crime. It should not be varied to suit the circumstances of the offender, nor should 'reformation' be thrust upon criminals (Radzinowicz & King, 1977). In the early nineteenth century the religious ideal of penitence was superimposed, but the age of Comte and Darwin saw attempts to apply scientific principles to the study of criminal behaviour. Recognising only positive facts and observable phenomena and the relations between them, positivists like Lombroso sought to explain crime by studying such aspects of criminals. Their generalizations, however, were based on the untypical minority of offenders who were caught and therefore available for study, and assumed that the causes of crime lay within the criminal. Positivist criminologists have had a field day linking delinquency with body build, glandular imbalance, XYY chromosomes, hypoglycaemia, IQ, and psychological maladjustment; subsequent attention has been turned to environmental factors such as poverty (or relative poverty), inconsistent parental discipline, mixing with the already delinquent, frustration and alienation induced by society, stigmatization, and the structure of society itself.

While the causes of crime were believed to be in the individual, the hope was that they could be 'cured', as in Samuel Butler's famous caricature of *Erewhon*: the persons who had the 'misfortune' to commit a crime would be referred to one of 'a class of men trained in soul-craft, whom they call straighteners, as nearly as I can translate a word which literally means "one who bends back the crooked".' The idea that the offender is 'sick,' neatly caricatured by Samuel Butler, had many adherents until quite recently; a newer trend is to seek explanations in the social environment, and in the structure of society which contains built-in inequalities of housing, education, employment and other opportunities. Both hypotheses are tenable, but both are in danger of denying the person's responsibility for his actions.

They also underrate the responsibility of other members of the community, both in their dealings with him and in the example they set him.

The argument over the 'rehabilitative ideal' is clouded by the desire for a simple explanation, and preferably one which finds faults in 'them', the convicted offenders, rather than 'us'. But crime is not a single type of behaviour, and it springs from origins which are equally diverse. Someone who breaks the law may be a well-brought-up person who thinks he can escape detection, or a member of a loving but criminal family, or his parents may have been too lax, or strict to the point of violence, or inconsistent; one or both of his parents may have been absent, or mentally ill, or alcoholic. He may be poor, with few skills or opportunities, or privileged, with a desire to increase his wealth and power still further, or bedevilled by an expensive weakness such as gambling. Or he may be a very ordinary person subjected to particular temptations and pressures. Perhaps if an analogy is to be drawn it should not be with disease but with malnutrition. A person's diet is determined partly by his own choice, partly by external constraints and pressures; if he eats too little, or too much, or a deficient or polluted diet, his body will not function correctly. To those who argue that crime can no longer be excused by poverty, the answer may be that, both physically and spiritually, individual malnutrition can exist alongside social obesity. Or a comparison might be made not with curative medicine, which waits until someone is ill and then tries to cure him (often by suppressing symptoms rather than causes), but with preventive medicine, which promotes an environment, diet and mode of life which are conducive to good functioning of the body. The trouble is that Nature, or God, or whatever creative force is responsible for the order of things, is very tolerant, and allows a long period of abuse before the ill-effects manifest themselves. Such a delay between stimulus and response is, as psychologists know, not conducive to rapid learning; consequently countries often take a long time to adopt preventive measures, whether medical or social. Whatever may be said of the 'medical model' as an explanation of the behaviour of individuals, the parallel with social hygiene is uncomfortably close in relation to collective behaviour. This is not to deny individual responsibility: the acts are committed by individuals, but others share responsibility for the conditions which put them under such pressure. It is therefore inappropriate to try to tackle prevention by measures, even rehabilitative ones, directed only at the offender and not at his surroundings also. If there is a known accident black spot, individual drivers who crash there are responsible, but improving the road design will be more effective (and often less expensive: *Times,* 21 June 1980) in cutting the number of accidents than punishing the drivers – or for that matter re-training them. Admittedly many accidents happen on adequately designed stretches of road: prevention there requires other strategies, but at least where there are obvious improvements to be made, they should be made.

The third objection concerns the length and nature of the would-be therapeutic intervention. Wootton recognised that 'the prospective offender must have a reasonably clear idea of the sentence that he is likely to incur,' and suggested that the courts should therefore fix the maximum (Wootton, 1963, pp.98, 114), but did not spell out the conflicting principles involved. In the name of 'treatment' a court can firstly deprive the individual of the safeguard that his sentence will be limited in proportion to his offence, and then interfere with his liberty more than avowedly punitive measures. A famous victim of this was George Jackson, author of *Soledad Brother,* who because he would not respond to 'treatment' spent eleven years in prison for the robbery of $70, and died there. In the late 1960s judges were still being encouraged to lengthen very short sentences so as to provide enough time for 'treatment' and training, and often they complied. In the 1970s, however, although 'treatment' was falling out of fashion, sentences continued to lengthen. Meanwhile under the welfare-orientated Children and Young Persons Act of 1969 a juvenile can be sent to a community home for up to six years after a minor offence (though in practice it is seldom for so long), and the fact that the release date is decided behind closed doors may cause additional feelings of unfairness. As an American judge has said, 'Experience should teach us to be on our guard to protect liberty when the Government's purposes are beneficient' (Brandeis, quoted by Fogel, 1978).

Fourthly, the 'treatment' model may lead to would-be therapeutic measures that are sometimes irreversible, and often demeaning. The most extreme example is psychosurgery. In 1947 a report on no less than one thousand cases of pre-frontal leucotomy was published, claiming that a third of patients were discharged, being recovered or improved, and a further third remained in hospital improved. But 1% became worse, 3% had fits, and 6% died, and the report ominously concluded that 'the question as to whether or not these results are achieved at the cost of the loss of some finer mental qualities is not yet answered and further study is needed on this most important point' (Board of Control, 1947). This operation now has few advocates; indeed, even the less drastic electro-convulsive therapy (ECT), which seems to a layman to be comparable with kicking the television set to make it go, arouses much unease, which is aggravated by allegations that some hospitals have used it for purposes of control rather than therapy.

Besides irreversibility there are problems of side-effects of 'treatment'. Hormone therapy for sex offenders, for example, can cause breast enlargement. In its defence it is said that the side-effects are fully explained and the prisoner's consent is obtained. It is, however, questionable whether consent can be freely given by a prisoner who knows that refusal will almost certainly mean that he is denied release on parole. The Howard League (1975) and MIND (National Association for Mental Health) (Gostin, 1977, pp.96–97), have proposed an alternative scheme for dealing with mentally abnormal offenders, namely, to provide for hospital orders of limited duration proportionate to the crime. If at the end of the order the patient is still considered ill or dangerous, civil procedures for restraint of the mentally ill would have to be used. For the small number who persistently commit very serious offences, however, individual liberty may have to be subordinated to public protection; but any such powers must be subject to rigorous restrictions. At the same time regardless of any medication that may be in use, every effort should be made to find ways in which the offender can adapt his circumstances so as to avoid situations where the prohibited behaviour is likely, for example, by moving to a job where there is less of a tradition of hard drinking, or taking up a leisure occupation other than youth work. Thomas (1979, p.28) tells of a man sentenced in Inverness in 1855 to fourteen years' transportation for having sexual intercourse with his wife's sister during the lifetime of his wife: his sentence was remitted on condition that he reside south of the River Tweed for fourteen years. (How this was enforced is not stated.)

Therapeutic measures do not normally involve physical methods, however. There is individual case-work, and as a variant group counselling, in which a member of staff, such as a social worker or prison officer, sits down with a group of inmates and encourages them to offer each other support and insight into ways of coping with their problems. At its best this method can be helpful, provided certain pitfalls are avoided. Enough time must be set aside for support for group leaders. It should not be assumed that every offender has problems of this kind, nor should people be coerced, for example, by the prospect of earlier parole, into going through the motions of some would-be therapeutic programme, outwardly complying, without any real commitment to it: this would be pointless and demeaning. A story has circulated that the advocates of group counselling tried to explain it to prison department top brass by arranging for them to participate in a group, but one senior official left the session abruptly and never returned. This could be taken to show the method's potential for pulling the veil off problems which an individual is unwilling to face or reveal; but it could also mean that it is an intrusive technique to which no one should be subjected without freely given consent after full discussion. Otherwise the result could be uncomfortably close to the group session depicted in the book and film *One Flew over the Cuckoo's Nest* (Kesey, 1962), where an unsympathetic nurse pried into the lives of her patients in the name of therapy.

The fifth objection to the rehabilitative ideal is that it doesn't work. Several reviews of research have reached discouraging conclusions. Cornish and Clarke (1975 pp.47–49) dismiss the very idea that institutional treatment might have much impact on juvenile delinquency, unless more effort is made to relate it to the homes and environments to which the inmates will return. A spell of custodial 'treatment' may actually slow down the process of marrying, finding a job, settling down and desisting from criminal activities (Trasler, 1976). Another review (Brody, 1976) concludes that 'Rehabilitative programmes – whether involving psychiatric treatment, counselling, casework or intensive contact and special attention, in custodial or non-custodial settings – have no predictably beneficial effects' (p.37). He did however put his point the other way: 'As "softer" sentences have apparently no worse effect on recidivism and still offer the chance of less tangible if as yet unknown advantages, they are seen as preferable by all schools of thought except perhaps the retributivist'. Moreover, some 'treatment' did work for particular offenders, and the personalities and skills of the therapists are also important. Sometimes the 'treatment' has failed because in reality none was provided (Brody, 1978).

One of the most quoted demolishers of the rehabilitative ideal is Martinson (1974): '*With few and isolated exceptions,* the rehabilitative efforts that have been reported so far have had no appreciable effect on recidivism'. The qualifying phrase which I have emphasised tends to be ignored; so also does the fact that he dismissed many studies on the ground that their research was inadequate, so that the

199

projects themselves were not necessarily all failures. Palmer (1975) showed that Martinson's analysis does not entirely support his conclusions: of 82 studies mentioned, 14 had a positive outcome and 25 partly positive, a total of 48% – not an overwhelming success, but better than 'with few and isolated exceptions'. The types of treatment which achieved good results included education and skill development, group counselling, milieu therapy, psychotherapy in the community, and intensive probation supervision. Sometimes the good results came from *less* treatment, for example with shorter sentences, or non-institutional or suspended ones. In one study parole agents who were 'adequate' produced improvements with a small or large case-load; inadequate ones had more failures even with a smaller case-load – not a surprising finding, but one that is often neglected. Offenders are interviewed and assessed, but how many studies take account of the personality profile, IQ, or even that other IQ the idleness quotient, of probation officers, psychotherapists, prison officers or volunteers? Has anyone compared the success rate of individual magistrates or judges, as reflected in the recidivism of those they sentenced? When a particular offender 'fails', how much of the failure is his, and how much is attributable to others in the system, or the system itself, or to the society which fails to give it enough resources? Palmer concludes (pp.149–150) that:

> Martinson's review strongly suggested that no known methods of treatment contain the "answer" for all offenders. Together with other data, it also indicated that some methods are nevertheless of value to at least *some* offenders. However this latter suggestion did not appear in his oft-quoted concluding remarks.

Martinson himself is reported as criticizing his 'survey of the literature' method for needlessly rejecting significant pieces of work because of imperfections in their research techniques; he had come to the conclusion that he and his co-authors 'threw out the baby but clung rigorously to the bathwater' (*Federal Probation*, March 1979, p.86).

Support for less pessimistic conclusions comes from a review by Romig (1978) of 829 juvenile justice studies up to 1976. In the years since Martinson's study research techniques had advanced; even so, some of the results have been clouded by the research techniques themselves. In one project with random allocation between the treatment and the control group no significant result was observed, but when youths considered amenable to this form of treatment were selected, their outcome was significantly better (pp.77–78). Techniques with unspecific aims did not do well; one of these was casework, defined as an effort based on personal friendship with boys and their families to make them understand themselves and the world they live in. Behaviour modification improved certain specific behaviours such as school attendance, but not delinquency. Attendance did not improve, however, when the project workers were consistently 'positive and warm', but only when their approval was contingent upon improvement.

Two main conclusions can be drawn from Romig's review. Firstly, rewards in the form of approval, visits to sports matches, or money, were effective in improving behaviour. This is a finding that could well be remembered by those whose idea of law enforcement is limited to punishment for misbehaviour. It could also be useful to those who want to improve attendance in a rehabilitative project without resort to compulsion. Secondly, the guiding principle throughout is specificity: if people have a clear idea of what they are trying to do, and of the specific needs of those they are dealing with, there is a reasonable chance of success. This too is a lesson that can be learnt by punishers as well as rehabilitaters. Punishment is unspecific (as well as being uncertain and frequently slow); nor does it teach any new skills. Like vaguely supportive social work, it neither sets clear goals nor helps to achieve them.

There can even be cases where the attempt to rehabilitate makes things worse. Walter Probyn (1977) feels that he was a victim of this process. At the age of nine he was placed on probation for a trifling offence, by a magistrate with the impeccably liberal intention of helping a child who seemed to be at risk, while his middle-class playmate was let off. For a breach of probation he was sent to approved school; after one of many escapes he was beaten up by policemen, who justified his bruises by saying he had assaulted them, so that at the age of fourteen he was sentenced to the first of a series of prison sentences which were to total more than thirty years. Carasov (1971) was another whose criminal career began with an approved school, in his case for stealing a bicycle in the course of running away from a hated foster-mother. The research of West and Farrington (1977) suggests that 'The experience of conviction usually led to a further hardening of anti-social attitudes and a worsening of delinquent behaviour.' Of course not all rehabilitative measures are such disasters: there are some success stories, but the question is whether the proportion of the latter is high enough to outweigh the former. It may be better to do nothing than to do the wrong thing. Any intervention in the life of an offender should be kept to the minimum compatible with other necessary objectives such as affirming the law and protecting the public.

Back to Punishment?

The strength of the rejection of the 'treatment' ideal in some quarters is probably due not merely to disillusion at its failure to live up to the hopes that were pinned on it, but to a feeling that it was hypocritical: while intending, or pretending, to 'treat' people it was in fact punishing them, by depriving them of liberty to an excessive extent. This was felt for example in the parole system where among the rehabilitative criteria for the decision to release there is a strong admixture of punitive ones. Secondly, the idea that the individual offender is frequently maladjusted or inadequate and should be 'adjusted' and rehabilitated into society is seen as being in many cases inaccurate and unfair. Delinquent behaviour can be a rational response, although a reprehensible one, to an unjust social structure: Jefferson and Clarke (1974) for instance point out that street robbery ('mugging') by rejected, unemployed adolescents provides not merely the chance of money and excitement, but an opportunity to express resentment at society. The conclusion is that neither preventive nor deterrent measures will work unless the structure that produces the deprivation is reformed: 'The construction of a just system of criminal justice in an unjust society is a contradiction in terms' (American Friends Service Committee, 1971, p.16).

Advocates of another school of thought criticize both the rehabilitative ideal and this response to it, from a different standpoint. They point out that sociological theories of crime causation may be correct but the measures they suggest, if any, are often long-term ones, which offer little guidance on what to do about offences occurring this week. J. Q. Wilson (1975), for example, acknowledges that a crime increase may follow a rise in the number of 14-to-24-year olds, because when there is a population 'bulge' there are more young 'barbarians' to be socialized; and that a child may become delinquent because of the influences of his family or his friends. But, Wilson says dismissively, such theories often fail to provide guidelines for policy: 'I have yet to see a "root cause" or to encounter a government program that has successfully attacked it.'

Both schools of thought, however, are reverting to the idea of punishment. Wilson does so from a rather simple deterrent stand-point: if you can't improve the rewards of virtue, maintain the differential by increasing the punishment of vice. Von Hirsch (1976, p.18) says: 'It cannot be rational or fair to sentence for treatment, without a reasonable expectation that treatment works.' But as has been argued earlier in this chapter, exactly the same could be said of punishment. Perhaps recognising this, though not admitting it, writers of this school take refuge in the classical belief that 'Certain things are simply wrong and ought to be punished. And this we do believe' (Von Hirsch, p.xxxix), which to my mind is just not good enough if they are using punishment in the sense, as defined above, of mere infliction of deliberate pain. They also appeal to the metaphysical Kantian agument (Von Hirsch, Chapter Six) that 'When someone infringes another's rights, he gains an unfair advantage... The punishment ... restores the equilibrium'; but, as will be suggested later, reparation could be used to the same end; denunciation, also, could be achieved in other ways. The advocates of punishment seem uneasily aware of the objections, for they seek to minimize the use of punishment and especially imprisonment, like the housemaid who had a baby and tried to play down her lapse by saying 'It's only a little one, ma'am.'

There is another danger in the assumption that the mistakes of rehabilitation can be dealt with only by abandoning it in favour of punishment: politicians who instinctively favour punishment may seize on the arguments, as for example, Sir Keith Joseph quotes Michael Zander (*Sunday Telegraph,* 28 May 1978) advocating 'the elimination of this kind of treatment for offenders and its replacement by a more honest punishment ethic'. Von Hirsch admits that 'Our solution is one of despair, not hope' and the last words of his book are 'As long as a substantial segment of the population is denied adequate opportunities for livelihood, any scheme for punishing must be morally flawed.' Indeed, this is hardly a solution at all, for three reasons. Firstly, by implication it refers only to the crimes of the poor, rather than of those who already have a more than adequate livelihood and resort to no less harmful behaviour in order to gain still more money and status. Secondly, it disregards the fact that for large segments of populations everywhere, opportunities for livelihood *are* denied: it is therefore inconsistent that much of the book is nevertheless taken up with schemes for punishment. Thirdly, as the present book tries to show, punishment has other serious disadvantages.

Social Control Without Repression

If then there are objections both to punishment and to the attempt at compulsory rehabilitation, is there an approach to law enforcement that can be put in their place? Life would be intolerable in a community without some form of social control. This phrase raises the hackles of some people, to whom it suggests authoritarianism exercised by a ruling minority on the rest of the population. There are two replies to this charge. Firstly, social control is only repressive to the extent that society is unjust. Western societies, and others, are unjust in various ways, with unequal distribution of resources and opportunities. Their law enforcement systems are open to grave criticisms, in particular for concentrating disproportionately on the crimes of the powerless, many of which are relatively minor; these countries nevertheless fall short of being tyrannies. Secondly, even an unjust society needs some form of social control. Ordinary people need protection against some who are much like themselves, as well as against exploitation by some of the rich and powerful: there will always be some harmful acts by one person against another, whatever the socio-economic structure of society. We may hope, and work, for social and political reforms, but law must be maintained in the meantime; indeed an important part of those reforms should be to make the law enforcement system more equitable, for example by bringing the harmful acts of the powerful within the scope of the law, and seeking ways to change the features of society that seem to lead people to harm each other more often.

There remains the problem of deciding the measures to be taken towards those who are found to have committed harmful acts. As was shown earlier, punishment can be demeaning, oppressive and ineffective. Rehabilitative measures are not immune from these defects; but despite misconceptions and misapplications of the rehabilitative ideal, the case for throwing it out with the bathwater does not seem to me to have been made out. Von Hirsch (1976) and his collaborators themselves concede that in some ways 'It was never really given a complete chance, [and] that it was only accepted in theory while in practice the system has insisted on maintaining punitive practices.' Those who design 'treatment' programmes have 'rarely allowed for individual variations, or "interaction effects", in their experimental designs, but have expected one particular programme to work equally for all offenders and to provide a universal remedy.' Expectations have been unrealistic: 'A few sessions of therapy cannot change the habits of a lifetime or counteract the influences on an offender once he is released from confinement and returns to his familiar surroundings and companions' (Brody, 1978, pp.135, 136). There has been too much readiness to generalize from those offenders – among the minority who are caught – who have social or individual handicaps and to ignore more universal human traits such as acquisitiveness, the desire to count for something, and weakness in the face of temptation. Until recently not enough stress was placed on environmental influences, especially those which are inherent in the structure of society. Blaming crime on deprivation does not account for those who are already flourishing comfortably in society, and yet act criminally. But when all that has been said, although it may be wrong to try to alter a person while failing to remedy deficiencies in his environment, it is surely acceptable, if reasonable efforts are being made to improve that environment, to try to persuade him to alter his attitude towards it.

Persuasion is a concept which appears surprisingly little in the literature of penology. This method of trying to influence behaviour is commonly employed among equals, and is therefore more appropriate in a society which claims some regard for equality; attempts at deterrence and compulsory rehabilitation rely ultimately on the use of force and are more likely to be used on members of the weaker sections of society.

In an ideal world the law would be upheld as far as possible by appealing to people's better nature, or at least to their sense of shame, rather than by threatening them. It does happen: whereas in Britain, to take a small example, posters on railway and underground stations usually threaten heavy penalties for fare dodgers, in West Germany and Switzerland the posters do not stress the penalties but urge passengers not to 'ride on other people's backs.' Nearly everyone will agree that when a person had broken the law, other members of society collectively have a right to intervene; but this right is not unconditional. There are certain limits beyond which they should never go, and even within those limits they should be proportionate to the offence. Other criteria which they should meet have been discussed in this chapter. Neither persuasion nor compulsion, of course, can succeed if a person is incapable of behaving in the way required of him; many of the objections to compulsory rehabilitation would be removed if it were made voluntary and regarded as enabling.

There has rightly been criticism of measures which impose excessive constraints in the name of 'treatment', such as care orders which result in unnecessary removal of children from home; but there is no reason to go to the other extreme, as some probation officers seem to do. We are all subject to constraints, and the offender need not be shielded from them, provided he is also offered fair social and financial incentives and, if he needs it, the compensatory education or other help that can equip him to claim his rights, shoulder his responsibilities, and develop his full human potential. There are also some who have been so damaged by their experiences that they need therapy in some form.

The implication of these two considerations taken together – that intervention is legitimate within limits and that help is often needed – is that offenders could be *required* to visit a probation officer, day centre or similar project, where they could be *offered* help with any problems they recognise. The problems would not necessarily be personality difficulties, as used to be assumed, but practical matters such as accommodation and employment. Those without special problems would merely have to report at stated times. The main objections to the rehabilitative ideal as described above would be met by restricting the length of time for which anyone was required to attend, in proportion to his offence. Even if he had deep-seated problems, he would not be required to attend for a long period if his offence was only a minor one; if he wished to continue voluntarily, he could. This could be regarded as a combination of punishment, to the extent that he was required to be in a certain place at a certain time, with enabling, which was the way the time was spent. Some probation officers are beginning to use a 'contract' between the probationer and themselves: the probation service undertakes to provide certain services, within its resources, and the offender agrees to make full use of them. The contract is not legally binding, and is used mainly for its persuasive effect; it can however be criticized for being one-sided, in that if the offender is totally uncooperative he can be taken back to court, whereas he has little redress if the probation officer delivers an inadequate service.

Some types of intervention do not, however, fit neatly into this relatively tidy framework: schemes such as the Kent Family Placement project, referred to in Chapter Four, in which foster parents accept difficult and disturbed adolescents into their families; or probation supervision by volunteers, which could be, as it were, a non-residential version of the same principle, providing 'aunts and uncles' instead of 'parents'. What these offer, particularly to young and disadvantaged offenders, is *caring*. This is a vital dimension in human motivation, but is too often left out of the argument: it often appears to be assumed that the only options are punishment, which is essentially coercive, and imposed rehabilitation or 'treatment', which can be manipulative. If caring is to be made part of a system it will require safeguards, of course: adequate skilled support must be provided for all concerned, and placements must be based on consent, including the individual's right to opt out if things are not going well. This is one of the reasons for concern at the proposal, in the White Paper *Young offenders* (Home Office and others, 1980), which would give courts the power to order an adolescent's *compulsory* removal from home and would include fostering as one method of removal.

Measures imposed on offenders make demands on them as regards their future conduct. There is not necessarily anything improper in that, but as a counterpart there should be something in the nature of a social contract. Citizens can make legitimate demands on the State, as well as *vice versa* – and those who have broken the law are still citizens. For one thing, the ideal is that social control should be exercised not in the name of the powerful forces in society, but of all the people who are trying to live together in reasonable harmony (Howard League, 1974). They may, collectively and individually, have to alter their life-style. In Western countries we have shops which want to cut shoplifting without increasing staff, public housing authorities who try to cut vandalism while reducing the number of resident caretakers, and people working overtime while others are unemployed – to take just three examples. Inevitably some individuals will fail to honour the social contract, but when they do the society which invokes the penalty clause should make sure that its own hands are clean.

When it does act to enforce the law, there are some methods which society should refuse to employ, whether or not they are effective. Disraeli, in *Sybil,* comments that if among the population of Wodgate there was 'less vice ... than might at first be anticipated, we must remember that excesses are checked by poverty of blood and constant exhaustion. Scanty food and hard labour are in their way if not exactly moralists, a tolerably good police.' We do not now try to starve the populace into submission; even when workers are on strike, a humane society provides social security for their families. We do not know how many people were deterred from extra-marital sex by the rigid old attitudes, but the suffering inflicted on illegitimate mothers and their children was so great that today we do not try to uphold the institution of marriage by making outcasts of them;

instead, we go some way toward helping them. To be compassionate may require more courage than to be tough, and in the short term it may seem to be ineffective; but as Solzhenitsyn has said (*The Times,* 2 April 1976): 'A moral stance can suddenly turn out to be more far-sighted than any pragmatism.'

9. Keeping Crime
in Check

If deterrence through punishment is not as effective as people like to assume, and since there are also grave doubts as to its morality, how else can crime be kept in check? Reformers are often accused of being too squeamish to inflict punishment; thereby putting the community at risk. Their reply is that on the contrary, if politicians are encouraging the public to put its faith in primitive methods which have been discredited, the time has come to draw attention to the fact; otherwise people will have a false sense of security, and will not give their attention to the search for more effective methods. But what methods offer any better protection against crime?

My proposal is this: that we should go a step beyond Wootton's premiss that deterrence of the general public is problematical, and accept that influencing the individual who has appeared in court, whether through deterrence or rehabilitation, is no less so. The process of bringing people to court may act as a deterrent, but the potential of court sentences for preventing crime is so marginal that we should no longer regard them as having a significant effect towards crime prevention. If they make an incidental contribution, that will be a bonus; but the primary effort towards prevention should be by means of specifically preventive measures, unrelated to the court (although it is to be hoped that magistrates and judges, as prominent citizens, would help to establish them). Although this may sound radical to those brought up on the punishment ethic, it is a well established principle. The opening paragraph of the regulations for Peel's new police, for example, state that 'It should be understood at the outset that the principal object to be attained is the prevention of crime. To this end every effort of the police is to be directed. The security of person and property, the preservation of the public tranquillity, and all other objects of a police establishment will then be better effected than by the detection and punishment of the offender after he has succeeded in committing the crime' (quoted by Rolph, 1962). Although theory is often punitive, in practice it will often be found that when a group of people sit down to work out ways of reducing the incidence of a particular form of crime, their thoughts focus mainly on preventive measures. The courts, relieved of the dispiriting task of attempting the impossible, would devote themselves to each individual case, concentrating on a question hitherto largely omitted from the theory of criminal law: what can be done by the offender or others to repair the harm caused by the offender's act, and make similar acts less likely in future? The two main aims, prevention and making amends, will be examined in the last two chapters of this book.

Although the expression 'crime prevention' is in common use, no one is suggesting that crime can be prevented. Even to approach total prevention would lead to oppressive social control, denial of liberty and intolerable over-policing. What can be done is to study the circumstances in which crimes occur, and then to use a variety of strategies aimed at reducing the number of crimes committed. This chapter will consider, first, measures aimed directly at crime reduction, in a general way and in relation to specific types of crime; secondly, the quest for a better society in which pressures towards crime would not be so great; and thirdly, the responsibility of individual citizens. The first concentrates on making it more difficult to commit crimes, or to escape detection; the second and third are ways of trying to make people less ready to harm each other.

General Preventive Strategies

Eight principal approaches are identified in a recent book of studies by the Home Office Research Unit (Clarke and Mayhew, 1980). The following is their list, but not all the examples are theirs; some further examples will be given later in the chapter when methods aimed at specific types of crime are considered.

TARGET HARDENING

The most basic way of reducing crime is to increase physical security with bolts, bars, steering column locks and immobilizing devices on vehicles, and similar methods.

TARGET REMOVAL

Cash in transit is notoriously vulnerable: paper transactions reduce the risk. It is high time more people accepted payment of wages by cheque. In its annual report for 1978, Barclays Bank states that 59%

of the British working population are paid in cash, compared with about 5% in Germany, France, Australia and Canada and 1% in the U.S.A. In 1978 security companies were subjected to 169 armed attacks on their vans and four people were killed (*Daily Telegraph,* 18 March 1979).

REMOVING THE MEANS TO CRIME

The use of screening devices to prevent weapons from being taken on aircraft has already been mentioned. Another example is the provision of plastic containers in pubs where violence is frequent, so that glasses cannot be used as weapons.

REDUCING THE PAY-OFF

This applies particularly to property crime. One method is to mark valuable property indelibly so that it is harder to dispose of. Another is the 'sting' operation in which some American police forces have posed as 'fences' so as to trap thieves and undermine the trust between thieves and fences.

FORMAL SURVEILLANCE

An example is patrols in public parks.

NATURAL SURVEILLANCE

This consists in making it easier for places to be supervised by members of the community as they go about their daily activities. A few years ago, for example, a group of tenants complained to the Greater London Council that the firm of contract cleaners on their housing estate was not doing its job properly; the tenants threatened to do the job themselves and send the bill to the council. It would have made good sense for the council to accept, and to employ local people wherever possible for cleaning and maintenance. They would have had a supervisory function simply by being around on the estate, would probably have got to know at least some of the children by name (an important factor in discipline, as schoolteachers will confirm), and could have checked up if, for example, they were not at school when they should be. There would be additional bonuses of other kinds: for example the cleaners could notice if old people had not taken their milk in and might therefore be in need of help. The neighbourhood councils or residents' association might act as a permanent body through which problems could be channelled. Other ways of encouraging people to be around can be suggested at meetings of local residents. Possibilities include: resisting any move to charge for admission to public parks, since that would reduce the number of people using them, as well as restricting children's play space. Buskers should not be bannned from subways, since their presence may discourage vandalism and robberies. Telephone kiosks should be in full view, to discourage vandalism (as well as making them easier to find), although Home Office research suggests that better protection is given by siting them in supervised premises such as shops, pubs and launderettes (Mayhew and others, 1979). Now that tower blocks are unpopular, it might be worth converting some of the flats into offices, which would discourage day-time vandalism by ensuring more coming and going during business hours. Milkmen and other regular tradespeople making door-to-door deliveries are an asset from this point of view too. Perhaps small shops and cafés could be encouraged to remain open late at night. Areas which have multiple purposes are safer, as Jane Jacobs notes (1961, pp.29ff.); furthermore: 'If people are afraid they remain inside behind locked doors ... A vicious cycle is created whereby crime forces people off the streets and out of the parks, and the non-use of streets and parks results in a further increase in crime.' When fear makes public places more deserted, and hence more dangerous, more police and powers will be called for; this will divert attention from the real nature of the problem.

SURVEILLANCE BY EMPLOYEES

It has been shown that the presence of caretakers on housing estates can reduce the amount of vandalism. Supervision is also one of the keys to checking shoplifting, which can be limited considerably by service from behind a counter; this has the further social advantage of allowing a more personal contact between the shopkeeper and the customers, but at the price of reduced turnover. In self-service shops some limitation of shoplifting is possible with a reasonably high density of staff, and all the more if staff are trusted and vigilant; but staff are expensive, and in self-service shops not only is theft easier but dedicated staff with strong loyalty are perhaps less commonly found (Walsh, 1978, pp.84–86).

Strategies of reducing opportunities to commit crime are beginning to be developed. One is to treat prevention as an aspect of management on a par with, say, marketing or stock control. Pease (1979) in his useful review of crime prevention strategies mentions that thefts of tobacco and wines and spirits in transit in the United

Kingdom have plummeted after these industries developed special departments responsible for security. In the case of the tobacco industry, the losses in 1978 were reduced to one-sixth of the value stolen in 1969 (adjusted to 1969 prices) and for wines and spirits from £1 million in 1971 to £48,000 in 1978 (prices not adjusted). Systems for handling money should be designed so as not to facilitate theft. This was recognised by a judge when five ticket collectors were convicted of pocketing excess fares: he refused to imprison them on the ground that British Rail subjected them to an excessive degree of temptation by not insisting that receipts be given (*Daily Telegraph,* 22 October 1976).

ENVIRONMENTAL MANAGEMENT

People's surroundings are one of the influences on their behaviour. Physically, they respond to noise, pollution and overcrowding; socially, to alienation, loneliness, anxiety and dehumanization (Jeffrey, 1971, pp.214–225). These effects probably extend to criminal behaviour, although conclusive proof is difficult, and architects and town planners should be required to study the social effects of their work and meet the people who have to use their buildings. It has been suggested for example that houses should be arranged so as to allow residents to establish contact readily, by being built in short streets and sharing common space (Alexander, 1964, p.44). Since some types of crime are more common on housing estates where there is a high concentration of children, this factor should be allowed for in housing allocation policies. Further examples will be given below, in considering specific offences such as vandalism; the possiblities of community action will be described in more detail in the next section.

Two further points need to be made in relation to preventive approaches generally. The first is that although a good case can be made for them, putting them into operation inevitably takes money and effort. It would therefore be good policy to devise incentives. At present, for example, the insured has little incentive to spend much money on security devices, since insurance companies, because of the cost of inspection, often do not insist on them. In Denmark, on the other hand, stores have a strong incentive to take measures against shoplifting, since the police refuse to prosecute for the theft of smaller items (up to 500 Kr), and there is no right of private prosecution in this area of Danish law (Pease, 1979). There is a need for further ways of inducing individuals, firms and local authorities to adopt preventive measures.

Secondly, some of the schemes described here could, if mis-applied, degenerate into a remedy worse than the disease. Super-vision could turn into surveillance; citizens keeping a look-out could become vigilantes. In building design, excessive pre-occupation with security could make the Englishman's home too much like a castle for comfort. Measures designed to keep people out of prison, or out of the criminal justice system altogether, could actually add up to an increase in social control as was seen in Chapter Five (Cohen, 1979, p.23–4). A typical instance of this is that minor offenders, or even youngsters deemed merely at risk of offending, who previously would have been let off with an informal warning, may be brought into 'diversionary' or 'intermediate' schemes, while more serious offenders for whom the schemes were intended remain as enmeshed in the system as before. But in making this point Cohen concedes that these programmes can be more humane, offering improved oppor-tunities and resources to groups that need them.

Community Action to Reduce Crime

Several forms of crime prevention are dependent on the co-operation of the community; but how is this to be secured, especially when in so many large cities there is little sense of community among those who happen to live in the same area? It is a sad fact that it often takes a tragedy to stimulate demands for action relating to crime (as also to road traffic, chemical contamination and other social dangers). In the case of crime the action demanded is all too often concentrated on the more severe punishment of the perpetrators, regardless of its effec-tiveness (or lack of it). A better memorial has been set up to one victim, a 90-year-old retired teacher who died in Indianapolis at the hands of a teenage purse snatcher. Thirty leaders of the city's major women's clubs held a meeting in March 1962, and formed the India-napolis Anti-Crime Crusade. The women spent six months studying the crime problem and setting priorities. They made a point of tack-ling problems initially on a modest, pilot basis. They 'curbed one crime, put one drop-out back in school, got one bright new light on one dark street, sat one day in court to observe, helped one problem child, assisted one father to get a job.' They worked with the auth-orities; for example they discussed the problem of truancy with school counsellors, and were given permission to contact drop-outs personally to discover why they did not attend school and to attempt to remedy the causes. Of the first 28 contacted, 26 returned to school.

The crusade estimates that it has returned 2,000 young people to school. It is prepared to criticize where necessary, however, and claims for instance to have brought about substantial improvements in the conduct of local courts – which is desirable in itself and probably enhances respect for the law among defendants (U.S. National Advisory Commission, 1973).

It is also possible to involve people in a district that has little sense of community. In Savin Street and Moreland Street, in Boston, Massachusetts, known as the Sav-More neighbourhood, the crime rate was the eighth highest of the 74 neighbourhoods of Boston. Residents feared attack not only at night but in broad daylight on busy streets. There is high unemployment, with 27% of the (mainly black) population of 5,000 below the poverty level. In 40% of families a woman is head of the household: few of them would have the time for the activities of the women's organizations of Indianapolis. This downtrodden district did, however, have a Neighbourhood Association and a centre run by professionals. Between them, they formed the Sav-More Community Security Program, defined as 'an effort to decrease crime in our neighbourhood through citizen participation and better police services,' by encouraging citizens' community spirit, and discouraging them from leaving crime reduction to the professionals. Workers in a car with two-way radio patrolled the streets and, though they had no power of arrest, they were able to report anti-social incidents, assist people who needed help, and generally exemplify the benefits of citizens helping other citizens. Residents became willing to report suspicious activities themselves, and the patrol was discontinued. A survey was conducted to discover people's attitudes towards crime; one response indicated dissatisfaction with police co-operation, and as a result monthly police-community meetings were instituted which increased mutual understanding. Neighbours agreed to watch each other's houses, they were urged not to buy goods suspected of being stolen, and a campaign was started in which people engraved their social security numbers on household goods and listed the items marked. A petition for improved street lighting was organized, but unfortunately the city was unable to provide funds for this. It was by no means plain sailing. Although senior police officers supported the programme, officers on the beat were not fully aware of it. Residents began to have excessive expectations of the range of problems that the workers could tackle. Within the project, too, there were problems of lack of communication, inadequate record-keeping, and staff turnover. Nevertheless it is felt that there is a definite improvement in community co-operation and an increase in the number of incidents reported to the police (U.S. National Advisory Commission, 1973).

In Eastern European countries the public is involved in crime prevention to a considerable extent. Local residents' associations include crime prevention among their tasks, and committees of employees consider crime prevention (including 'white-collar' offences by management), apparently in much the same way as works safety councils try to reduce accidents.

The number of projects is countless, and probably growing; perhaps in time they will be as much part of the scene as, say, Residents' Associations. It is encouraging to note that the initiative may come from several different sources. In Indianapolis it was a group of women, probably fairly middle-class and well-heeled; in Boston it was professional social workers in conjunction with local residents. Three more types of initiator will be described: a voluntary organization, a school, and the police. In Kentish Town, London, Inter-Action is a charitable trust specializing in community arts and in developing new forms of youth and community activities. One of these is City Farm, which started with gardening on a piece of rubble-covered land and developed into a farm with 12 ponies and several other farm animals; there is a riding school which sells lessons to the local authority and to organizations for the disabled and handicapped, earning fees which help to make the project self-supporting. In its first year the bill for vandalism was £20, compared with £24,000 on a nearby local authority playground; this may be partly because the animals seem to have a gentling effect on even the roughest boys who were often the first to defend and care for them, and partly because the rough-hewn finish of sheds, etc. gives a minimal target for vandalism, whilst also being attractive and in character as a farm. By 1978 there were about 20 similar projects (Donovan, 1978). Unlike steel-and-concrete municipal playgrounds, City Farms give children an opoortunity to take part in activities with adults. In a competition organised by South Yorkshire police for schoolchildren on how to stop vandalism 'the children themselves asked for more parental discipline, not in the form of strict fetters but in the form of oversight, interest and communication' (Cross, 1978). Those three words sum up what projects like these have brought to the communities in which they work.

Schools can initiate changes, by transforming a poor ethos into a good one. I am taking 'ethos' to imply institutional pride and morale.

These can suffer if, for example, discipline is lax or is enforced in a rigid, uncaring way; nor are they helped if the curriculum is based on examinations which many of the pupils see as irrelevant to the labour market into which they will go on completing their education (Phillipson, 1971). Community involvement is also important: it helped to achieve such a transformation in the Cortes Street School in Los Angeles. In 1961 it had one of the worst crime problems in the city, including violence, theft and vandalism. Most of the children were Mexican-American, yet the Spanish language was discouraged and children with language difficulties were often placed in classes for the retarded. The school was not open to parents, who not unnaturally avoided it and demanded a Mexican-American principal who understood their needs. The principal, however, took a conversational course in Spanish and spent the summer walking and visiting throughout the community, giving the message to anyone who would listen: 'Cortes is your school – let's get to know each other.' Teachers visit parents to invite them to the school, which now admits them not merely to the school but to their child's classroom. Parents and senior citizens living in sight of the school have been invited to join 'Operation Security Watch' to keep an eye on the premises out of school hours. It is claimed that vandalism has all but disappeared, though the report (Cross, 1978) does not mention the effects on other forms of crime.

The initiative of the police in the field of general prevention is growing. For example in a South Yorkshire scheme two officers recruited children aged 6 to 12 as 'special agents' with 'identity cards' including details of their bicycles; they were also given four 'Don't' warnings and encouraged to report suspicious actions such as people trying car door handles. It is to be extended to other parts of England and Wales (*Justice of the Peace*, 28 April 1979, p.237). A more comprehensive concept of police initiative has come from John Alderson, chief constable of Devon and Cornwall. He formed a Community Policing Consultative Group with representatives of education, transport, planning, magistrates, the church and voluntary organizations in addition to commercial and trade union interests. This began by examining facts and statistics about crime trends and relevant community problems (with police and local authority resources used to help in compiling the information), and went on to invite voluntary and statutory organizations to join in working out self-help methods. (Alderson, 1978, 1979). In his Howard League lecture Mr. Alderson quoted encouraging preliminary results: during the first three years of the experiment (1977–79) the police area concerned showed an overall reduction of reported crime by 5.8% as against a increase in the Force area as a whole of 8.1%. Some police colleagues are sceptical as to whether the approach could be transferred from a small provincial town to the inner city, but it is precisely in the inner city that the dangers of police alienation from the local community are greatest. Like other city dwellers, Alderson points out, policemen often no longer live near their work; rapidly changing populations, combined with the practice of drafting in police from other areas, sometimes in squads such as the Special Patrol Group of the Metropolitan Police, increase the risk that police and public will see other as stereotypes, not people. This appears to have been recognised in the SPG's reorganization on more decentralized lines, with service limited to four years (*Guardian,* 11 March 1980). Other apprehensions have been expressed on Mr. Alderson's initiative by those who fear the growth of police power, but he is insistent that although the initiative came from the police this was not essential to the scheme: the project belongs to the community and the police are only one of the agencies who co-operate in it.

The emphasis on community measures in this section should not be taken to suggest that crime is merely a product of social disorganization and the community's inability to police itself. The determinants of crime have such fundamental political, economic and social origins, as well as personal ones, that they are often too general to be tackled by policies aimed specifically at crime reduction – a point which will be considered later in this chapter. Nonetheless, the impetus and initiatives introduced in the name of crime reduction may prove beneficial to communities and encourage the development of self-help. Some critics would object to 'do-gooders' descending on a community and instigating sweeping changes; they see this as paternalistic. But there is no reason why it should be, if done properly. Most of the projects described here go out of their way to involve local residents, showing those who have not had the experience of controlling their own destiny how to set about it, in which they have sometimes been too successful for the authorities' liking. In large urban areas, often lacking such basic facilities as a meeting hall and a duplicating machine, it is difficult for communities to evolve naturally. But with initial outside support roots can be established and the community can produce its indigenous leadership.

Community self-determination has been given prominence here because it is possible to develop within an existing social and political structure; it does not imply unquestioning acceptance of that structure. The proposal to encourage the development of communities should not divert attention from ordinary political efforts to secure improvements. On the contrary, one of the benefits of strengthening community organizations is that they can help to raise people's consciousness of the power over their own lives that they are entitled to claim. Groups like these could share in local government decision making, and even press for legislative changes.

Strategies Against Specific Crimes

It may be worth looking at the problem from the other point of view, by considering action which could be taken to try to reduce particular forms of crime. It seems reasonable to expect that methods specifically designed to tackle a crime at a time will afford better protection than indiscriminate brandishing of the blunt instrument of deterrence. Some of these examples will illustrate further applications of approaches described earlier in this chapter. The examples are very selective, concentrating on a few of the types of harmful acts that are conventionally thought of as crime. Nor do they attempt a complete strategy for the reduction of each type. But if methods can be devised for these highly visible crimes, it should be possible to find others to protect people against risks of which they are less aware.

A general point illustrated by some of these projects is the importance of measuring their effectiveness wherever possible. Some have been evaluated quite rigorously, such as the Exemplary Projects of the Law Enforcement Assistance Administration in the United States. If they are successful, the assessment will help to make the case for starting others elsewhere; if not, people should not be lulled into believing that something effective is being done when it is not (one of the major objections to punishment, after all, is that it does just that). It should be noted, however, that the reduction of crime is not the only objective: the reduction of fear and anxiety is at least as important. Research might therefore not concentrate exclusively on estimating the number of offences, but could also enquire whether residents *feel* that crime has decreased and their area become pleasanter. In some cases the benefit in one area must be weighed against the fact that some of the criminal activity has merely been displaced to another: from robbery, say, to frauds using credit cards or computers, or from underground stations with closed circuit television to those without it. But it may be considered that so long as the benefits of crime prevention projects outweigh their social costs, they are justified (Clarke and Mayhew, 1980).

Burglary

Burglary is one of the commonest crimes: in England and Wales it accounted for more than one in five of all indictable offences recorded by the police in 1978. One American city mobilized public concern into action: the Community Crime Prevention Program (CCPP) in Seattle, Washington, used full-time staff to distribute informative materials, cultivate a sense of community, and promote security inspection of dwellings. Residents were also encouraged to mark their property and to organize 'block watches'. These are groups of neighbours, organized to work in co-operation with the police (*not* as vigilantes) for example to call the police and warn each other if they see any suspicious activity (NILECJ, 1977), and thus to reduce vulnerability to burglary through co-operative action. The results were monitored not by the number of crimes reported but by victimization surveys, which indicated that in the 5,280 households using the CCPP services the number of burglaries was reduced by as much as 48 to 61%, at a total cost of less than $50 per household per year. It is claimed, too, that more burglary-in-progress calls were made to the police, that the program met or exceeded its goal of involving 30% of the households in each neighbourhood, and that there was no increase in burglaries among non-participants or adjacent neighbourhoods (NILECJ, 1977). Another carefully evaluated project was in Atlanta, Georgia, which coordinated security surveys for homes and businesses, an emergency contact system for business owners in the event of a burglary, and standards for buildings and security devices. Goals for percentage reductions in burglary and robbery were set and in most cases exceeded (on the basis of recorded crime figures, not a victimization survey). Commerical robbery was reduced by 42%; there was apparently some displacement to residential robbery, however, which increased by 17% (Newton, 1978, p.254).

Vandalism

Among the types of crime which arouse strong resentment is vandalism. One attempt to reduce it on a demoralized housing estate is the Cunningham Road Improvement Scheme in Widnes, where small groups of residents were paid a token fee to attend meetings and discuss possible improvements. In contrast to many American approaches, the scheme did not have a programme or goals which the coordinators were trying to get the residents to accept. Rather, they were merely there to help the residents decide what they wanted; to communicate that to the local council more effectively than they could hope to do unaided; and to prod both the authorities and the tenants themselves to stick to the job of achieving what they set out to do (Hedges and others, 1980). A major problem was found to be the maintenance and repair of council houses; negotiations with Chief Officers led to an integration of policy between the local authority departments responsible for housing and for repairs. A youth centre was opened. Many other suggestions were made by residents, and although not all of them were implemented, substantial improvements were made, especially to rubbish collection and other council services. The final report concludes that, all in all, 'this broad approach is effective in tackling seemingly intractable problems of estate regeneration; and that this in turn reduces but does not abolish vandalism.' The quality of life on the estate has been improved in a number of other ways. A Residents' Association was set up and is thriving; there are fewer visible signs of vandalism and litter; more tenants are tidying up their front gardens, in some cases paying local teenagers to help; tenants are no longer afraid, when teenagers are causing a nuisance or smashing things, to go out and tell them to stop, because they know them individually and can rely on their neighbours to come out and support them. Despite predictions, most newly planted trees have survived. Relations with the local council have also been transformed. The council has recognised the possibility of improving conditions without massive capital spending, and is developing better channels of communication with the Residents' Association. A beat policeman has been introduced; although the police originally believed that officers would not want to regress from patrol cars to pavement pounding, the local constable became accepted, particularly by the young children, and said that 'it would take crowbars' to get him off the beat again. He has promoted 'crime parties' to bring neighbours together to co-operate in preventing crime; in the process they have got to know each other better (Spence and Hedges, 1976; NACRO and SCPR, 1978).

In New York a less elaborate approach to vandalism has been a 'beautification program.' Tenants have been encouraged to 'beautify their buildings in various individualistic and innovative ways', at their own expense apart from paint and related materials. What the arbiters of taste say about it is not recorded, but it is claimed that vandalism has been reduced. Other ploys are to fine owners of empty properties if they do not repair broken windows; instead of posting notices on them threatening penalities for vandalism, they are encouraged to disguise the fact that they are empty, for example by leaving curtains visible (Cross, 1978).

Football Hooliganism

Another type of crime which lends itself to specific prevention is football hooliganism. There can be no 'solution' to the problem. When thousands of people, mostly young, are gathered together in an excited state, there are bound to be incidents. The line between deliberate aggression and spontaneous flare-ups cannot be clearly drawn, so attempts to be tough with the former are likely to punish unfairly some of those involved in the latter; they may also provoke a show of toughness in return, especially when accompanied by exaggerated press reporting (Ingham, 1978). Encouraged by the National Federation of Football Supporters' Clubs, football clubs are trying to take preventative action at matches and during travel to and from them. The Aston *Villa Times* of 28 September 1978, for example, has a banner headline 'BEHAVE—OR STAY AWAY'; it announces that admission to a big match with Manchester United will be by ticket only, and that as 'drink causes a problem too,' bars will be closed while play is in progress – and if things do not improve, closed altogether. (But at the top of the same front page is an advertisement for whisky.) British Rail, after a year in which damage to trains by football fans reached £100,000, instituted a coordinated plan: special trains were run, on the ground that 'boisterous young men and quiet elderly ladies don't mix'; alcohol was not on sale; two stewards were to be provided by the club for each coach, and extra railway police were provided, with the same officers escorting the same club each time; and if possible coaches would be provided from the station to the ground. The bill for damage was reported to be reduced to £5,000 (*Times,* 4 July 1977). Other proposals have included providing bands and other entertainments before and after the match, and at half-time, and creating a more civilized atmosphere by providing seats and improving the refreshment facilities and toilets.

Clubs have also taken action of a more general kind. In Liverpool professional footballers ran four two-hour training sessions for unemployed youths, but it was impossible to continue for reasons of cost.

Shortage of money is also reported to have prevented Chelsea Football Club, which has had a bad reputation for violence (see for example *Evening News,* 3 October 1975) from opening their stadium and providing facilities seven nights a week to the general public in the hope that this would encourage users to take better care of it (*Guardian,* 26 May 1978). Those who read of the constant transfer of players from club to club at fees which have now reached a million pounds may wonder whether the problem lies in the shortage of funds or their allocation; be that as it may, the Government allocated an extra £2 million in 1978/79 to tackle hooliganism, half for developing opportunities in inner cities and half to encourage about a dozen clubs to increase their supporters' involvement. A levy on transfer fees would provide a continuing fund to develop ideas like these, and it is to be hoped that an adequate proportion of the money would be devoted to proper evaluation.

Crimes of Violence

'Crimes of violence' are commonly referred to as a single category, although they include a wide range of acts from homicide to assault. It could be argued that the term should be widened to include other acts endangering life and health, such as those committed by industrial companies. But even taking the narrower conventional definition of physical injury inflicted directly by one individual on another, such crimes are too varied to be dealt with by a simple policy of deterrence. There have been two recent examples of an integrated approach, in Scotland and in France. The Scottish Council on Crime (1975) stresses the importance of preventive social action, including the rôle of the school (paras. 206 ff.) and planning and remedial work in deprived areas (paras. 211 ff.). By analysing the instruments with which injuries are caused, it found that 37% of assaults involved the use of a knife or other sharp instrument, and in 22% the weapon was a bottle or glass tumbler. It suggested limitations on the availability of the former, and replacement of the latter with metal or plastic containers.

Similarly, a French report on violence was followed by a range of social measures to 'encourage the free development of the individual's personality in family life, leisure and sport.' Special attention was given to planning new towns: a policy has been adopted which rejects 'gigantism' in favour of towns of less than 200,000 inhabitants, smaller buildings, more individual houses, and design aimed at reducing isolation. The Ministry of the Environment has issued directives aimed at reviving local spirit; other measures encourage local organizations, with increased participation by women and young people. Some youth activities are being subsidized. A code of ethics was adopted in October 1980 by the TV networks to restrict the exposure of young people to violence. A law on improved sound insulation is in preparation. Each *département* will set up a violence prevention committee with elected representatives, civil servants and specially qualified persons; their activities will be coordinated by a national committee (Council of Europe, 1978, p.9).

The proposals are not entirely progressive: the majority of the Scottish committee recommended increased police powers to detain suspects and search people in public places for weapons, and court powers for 'the continued detention of a violence-prone offender until it is safe for him to be released.' The subsequent Criminal Justice (Scotland) Bill of 1980 was strongly criticized for eroding civil liberties. So was the French 'Security and Liberty Bill' which while reducing penalties for minor offenders, contains heavier punishments for serious crime and restrictions on parole (France, 1981; Perier-Daville, 1981). The preliminary report of this initiative makes no specific mention of assessing its results. Nevertheless the official recognition that crime prevention extends beyond the apparatus of control and punishment into social conditions and the quality of life is welcome.

Crime control often involves restrictions which affect large numbers of law-abiding people. There is a case for stricter controls on the acquisition and possession of firearms by individuals, for example, and in 1978 the Council of Europe introduced a convention on that subject. It has been suggested that control might only divert criminals to other weapons, besides creating resentment among legitimate owners (which has certainly been one response to gun-control proposals in the United States). But there can be no serious doubt that the easier the access to firearms, the more people will be wounded and killed by them. It is almost certain that the use of 'deadly force' (as it is euphemistically called) by police in the U.S. has encouraged criminals to arm themselves, and it is possible that the increasingly frequent issue of weapons to police in Britain has been having a similar effect; the point needs serious consideration (Harding, 1979). In this country, where a considerable degree of control already exists and is accepted, restrictions are especially urged for shotguns, which were used in twice as many robberies in

1978 as in 1974; and many Americans, as well as foreign observers, are convinced that limitations on the availability of firearms must be accepted if the mayhem is to be checked.

One factor in the increase of violence against people in robberies is that they have become the most vulnerable point in the protective armour which modern technology provides for money and goods. A criminologist has commented:

> When we bewail the increased use of violence in modern thieving, . . . we should remember that these changes do not result from a general lowering of moral standards that can be corrected by stricter schooling or harsher punishments. The changes result rather from changes in the nature of property and of our protection of property. . . . I do not suggest that we can avoid having some concentrations of valuables – though the extension of credit card banking may help – nor do I suggest that we should stop bothering about protecting property; but we must recognise that in doing so we create the conditions for escalation in criminal technology and organization (McIntosh, 1971, pp.123, 130–131).

Sexual Crimes

In combating sexual crimes a number of strategies have been proposed. There is little evidence of their effectiveness in prevention, but, in combination, they may have some effect on the incidence of these offences and, also of great importance, on the level of anxiety about them. There are broad social ones, such as educative programmes aimed at increasing men's understanding of and respect for women. Secondly, there are measures directed at deterring potential rapists (such as threatening to publish names and pictures of any that are convicted) or at rehabilitating convicted ones (such as psychotherapeutic treatment and sex education). Thirdly, there are assertive methods, in which women are encouraged to attend self-defence classes or to carry alarm devices. Fourthly, there are the familiar restrictive ones, such as warning children not to go with strangers or get into their cars, communicating to adolescent girls the dangers of dressing or behaving provocatively, and encouraging them, and their parents, to make reasonable arrangements about where they are going and when and how they will come back. (Parental supervision is of course also relevant to preventing children from committing offences: see for example Wilson, 1980.) Lastly, there should be constant study of new preventive strategies. When an offence is committed it should be studied from a preventive point of view, for example to discover ruses employed to tempt children. Thought also needs to be given to ways of getting the information across; one way might be to encourage local groups such as parent-teacher associations to arrange meetings at which parents could exchange experience on, say, how to withstand children's instinctive tactic of blackmailing them into feeling that they are spoilsports.

Even within a single type of sexual offence, rape, there are wide variations. It may be committed out of lack of respect for other human beings, or lack of knowledge of how to relate to them, or simple ignorance about sex. The assailant may be more interested in dominance than in sex; he may be acquainted with his victim, or even married to her. To some extent schools could be asked to educate children about relations with the opposite sex; but this is one more in the list of tasks which are all too readily suggested for schools, and will have to depend upon resources – or is this an aspect of social upbringing which should even have priority over academic subjects, if there has to be a choice? As regards disseminating information about sex, it is gratifying to see the media making amends for some of their shortcomings through their often educative features, advice columns, and radio phone-ins.

The sexual assault can be influenced by the victim's reaction. Gunn (1976), in a useful review, points out that some women may be able to talk attackers out of their intentions, but others may resist in a way that provokes violence. He illustrates this by a case in which

> A young man who was dominated by a possessive and disturbed mother eventually found a girlfriend (but she) rejected him and in his anger he attacked three women over a short period of time. Each one he threatened with a knife. The first refused intercourse but agreed to masturbate him and he accepted that; the second ran off screaming and he let her escape; the third submitted to intercourse, but spent a long time talking to him afterwards trying to persudade him to go to the police.

(This is not of course to suggest that victims will often be able to mitigate the attack as these women succeeded in doing; but it shows that in some cases the victim's response can affect the outcome.) The threat of punishment complicates the task of prevention. A woman may feel that it is safer not to resist, but if she doesn't resist it may not be possible to secure a conviction. The defendant's lawyer sees his job as preventing his client's punishment, and may therefore cast doubt on the woman's word and character rather than try to arrive at the truth from which might be learnt something relevant to the treatment of his client or general preventive policies. Some offenders would seek counselling or psychiatric help, but are deterred from this by the threat of punishment – without being deterred from the act itself. This is not to deny that it may be necessary to restrict or remove the liberty of some offenders, in order to protect the public or allay fears. But it may be counter-productive to place sexual offenders in most present-day prisons, with no research into possible preventive strategies, no opportunity for amends, little or no attempt to help them towards insight into what they have done, and a risk of serious aggression from other prisoners.

A number of preventive measures that can be taken by individual women and by the community are suggested in a leaflet by the Rape Crisis Centre, London, now called the London Rape Counselling and Research Project. Other centres have been started in Britain and the United States; their primary purpose of helping victims will be referred to in the next chapter, but they also add to knowledge about rape. In some cases women gain the extra confidence needed to report the offence (although no pressure is put on them either way); this should contribute to ensuring that more offenders are detected and helped or punished as the case may be. With this offence it is particularly important that any care service should be well run; independent evaluation is essential.

Cruelty to Children

Punishment is a particularly inappropriate response in cases of incompetent parents who neglect their children. Two obvious criticisms are: punishment does not teach them how to be better parents; nor can it be defended on grounds of general deterrence, since it is not fear of punishment which spurs most of us to take reasonable care of our children. The same is true of many of those who batter their children. The fear of punishment, or even censorious disapproval, can deter desperate parents from seeking help. Preventive services can be of various kinds. The National Society for Prevention of Cruelty to Children (NSPCC) pioneered centres offering a 24-hour on-call 'lifeline' to which parents could turn in moments of stress; one of these provided in a year 2,600 therapeutic sessions for children and 952 for their parents, in addition to casework services to 47 children and their families (Castle and Kerr, 1972; NSPCC, 1979). The NSPCC and local authorities are constantly looking for new methods, so that when emergency calls are received, by a NSPCC branch or the local authority social services department, those concerned can consult to decide on the best action – which may include removing the child from home. In many places parents' associations have been set up, with telephone services or walk-in centres or both; they are run by parents some of whom have themselves experienced violent impulses, and the dividing line between helpers and helped is deliberately indistinct. Some groups collaborate with statutory social services; others have been formed where few services exist, for example in rural areas, or where people are not satisfied with the authorities or actively mistrust them. In England a National Co-ordinating Committee of Parents under Stress has been formed. Similar initiatives are taking place in other countries, including the Netherlands, Switzerland, France and the United States. Some involve the help of individual volunteers, 'adoptive grandparents', 'godparents', etc., some of whom may have illtreated their own children before undergoing therapy; they offer psychological or in some cases practical support such as taking in the child during periods of high tension. One Swiss experiment offers a telephone service to children about ill-treatment, their rights, and other questions (Council of Europe, 1980). Another approach is to maintain registers of 'non-accidentally injured' children and those considered to be a risk (Pickett, in press).

A carefully graduated system for protection of children is operated in the Netherlands, largely through the civil law. It works on the preventive principle of restricting parental responsibility, but only to the degree necessary. The available measures include, firstly, immediate intervention in crisis situations to place the child in the temporary custody of the Council for Child Protection. Secondly, a family guardian may be appointed: this is a volunteer or social worker of a family guardianship agency, accountable to the judge for assisting and advising the parents in rearing the child, for a period of not more than a year at a time. Thirdly, where parents appear unable to care for a child, they are released from parental responsibility – generally with their consent. Lastly, in extreme cases such as abuse or gross neglect, the court deprives parents of parental responsibility; the child is placed in a foster family or institution, under a legal guardian which is usually a guardianship agency. (United Nations, 1981, pp.32–33).

None of these is 'the' answer, of course. Self-help groups are not suitable for parents who are severely disturbed or incapable of joining in discussion, and have dangers such as one-sided perceptions and lack of qualification leading to inappropriate action. Registers bring the danger of the 'false positive', that is, the person wrongly predicted to be likely to re-offend. For fear of a public outcry when a child is injured or killed by its parents, social workers can be under pressure to remove children from home when it is not necessary, thus risking traumas of a different kind. The one method which appears to offer nothing but disadvantages is imprisonment; the NSPCC, recognising this, uses courts only as a means of ensuring, for example, proper treatment for a mentally ill parent.

Crime and the Social Climate

The above are only a few examples of specific approaches; it is hoped that they will suggest many others. Next, some more general ones need to be considered. The term 'general prevention' is sometimes used as synonymous with general deterrence, but here it will be taken to mean the general principles underlying the effort to prevent (some) crimes by changing those circumstances which make them more likely to occur.

The reduction of crime has much in common with industrial safety. A good management studies the background of accidents: poor lighting and ventilation, fatigue, noise, obstructed gangways, monotony of work, domestic anxieties, and so on. It will make sure not only that its workshops come up to high standards, but that everyone regards his job as helping to maintain those standards, as well as operating his machine. A safe factory is likely also to be relatively pleasant one to work in, and efficient. Although the analogy cannot be taken too far it points to the attitude which a community can take towards crime prevention.

It is inevitable that a chapter on crime reduction should touch on social and economic reforms. But although these ideals are difficult to specify, and even more difficult to achieve, we must come much nearer to attaining them if society is to be worth living in. Social explosions (which these days all too often include literal explosions) have a way of building up unnoticed until a small spark detonates them. Shaw draws an anology in the Preface to *Heartbreak House* (1919):

Nature's way of dealing with unhealthy conditions is unfortunately not one that compels us to conduct a solvent hygiene on a cash basis. She demoralizes us with long credits and reckless overdrafts, and then pulls us up cruelly with catastrophic bankruptcies. Take, for example, common domestic sanitation. A whole city generation may neglect it utterly and scandalously, if not with complete impunity, yet without any evil consequences that anyone thinks of tracing to it. In a hospital two generations of medical students may tolerate dirt and carelessness, and then go out into general practice to spread the doctrine that fresh air is a fad, and sanitation an imposture set up to make profits for plumbers. Then suddenly Nature takes her revenge. She strikes at the city with a pestilence, and at the hospital with an epidemic of hospital gangrene, slaughtering right and left until the innocent young have paid for the guilty old, and the account is balanced. And then she goes to sleep again and gives another period of credit, with the same result.

Shaw's comparison is with political hygiene; but our failure to tackle the aspects of society which are known to be linked with crime and misery deserves equal castigation. In a similar way there can be long periods of mismanagement and oppression before a colony erupts into revolution, a prison into a riot, or a community into endemic crime.

The first part of this chapter has been devoted mainly to initiatives in local communities; but the effort needs to be backed up not only by national government, but also by individual citizens. These ideas are beginning to find a place in the vocabulary of public debate. Thus Mr. James Callaghan, as Prime Minister, spoke of schools, parents and caring communities sharing their problems (speech at Isleworth, 26 April 1978); and Mr. Merlyn Rees, the ex-Home Secretary, said that 'we cannot shuffle off onto the agencies of law and order all our responsibilities for preventing and dealing with crime.... We must all get involved..... We must set an example in our own lives of integrity and honest dealing' (speech at Bromley, 19 September 1978). But in both cases these remarks were tucked away at the tail-end of their speeches, and neither said anything about how to bring about these changes of attitude. The director of the Canadian Association for the Prevention of Crime was more specific (McGrath, 1978):

> Usually when we speak of prevention we have in mind programs aimed at individuals who do not fit easily into society and who therefore are seen as potential offenders. This is not the kind of prevention I have in mind. I am thinking of prevention that involves the population as a whole on a continuing basis.... The main point to be recognised is that the vast majority of crimes are committed by that portion of the community who are seen

and who see themseves as law-abiding, those who make up the public we would like to see active in crime prevention. Involved are such crimes as employee theft, smuggling, cheating the welfare or public insurance systems and on tax returns, and graft in government and business.

... the recognised outlaws get away with stolen money and even kill a number of Canadians each year but there is no danger of society's collapse from their activities. It is the undetected or condoned rot at the root of the tree that poses the real threat.

What we must accept is that the responsibility rests with each of us as individuals.

The hypothesis being advanced is this: that just as there are societies which are liable to rebellion because they are repressively governed, and those in which corrupt practices flourish because there is corruption or at least weakness in high places, so there are societies which are more prone than others to harmful acts, including those which in many countries are defined as criminal. The nature of the crimes is very diverse, and the conditions which make them more likely to occur are still more so; the hypothesis is therefore difficult if not impossible to test. All that can be done is to identify a number of features of society which there is reason to believe may be conducive to a high crime rate: it may then be claimed that the possible link with crime is an extra reason for trying to reduce them to a minimum, but that the effort is worthwhile in any case on general social and ethical grounds. Among such undesirable features are the lack of legitimate opportunities for substantial numbers of people to lead reasonably rewarding lives; unemployment; the break-up of communities, for example through slum clearance or mobility in search of jobs; inadequate care for casualties of bad upbringing, such as the children of neglectful parents; people at high and middle levels of society setting an example of ruthlessness or dishonesty, and pursuing profit or pleasure regardless of the effects on other members of society.

None of these are advanced as 'causes' of crime: criminology is littered with over-simplified theories of that kind. They are merely put forward as conditions under which crime is likely to increase; some of them are themselves crimes, or ought to be. Nor is it suggested that by putting them right, crime could be eliminated: for one thing they never can be entirely put right in an imperfect world; for another, even if unemployment and other hardships were drastically reduced, this would not necessarily affect the extent of the harmful acts committed by some who suffer no such disadvantage.

231

What are the implications for crime prevention? Some of these social ills could be tackled through social engineering, such as housing policy, provided the political will existed; others need not so much political will as knowledge of how things could be improved. There are those who believe that a change in the political structure, which leaves so many citizens virtually powerless, is needed; but even if such a revolution could be effected, there is no guarantee that the new structure would not have other defects that were no less serious. These approaches are liable to entail increased restrictions on citizens by the authorities – a price that may have to be paid for security, but one that needs constant scrutiny, to make sure that the possible benefit in crime reduction is worth the certain increase in social control. It is often implicitly assumed that the restraints will affect *other people* but not 'people like us'. But in a just society they must be imposed equally, and in a free society (insofar as such a thing is possible) they would be self-imposed rather than enforced by the state. It has been said of Aristotle, when he was trying to justify the use of other men as slaves, that 'He seems to have taken it for granted that there must be an answer to any question about the way men behave which would be in accordance with his moral principles and yet not involve a radical alteration of his mode of life' (Stebbing, 1939, p.24). The thesis offered here is that members of a society, wanting to reduce crime, *will* have to alter their lifestyle. We have already seen how this is done in relation to specific crime prevention measures: passengers submit to time-consuming security checks before entering aircraft, and – a much more substantial restriction – women and children do not move around freely alone after dark. There are reasons for believing that society would be not only healthier but less prone to crime if there were a similar readiness to accept other constraints voluntarily. This would be difficult to bring about, since much of the population would be asked to alter its attitudes substantially, and the pay-off would not be as direct or certain as in the examples given earlier. It is also difficult to describe, without lapsing from moral arguments into moralistic ones, or making naïve statements that boil down to the proposition that if everyone behaved well there would be no crime. The reader will have to be the judge as to whether these pitfalls have been avoided in the following, which will consider the possibilities of self-restraint, first by members of the public collectively, in the economic sphere and in relation to violence and sexual offences; and then by individuals. The proposals are presented not as substitutes for any other social or political policies, provided these are compatible with them, but as complementary.

One approach could be through increasing participation, if those in authority are prepared to delegate responsibility, and the participants to exercise it. Examples of the possible impact on local communities have already been given; the principle could be extended to industry, for example by involving employees in such questions as incentives to cut pilfering and 'fiddles'. Participation of this kind will not always be welcome, nor will it resolve all problems, since on some matters there will obviously be a conflict of interests. Nevertheless it offers one possible way of improving on the present situation. It would give people a greater share in the decisions that affect themselves and each other, on many matters including crime prevention; and perhaps a greater awareness of economic choices.

It is hard to resist the conclusion that unemployment, besides undermining the self-respect of many people, has a bearing on the extent of some forms of crime. This is not the place to discuss economic policy, but there does seem to be scope for personal and collective action to seek a fairer sharing out of what work there is, and government action to facilitate this. In some firms the employees already accept short-time working rather than see some of their number laid off. While there is high unemployment it does not seem fair that some industries still make such regular use of overtime. Sooner or later it will have to be realized that 'moonlighting', or spare-time work often at cut rates and without paying taxes, is not only an economic problem but a moral one, if it aggravates unemployment. It is not of course suggested that any such changes should affect only trade unionists: management and the professions should accept their share. There are of course arguments against such a proposal, quite apart from views as to the likelihood of its being accepted. But for present purposes it is sufficient to say that there is a case for a shorter working week, and it is supported by the possibility that it would lessen some of the pressures towards crime. Although obviously not all the extra leisure time would be devoted to worthy objects, people could spend some of it on their families, or helping other families, or community work for which too often there is not time at present.

Again, there is a connexion between crime and deprivation, as for example the effects on children of neglectful parents, sub-standard schools or understaffed children's homes. Some methods of helping to overcome these problems are known, and others are from time to time developed. But they need resources, and one constraint which

233

members of the public must accept is that these resources can come only from them: either through their rates and taxes; or, if they insist on low taxation, through charitable donations to support voluntary organizations; or in appropriate cases by undertaking the work themselves, as volunteers. In practice, of course, caring services are provided by a combination of these; but any improvement in these services with their crime-reducing potential is in principle possible only through increased contribution by the public in one of more of these ways.

The foregoing has been concerned mainly with economic self-restraint, which might help to create a society in which there would be fewer pressures towards crime, particularly property crime; other forms of personal restraint might contribute towards the reduction of other forms of harmful behaviour. The question of whether to restrict the availability of alcohol illustrates the gains and sacrifices which may follow from policies of personal restraint. For a long time the English have tolerated much-criticized licensing laws and taxes on alcohol, originally designed to check drunkenness; recent evidence that increased availability of alcohol in supermarkets has been associated with increased alcoholism suggests that the policy had some effect. The issue is a balance of interests: the probability that a minority will succumb to alcoholism versus the convenience of the majority buying it whenever they want it (and the profit of the vendors and manufacturers); or the link between the consumption of alcohol and violence (as for example with football hooliganism) versus the argument that longer licensing hours could lead to more sociable drinking instead of drinking to get drunk. Everyone knows the result of prohibition in America; but without advocating anything of that kind, there is a need for further experiment.

One of the most controversial questions of restraint in the name of crime reduction concerns crimes involving sex and violence. Some of these crimes, or the fear of them, seriously impair the quality of life for large numbers of people, especially women. If there is a possibility that these could be checked by the exercise of restraint, it should be considered, even if decisions have to be made without conclusive information. For example, at least one extensive review of research on the effects of screen violence concludes that viewing violence increases people's aggression (Eysenck & Nias, 1978). But although research has not conclusively proved that television violence aggravates violence in real life, the codes adopted by the broadcasting authorities in Britain are based on the argument that this is a strong enough possibility to warrant some self-imposed curbs. In some areas of life it is generally accepted, albeit grudgingly, that everyone recognises certain limitations because otherwise a few would suffer. Speed limits on roads do something to limit injuries and deaths; licensing laws and high taxation constitute a small brake on the spread of alcoholism, which in turn is linked with some road accidents and family violence. These are arbitrary compromises, since only a compete ban on vehicles and alcohol would eliminate all road accidents and all alcoholism. There is no need for compromise, however, in eliminating the institutionalized violence which persists in many British schools: the use of physical punishment on children makes them regard it as legitimate when they become parents in their turn. Sweden has taken the courageous step of prohibiting parents from assaulting their children in the name of punishment (*Guardian,* 30 June 1979): although it is not possible to enforce such a law comprehensively, it is to be hoped that it will reduce tolerance of violence, and that it will be introduced in other countries, as was recommended by the recent Council of Europe colloquium on child abuse (Council of Europe, 1980).

The link between sex crimes and pornography is of the same kind as that between violence and television: plausible but unproven. No one likes censorship, which is so often repressive and ridiculous (not least in prisons); but in her reflexions on the Moors murders Pamela Hansford Johnson (1967) puts the case for self-restraint, at least with the 'hard', sadistic variety of pornography. Well educated people may not be harmed by it, she says, but 'It is no use for us to pretend that we are an ideal society, fully mature. . . . when we are so, there will be no need for censorship of any kind whatsoever' (p.29). After listing some of the books found among the murderer Brady's belongings, including *Origins of Torture and Brutality, The Life and Ideas of the Marquis de Sade, Cradle of Erotica* and *The Mark of the Swastika,* she comments: 'I cannot help but wonder whether, by making all books available to all men, we do not pay too high a price, if that price should be the death of one small child by torture. No one can prove a causal connection between what these two people read and what they did. It might have happened anyway. But if there were a causal connection – how does one weigh in the balance the libertarian principle of making all books available to all men, and the death of a child in such a fashion?' (pp.31–32). 'We ourselves have the freedom to write, in any political terms, and to a large extent in any sexual terms, without being in danger of jail, or even of social disapproval. Therefore, is there no obligation on us to pay for these privileges, by the exercise of some sort of moral responsibility? Do we want everything for nothing?' (p.82). She compares the free sale of sex to the free sale of firearms in the USA. These are only the most extreme of a whole number of examples (alcohol, gambling, motor vehicles . . .) where the convenience and fairly harmless indulgence of the many have to be weighed against the tragedy of the few. Bernard Levin (1970, p.385), unwilling to concede the argument for any form of censorship, even self-imposed, takes Hansford Johnson to task on the grounds that 'crimes as horrible as those committed by Brady and Hindley had taken place in societies far less permissive than ours, and had been committed by people who . .. had never head of de Sade.' This does not, however, demolish her case: she is not saying that pornography is *the* cause of sadistic murders, merely that it might tip a handful of perverted individuals over the brink from fantasies into atrocities, and that this is a risk which we should not take. She is writing of self-censorship, and does not spell out what should be done if that does not work; the implication is that limits should ultimately be set by law just as, with equal reluctance, limits have been imposed on free speech by prohibitions against inciting racial hatred. The effort should not of course be devoted entirely to restricting people from committing harmful (or potentially harmful) actions, but rather to doing whatever is possible, for example through education and counselling, to help people overcome any barriers which may prevent them from enjoying a responsible sexual relationship.

There is an argument for total freedom, on the grounds that it is the prohibition that lends attraction to pornography and the dangerous forms of sado-sexual deviance; since relaxation of the law in Denmark in 1965, it is claimed, sex offences have become less of a problem, and the pornography trade is only kept alive by exports to countries like Britain where it is still prohibited. The Williams Committee on Obscenity and Film Censorship felt that the figures on sex offences in Denmark were inconclusive, but gained the clear impression that since the new law the Danes were no longer concerned about the pornography problem (Home Office, 1979, para. 110) – which could be regarded as achieving one of the major purposes of legislation. For the record, it should be noted that even in Denmark it is still an offence to exhibit or distribute offensive publications in a public place, to sell obscene pictures or objects to a person under 16, or to engage in obscene behaviour so as to cause affront: under the latter provision, live sex displays have been closed down.

The solution proposed by the Williams committee was to distinguish between prohibition against producing pornographic materials, and restriction on their display and sale. The latter was justified to protect citizens from being affronted against their will. But prohibition should be employed only where there was evidence, or very strong presumption, of actual harm. The Committee was prepared to accept this only in relation to the persons used in the production of the pornography, that is if actual physical harm was inflicted or a child under 16 was exploited. The case for harm to the viewer or the objects of his violent or sexual practices was not thought to have been sufficiently proved yet. This is a tenable case against the attempt to control pornography by means of the apparatus of criminal law enforcement. It does not invalidate Hansford Johnson's argument that, proved or not, it would be better not to risk precipitating such acts of barbarity; but it would mean that such restraint would have to be brought about by persuasion and social pressures. This is harder to achieve than passing laws, but *if* it could be done it would avoid the imposition of the views of an unrepresentative minority, and would probably be more effective.

The complexity of the question is illustrated by the history of the Commission on Obscenity and Pornography in the United States (1970). The majority of the Commission, having recommended improved sex education, proposed also that legislation prohibiting the sale of pornography to consenting adults be repealed; but a third of the commissioners disagreed, some of them complaining about the way the inquiry handled evidence, while two thought the report did not go far enough. Part of that evidence consisted of studies of sex crimes in Denmark after the repeal of restrictions in 1965 (Kutschinsky, 1971; Ben-Veniste, 1971); but the reduction was most marked in less serious offences, and may be due partly to a reduced tendency to report such offences in the prevailing climate of tolerance. Rape and attempted rape were reported at about the same level as before, and Ben-Veniste warns (p.252) that 'Not to be ruled out at this stage, however, is the possibility that pornography portraying some forms of deviant sexual behaviour, especially sadism, may adversely influence potential offenders.' Despite this he concludes that 'While there may be some valid reasons for the prohibition of Danish pornography in our society, fear that it will inspire potential sex offenders to act criminally should not be one of them.' Be that as it may, the case for restraint deserves continuing attention.

Individual Restraint

Whether or not there is any move towards collective self-restraint, economic or otherwise, action is also possible at the individual level. Extending the principle that a dirty railway carriage is the fault of the passengers as well as of the cleaners, any person or firm can make a commitment not to break or bend the law, and indeed to set a higher standard than 'doing anything so long as it is not illegal.' Of course people fail to live up to these standards for at least some of the time, for reasons ranging from ordinary human weakness to fear of seeming self-righteous; and some make little attempt to do so. Nevertheless the raising of standards is not a hopeless quest: there are substantial numbers of people who are willing to make sacrifices, if the reason for doing so is made clear. Conservationists forgo collecting birds' eggs and wild flowers and wearing fur coats; motorists abstain from drinking and driving; people resign from their posts for reasons of principle. Public education gradually explains why these things are important, sometimes with the help of laws, although these may in practice be difficult to enforce. Double standards will have to be exposed: for example, there are solid citizens who would never dream of committing burglary, but have bought things at suspiciously low prices with 'no questions asked', or paid a reduced price in cash knowing that this enables the supplier to evade tax, or had extra car repairs added to an insurance bill. No one who connives at these or similar forms of dishonesty has a moral right to demand that thieves be punished.

There are Do's as well as Dont's. They may include not only refusing to condone practices such as those just mentioned, but letting a room, arranging activities for young people, or other voluntary work, according to one's situation and talents. One example with wide implications is perhaps worth considering in more detail: if it is accepted that employment is one of the keys not only to crime reduction but to the health of society, individuals should consider what they can do personally, with or without the encouragement of government policies such as those mentioned in previous section, to promote it. People can aspire to be something more than 'economic man.' They can, for example, prefer to buy goods that are hand-made and services that are labour-intensive (crafts and the arts are among these – and have the further advantage that they use few raw materials and cause little pollution). Those who invest their savings can try to discover something about the employment practices of the firms in which they buy shares – something which, incidentally, unit trusts make it impossible to do. They may even combine with others to forgo a salary increase so that their employer can take on more staff (provided they are needed, of course); this is after all what is expected of trades unionists every time they are asked to moderate their wage demands on pain of causing redundancies. Or they can accept the pay increase and covenant part of it to voluntary organizations, including those whose work is relevant to crime prevention. Citizens can help to keep down inflation by paying taxes and bills promptly; so as not to be too idealistic, perhaps the suggestion should include a discount for doing so. In short, individual citizens who wish to play a small part in combating unemployment can heed the lesson of Hilaire Belloc's Lord Finchley:

> Lord Finchley tried to mend the electric Light
> Himself. It struck him dead: And serve him right.
> It is the business of the wealthy man
> To give employment to the artisan.

Those who, even if not so wealthy, come closer in their personal lives to upholding these standards will have contributed, however obliquely, to crime prevention, by reducing the temptations and pressures for a number of people. If we refrain from an illegal act we have prevented a crime, as well as set an example and in a small way affected the moral climate. There is no guarantee that such forbearance will be reciprocated: if a passenger pays his excess fare the ticket collector may pocket it, if a customer employs a local firm and pays the bill promptly, the owner may not pass on the saving to his employees and customers. But at least those seeking excuses for their actions will not be able to say 'everybody does it.'

10. Making Amends: A Two Way Process

I hope that readers will not turn first to the last chapter of this book, as a short-cut to its conclusions, because the argument depends on what has gone before. This may be summarized by saying that there are ethical and practical problems in basing law enforcement policy on deterrent punishment, or on rehabilitation, or on an attempt to combine the conflicting demands of both. It is suggested that a way out of this dilemma is to separate society's efforts to prevent crime from its reaction to crimes when they occur. The preceding chapter outlined an approach to crime prevention, or rather a series of approaches adapted to particular forms of crime. This would make it possible to abandon the attempt at deterrence through severity, whose effectiveness and morality are dubious; although the measures proposed in this final chapter will be unpleasant for some people, and may help or persuade others to change their ways, these are not their primary aims. The other type of deterrence, which follows from probability of detection, would probably be enhanced. But in first place would be a different philosophy: instead of the classical view that harm caused by the offender should be matched by further harm inflicted on him, it is proposed that the damage should be counterbalanced by, as far as possible, putting it right or making up for it. This would not merely denounce the offence, but affirm society's values.

The previous chapter described a few of the range of preventive policies that could be developed to counter specific forms of criminal activity. But in the nature of things they will not be entirely effective, and the question has to be faced: how should society react when an offence is committed? This chapter will summarize objections to a policy based on punishment, and will consider instead what a system would be like in which the guiding principle was the restoration, as far as possible, of the state of affairs before the offence was committed. The means of reaching this solution will be examined, since they might well be different from present-day criminal procedure. Examples will be given of ways in which the offender could make amends, and of other consequences of his act which he could be required to meet. The problem of enforcement in case of non-compliance will have to be considered, and finally the obligations of the community which complement those laid upon the individual (or corporate) offender.

Drawbacks of Traditional Practice

It has already been suggested that the use of punishment has several important disadvantages. In addition, if the threat fails to deter and it has to be inflicted, the effects of the punishment are often damaging. When punishment becomes disproportionately severe, it may deter victims from reporting offences, offenders from confessing and juries from convicting. Its drawbacks extend to criminal procedure, where it can be an obstacle to the discovery of the truth. Because of the seriousness of punishing an innocent person, the procedure is elaborate and a very high standard of proof is demanded; hence the burden of the prosecution may be 'so onerous that many are acquitted who, by reasonable standards of judgment, ought to be convicted' (Blom-Cooper, 1977), or the suspect may not even be brought to trial because the police feel the evidence would not stand up in court. Moreover, the prosecution's difficulty in reaching the standard of proof required, combined with the defence's interest in minimizing punishment, leads to their complicity in plea bargaining: the prosecution drops a more serious charge, and in return the defendant pleads guilty to a lesser one, with the result that the full seriousness of his act is not brought into the open. In all these ways the more severe the threatened punishment, the greater the danger that the facts will be obscured.

The facts which the traditional process seeks to establish concern the offence itself; other aspects of the background to the offence are largely relegated to the plea in mitigation or the social inquiry report. This does not help the court's or the public's understanding of how the offence came to be committed; the victim and the offender are not encouraged to see each other as individuals, nor to forgive and to be forgiven, respectively. The victim does not benefit by the punishment of the offender, except possibly through gratification of his retributive feelings; if a fine is imposed it is paid to the state, not to the victim, and even compensation may be delayed if the court decides to give a custodial sentence as well, because the latter takes precedence. The offender and especially the victim are allowed little part in the proceedings: the conflict has been 'stolen' from them by lawyers and social workers, as Christie (1977) perceptively argues. The solution reached is fitted into the requirements of the system, rather than of those personally involved. We shall return to this below.

It is usual to speak of dealing with 'the crime problem' through the criminal justice 'system'. In fact, however, as we have seen, the label 'crime' is attached to all kinds of different problems, which should be tackled by a variety of preventive measures. To use punishment on all of them is comparable to treating all kinds of illness with leeches. Moreover, criminal justice lacks essential attributes of a system; on examination it has been found

> that there are few common aims, that there is considerable diffusion of duties and responsibilities and little or no co-ordination between the subsystems, and that there are often differing views regarding the role of each part of the system. ... Yet, when people talk about the criminal justice system as a whole they ... assume that the system functions well and is effectively controlled. They also assume that it is a system oriented towards goals which are designed to meet the needs of the community.

Quoting this extract from a United Nations working paper, Hulsman (1978) points out that in a system there should be a plan with stated objectives, regular assessment to see whether they are being met, and when they are not, power to make changes to improve matters: instead, in Britain and no doubt elsewhere, the objectives are diffuse, the assessment patchy, and the power fragmented between central government (the Home Office) and other departments, courts, police, and to a lesser extent probation and social services.

The final objection to the criminal justice 'system' is that it is the only department of state (except the military in time of war) which deliberately inflicts deprivation of liberty, stigmatization, dispossession, and in many countries torture and death. It 'deliberately produces "anti-welfare" on a large scale. ... Throughout history the greatest threats facing man have been natural disasters, war, and the dispensation of criminal justice' (Hulsman, 1973/74, p.8). This is a strong statement and needs qualification. It is levelled at the system as a whole, not at those working within it, who with few exceptions cause suffering only because the system obliges them to, and do what they can to mitigate it. Many crimes are indeed serious; but the extreme reactions of the law enforcement agencies are often not confined to the worst crimes, and bear particularly harshly on those sections of the population who are already poor, confused and otherwise at a disadvantage in life's struggle.

The Aims of the System

Despite this, many justifications for punishment have been advanced. Some assume it to be axiomatic that crime justifies retribution; this is particularly surprising in adherents of the Christian ethic, for the New Testament contains repeated injunctions not to return evil for evil. Others endorse it on the assumption that it deters, but the evidence for this is equivocal, as was seen in Chapter Eight, and it would in any case be necessary to show that it was *more* effective than other methods. As a method of denouncing deviance from the law it is effective, but again, not uniquely so. Lastly there are those who advocate it in a spirit of 'despair', like Von Hirsch, because rehabilitation has not been shown to work and one must do something; but they ignore the fact that punishment has not been shown to work any better.

What would be the effects if a different principle were given priority? Hitherto courts have had first to impose a penalty before ordering compensation (though the Criminal Justice Bill 1981 will change this), even if this means that the victim must wait before receiving anything until the offender has served a custodial sentence. Lord Justice Scarman, for example, said in 1975, in the case of *R. v. Inwood*, that compensation orders were 'not intended to enable offenders to buy themselves out of other penalties.' The courts do not, admittedly, very often combine compensation orders with custodial sentences, but when they do, Home Office research (on a small sample) suggests that most of the victims receive little or none of the compensation due. Of 27 offenders, only four had paid in full two or three years after their release, and eight had paid part (Softley and Tarling, 1977).

Suppose instead that making amends were elevated into the first place in the order of priorities: restoring as far as possible the damage to individuals or their property, or compensating them. (For the sake of simplicity the discussion will deal mainly with crimes where the victim is an individual or a corporate body, but the case can be extended to others, which can often be regarded as crimes against the community.) By concentrating on the needs of the victim this would remedy one of the main shortcomings of the present process. The second main priority should be to consider how similar acts might be prevented in future, either in the light of the individual case, or through organized research into larger numbers of cases: the procedure and records should be expressly designed to collect information which would assist such research, instead of concentrating on the offender's culpability. If research suggests any measures which could reduce the number of harmful acts in society, including those commonly defined as crime, they should be put into effect, provided there are no ethical objections. There would however be difficulties, including not only the cost but the fact that as was suggested in the previous chapter many of society's 'haves' would have to be called upon to alter their life-style (and here the 'haves' may include not merely those who have power and property, but those who have a tolerable job).

What of the other aims usually mentioned in discussions of sentencing: retribution, deterrence (individual and general) and incapacitation? Retribution, in the sense of repayment of one harm by another, would not have a place; instead the offender would be required to face what could be regarded as the natural consequences of his acts. It is natural to expect that if a person damages someone else's property, he should make it good as far as possible, and that one who has been found to be untruthful will not immediately be believed again; the extension of this principle will be considered below. The aim of deterring the individual from repeating his offence would be met primarily by the stigma of being brought to court, in other words by denunciation, which would be achieved under this system no less than under the old one. The effort at present devoted to general deterrence would be transferred to preventive measures. Incapacitation, or physical restraint, is not strictly speaking a punishment, though in practice it is often indistinguishable. It would continue to be necessary in a small number of cases; wherever possible it would take the form of non-custodial supervision, but in the few cases where that was insufficient some form of enclosed community very different from most present day prisons should be created.

Restoration has the advantage that it requires only a physical act on the part of the offender, which is easier to ensure than the change of heart on which rehabilitation depends. It is likely to have fewer side-effects than punishment, in the shape of resentment and reinforcement of anti-social attitudes. If deterrence and rehabilitation are to succeed, they must reduce the amount of crime, or at least recidivism, and they have not been shown to do so to any substantial extent. But a restorative policy aims at no more than inducing the offender to make an act of restoration and succeeds as soon as he does so; if it achieves any crime reductions or changes of heart, those are bonuses. Moreover, the removal of the threat of punishment should, as suggested above, improve the chances of arriving at the true circumstances of the case, and this in turn should give valuable help to preventative planning.

At this point I will digress to consider a possible semantic objection. This chapter is presenting a system based on asking, and if necessary compelling, the offender to make restoration and to accept certain consequences of his acts. But this can involve payment of costs, supervision, interference with liberty, and in the last resort detention; these seem to bear a close resemblance to existing punishment. Does this amount to bringing punishment in again by the back door? To this it may be answered, firstly, that this scheme must include as great a voluntary element as possible in agreeing the total of the amends and the form it should take. Secondly, it is fair to claim that the intention behind the requirements laid upon the offender makes a significant difference. To punish, in the dictionary sense, means to make someone suffer: the punishment has failed and its deterrent and denunciatory effect is undermined, if he does not suffer enough. This may happen inadvertently, as when a person settles down to endure the rigours of life in prison in preference to those which confront him outside; or deliberately, when a society has scruples about inflicting severe pain and moderates it by, for example, trying to combine it with rehabilitative programmes. The aim of restoration, on the other hand, is to make up for the harm done, without necessarily causing suffering at all, unless it be the pain of regret for the offence committed. Many offenders, for example, enjoy doing community service, and a few are glad to be given the chance to atone, but in neither case is the purpose invalidated – on the contrary the offender's reintegration into society is likely to be, if anything, helped. This is in accordance with the definition of the American criminologist, E. H. Sutherland: (quoted by the 'Six Quakers', Arthur and others, 1979):

> Punishment means pain or suffering produced by design and justified by some value the punishment is supposed to have. It the pain is merely incidental, to be avoided if possible, that is not punishment ... Some authors are attempting to stretch the meaning of punishment to include any method that is used by the courts in dealing with criminals, but it seems better to limit it to the infliction of suffering when that suffering is seen as valuable in itself.

It has to be remembered however that some measures that are not intended to be punitive, such as sending a youngster to a community home, or keeping someone in prison for a longer period because of the treatment he is supposed to receive there, are indistinguishable from punishment from the offender's point of view. For this reason it is important that, whatever the good intentions of the authorities, no measure imposed without the offender's consent should be out of proportion to the seriousness of the offence.

It is true that many offenders may be reluctant to make amends, and still more to undergo the restrictions which will be considered below under the heading 'natural consequences'. But in the absence of deliberate intention of hurting this could be defined not as a punishment but rather as a penalty, in the sense of 'a loss, disability or disadvantage of some kind, either fixed by law for some offence, or agreed upon in case of violation of a contract' (*Shorter Oxford English Dictionary*). Some may feel that such measures still fall within a broad definition of punishment, but if so it is of a different and constructive kind.

Suiting the Means to the End

If the aims of society's intervention after a harmful act are modified, changes in the way they are reached may also be appropriate. It is interesting to compare the way the community reacts to crimes and to accidents. After a crime, apart from first aid if the victim is physically injured, the emphasis is on catching the offender; if he is found, the seriousness of his offence is marked, usually, by a punishment. After an accident – a train crash, for example, or a fire – the welfare of the victims is the first priority, and sometimes a public appeal is launched to help pay for the damage. In due course there is an investigation to try to discover the cause, so that precautions can be taken to prevent a recurrence. Only later is attention given to the question of whether, say, a signalman or driver was at fault, and to possible disciplinary action against him. The purpose of comparing crimes and accidents is not to minimize the responsibility of the offender by suggesting, as some criminological theories seem to do, that his act was more the product of social forces than of his own will. The point here is to contrast society's response: when the disaster is, or appears to be, an accident, concern for victims and prevention has pride of place. It is suggested that this should be the case after crimes. Indeed it would form a major part of the denunciatory process: public condemnation of the crime and concern for the victim would be expressed by the help offered to him or her, rather than by the extent of the punishment inflicted on the offender.

With this in mind, three recent ideas will be considered in this section: that some cases could be resolved by using mediation, or if necessary arbitration, to discover the facts and arrive at a settlement between the offender and the victim; that the matter could be treated as a civil wrong, instead of employing a special criminal law and procedure; and that the community could be accorded a greater part in the process. In case it is felt that these suggestions constitute too radical an overturning of the old familiar methods, it is worth pointing out that they need not be introduced all at once. Existing courts could continue, with mediation tribunals introduced as a new 'bottom tier' to deal with certain types of case, as in several American projects. Courts' procedure and sentencing policy could be modified gradually to reflect changing attitudes. At first they would use civil procedure only for certain types of harmful act; the more serious could be left until experience had been built up and the principle had gained public acceptance.

Mediation

Mediation and arbitration schemes have been established in several places in the United States. Their origin lies in the realization that in a substantial number of crimes, especially minor crimes of violence, the offender and the victim are known to each other. Two tenants in a block of flats come to blows over noise or the behaviour of each other's children. A man and a woman live together for several years, but he moves out and later returns for his belongings: the woman gets angry and has him arrested for burglary. What is needed is not prosecution but a settlement of the dispute or a fair distribution of property. Criminal courts are not suited to this type of case. Their procedure is designed to concentrate on the incident in isolation, and does not give people an opportunity to explain the ramifications which lie behind it. Imposing a penalty on one of the parties is no use; indeed it is worse than useless, because people are often reluctant to be responsible for punishment inflicted on someone they know, and they therefore refuse to press charges or testify, so that the situation is left unresolved. Another encouragement to frankness is the guarantee of confidentiality; notes made during the hearing are destroyed, and only the agreement is recorded.

One scheme among many is the Dispute Center established in New York by the Institute for Mediation and Conflict Resolution (IMCR) in 1975 with a grant from the Law Enforcement Assistance Administration. The aim is to settle disputes, where possible before they have had serious consequences. Cases may be referred by the police, courts, or the parties themselves. The preconditions are that both parties must agree to submit their case, and that they were previously known to each other, although some schemes are beginning to accept cases involving strangers. The techniques are those of conflict resolution commonly used in industry and commerce: mediation, which is a voluntary conciliation process aiming to bring the disputants into sufficient accord to reach an agreement by themselves; and arbitration, in which the parties voluntarily place their dispute before an impartial person or persons, whose decision is binding and court-enforceable. In the IMCR scheme resort to arbitration has seldom been required. The scheme does not compete for resources in an overburdened criminal justice system; rather it uses members of the community, suitably trained, as mediators and arbitrators; in the New York scheme they are each asked to serve one evening a week. A hearing can be arranged within a fortnight. Also, as one scheme is capable of mediating 200 cases a month or more, the workload of the criminal courts is considerably eased, which makes for a better standard of justice in the cases which do go to court (Paterson and others, 1978; Chinkin and Griffiths, 1980; McGillis and Mullen, 1977).

No method is proof against distortion, and one radical writer has pointed out that a weak party may feel unable to insist on a fair deal from a more powerful one (and in criminal cases it could be either the offender or the victim who was at a disadvantage). He believes, however, that mediation programs based in the community have the potential not merely to resolve disputes but to help the community to discover ways of tackling its wider problems and to bring about changes (Wahrhaftig, 1981).

I was allowed to sit in on a mediation session, in which a wife accused her husband of harassment. The hearing was in complete contrast to what would have happened if there had been a criminal prosecution. The procedure was informal: almost the only rule was that while each side was giving his or her version of the incidents and their background, the other must not interrupt. The mediator may hear either person alone, if it seems advisable. There were no lawyers, witnesses or cross-examinations. Above all, there was no attempt to apportion blame, still less impose a penalty: the mediator's task was to help the two people to reach agreement about how their conflict could be resolved. This seemed to me to be in accordance with the New Testament precept that human beings should not judge one another. In this case they agreed to separate; other typical settlements include agreements to end harassment, stay away from each other's home or place of work, or make restitution – the latter being an obvious choice where property has been stolen or damaged. In one project which has been evaluated by comparison with ordinary courts, the Brooklyn Dispute Resolution Center, more complainants and defendants felt that their side of the story had been heard, and fewer complainants felt anger at the defendant or feared revenge (Vera Institute of Justice, 1979?, pp.50–58).

'Civilized' Legal Procedure

The second proposal for adapting the procedure arises because, in cases where the aim of securing appropriate amends for the victim replaced that of prosecution with a view to punishment, the methods used in civil law would be more appropriate than those of criminal law. The process could become more 'civilized', as Professor Hulsman suggested in his Howard League lecture (1976). At present, in the English system, when a person becomes the victim of an offence he can report it to the police, who then take the matter out of his hands: they investigate and decide whether to prosecute, and when the case comes to court the victim is not involved unless he is required as a witness. In the civil procedure he could be involved throughout. After the offence he would take the case to the mediation panel; if he did not know the identity of the offender he would ask the police to try to trace him. At the panel hearing, agreement would be reached as to how the offender should make amends; if it were not reached (or if after agreeing the offender failed to comply) civil proceedings could be instituted in court. It will be seen that the procedure would be very similar whether or not the act contravened the criminal law: it would resemble that used in cases of tort. This would de-mystify much of the theorizing that at present surrounds the subject of crime, which is elevated into a special kind of human behaviour with endless theories about the 'causes of crime': there has been no similar investment of psychological and sociological expertise in the study of the causes of tort. In some spheres the boundaries between civil and criminal law are already becoming blurred: as was seen in Chapter Four, there are suggestions that certain behaviour, even if undesirable, should not be regulated by means of the criminal law, and there has been public debate as to whether legislation to control trades unions should be enforced by means of civil or criminal law.

The existing and suggested processes may be illustrated by means of a diagram.

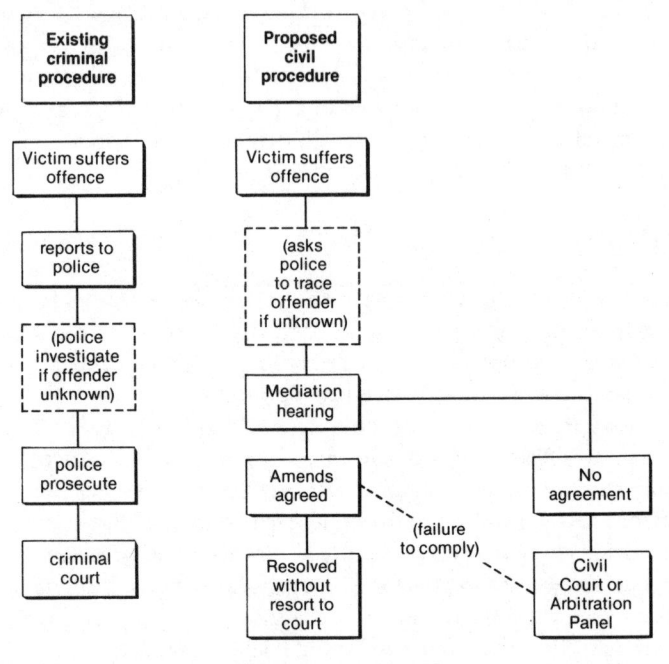

The two are not mutually exclusive; for example, failure to comply with an order in the civil court could be made a criminal offence, and the proceedings could then be transferred to a criminal court. The advantage would be that many cases would be filtered out before they ever reached the criminal court. This principle would be similar to that used by the Inland Revenue and the Factories Inspectorate: action would be directed not to obtaining a conviction but to collecting money or securing compliance, and prosecution would not be the standard method, as noted in Chapter Four, but it could be held in reserve as the penultimate sanction for non-compliance, making it less often necessary to impose the ultimate, criminal sanction. Alternatively, the civil procedure could be used for less serious cases, leaving the criminal one for the rest, at least until more experience has been built up.

Giving Justice Back to the People

The third of these suggestions is that the process should involve not only the main protagonists but members of the community (Christie, 1977). At present the system is largely out of the control of those it is supposed to serve. Professionals run it, and the interests of the victim and the offender have to compete with the need for smoothly running procedure. (It is also likely that, if serious attempts are made to change the system, the professionals will fight to keep control.) Local groups could take part by initiating the process described above, either on behalf of an individual who was unable to do so, or on behalf of the community as a whole: for example, a residents' association could use it with vandals, a football club with hooligans, a local council with speeding motorists, and so on. Local people would also be involved in mediation as we have seen, and it is likely that some capable people who shrink from being magistrates because they are unwilling to judge and punish their fellow men would be glad to undertake the mediating role. In England, with its lay magistrates and juries, there is more participation than in many countries; but magistrates are not sufficiently representative of the various sections of the community, and juries perform only a limited, though important, function of determining guilt or innocence.

It may be objected that these methods would not be suitable for serious offences, especially since they are often committed by people with low earning power and hence limited ability to pay compensation. This will be considered in more detail below, but to see the picture in perspective it should be recognised that the great majority of known offences are not in fact very serious. Of the half-million recorded burglaries in England and Wales in 1978, about 70% involved under £100, and so did the same proportion of the 1.4 million recorded thefts; while of the 87,000 recorded offences of violence, 93% were classed as 'less serious'. The numbers that are cleared up and reach the courts are of course much smaller; nevertheless, half the indictable and nearly all the non-indictable offences in magistrates' courts are dealt with by fines of £100 or less, so it is reasonable to assume that even if the mediation and restoration approach were restricted to less serious offences, a substantial number would be eligible.

These new models raise all sorts of other questions of detail. Could information for preventive research be collected without prohibitively time-consuming paper-work? How should the hearings be conducted so as to ensure fairness? Would legal representation be unnecessary, provided they had power only to reach agreed settlements, not to impose them? The question of the offender who refuses to make amends or to comply with restrictions will be considered below, but what should be done if the victim refused to attend, or if there were a large number of victims (of, say, a persistent burglar or a fraudulent company)? Nevertheless, it is worth reviewing time-honoured practices periodically to see whether they could be made to serve better the interests of the community, victims and offenders.

The Basis of Making Amends

The principle that a person should make restitution to someone he has injured is a very old one. In the book of Exodus it is laid down that restitution shall be made if a man steals an ox or a sheep, or puts his cattle to graze in another man's field. Saxons and Britons used the same principle of putting right the wrong; so did the British government, more recently, in legislating for the natives of New Zealand (Tallack, 1900). During the middle ages kings, barons and ecclesiastics claimed the right to fines and the property of felons, which meant that there was little chance that the victim could claim compensation (Softley, 1978). The Forfeiture Act of 1870 stopped this and reintroduced the principle of compensation, while in our own day the principle was greatly extended by the Criminal Justice Act of 1972, and now about 100,000 compensation orders are made annually, both for property offences and crimes of violence. A useful review of the history of restitution, and the case for it and against imprisonment, is given by Colson and Benson (1980) and Galaway (1977).

(For convenience, the following terms will be used. When the offender returns stolen property, it will be called restitution; when he contributes money or service to the victim, individual compensation; to community or state organizations, reparation. The general term will be 'making amends'. When the state makes payment to the victim it will be called state compensation.)

The return of stolen goods, where possible, is obviously appropriate; and a cash value can be placed on theft or damage of property and the pain and suffering of physical injuries, as well as loss of earnings. Civil courts have long been accustomed to make this kind of computation, and so more recently has the Criminal Injuries Compensation Board. In 1980 the Magistrates' Association suggested a scale starting at £20 for a graze, and going up to £300 or more for serious scars, in addition to the victim's actual expenses and loss of earnings, subject to a maximum representing the total amount the offender could be expected to pay in two or three years (*Magistrate*, October 1980, pp.156–157). The problem has always been to find a way of exacting compensation from individuals without means. Tallack, the secretary of the Howard Association, in his pamphlet *Reparation to the Injured* (1900), saw that, so far as the interests of the victims were concerned, the state should assume responsibility for seeing that they did not suffer because the offender could not or would not pay a sufficient sum. As for the offender, he thought it might be possible to use a system of sureties to try to guarantee that he would work to earn the money. But here again there are difficulties: this presupposes that an employer, or the state, will provide work, and that the offender is capable of it. If work is in short supply, some might argue that offenders should not be given priority over non-offenders; others, however, would say that those offenders who have hitherto experienced disadvantages should receive some positive discrimination. If a time comes when work is made equally available to all who are willing and able to do it, the addition of some unemployed offenders to the workforce would make only a marginal difference to the average number of hours which each person works annually. Until then, occupations will have to be found which are not in competition with those who have jobs already: those where there is a shortage of manpower, or perhaps work for voluntary organizations, paid for by the employment ministry. Ultimately, however, Tallack thought that the remainder of those unable to pay would have to be sent to prison, so as to ensure that they did not escape scot-free; thus he failed to show how to avoid inflicting more severe sanctions on the have-nots than on the haves.

Various ways of resolving this dilemma have been proposed. One is used in Sweden and elsewhere for fines, but could be applied as well to making amends. The amount to be paid would be based on the level of earnings, multiplied by a figure representing the seriousness of the offence (as described in Chapter Four). The problem of the offender without means is resolved by setting the lower limit so low (about 20 pence) that it is possible even for someone living on social security to pay a serious fine over a period without excessive hardship to him or his dependants. At present criminal courts disapprove of making compensation orders payable over very long periods, but civil courts have no such inhibitions.

One method of reducing the inequality of treatment of rich and poor could be not merely to allow, but to require, payment weekly or monthly over a long period. This would serve the subsidiary aim, suggested earlier, of constantly reminding the offender of what he had done; if he were required to pay in person it would also provide an element of supervision. If compensation to an individual victim were not appropriate, it could be paid as reparation to the community, or to a fund for crime prevention and victims' compensation – a more constructive, and perhaps instructive, requirement than a simple fine. This principle is already used in the Federal Republic of Germany (Section 1:56 b of the Penal Code of 1.1.75), and normally the court refrains from making an order if the offender has voluntarily offered to make suitable amends. In the case of juveniles, this can take the form of a personal apology to the victim (Section 3.15). A growing number of schemes based on restitution are being established in the United States, especially for young offenders.

Another way of resolving the problem of the offender without means is to require amends to be made not in money but in community service. This innovation (already described in Chapter Five), was another of those introduced in England and Wales by the Criminal Justice Act 1972, following a suggestion of Baroness Wootton. The rationale is that, just as the community assumes the responsibility of the welfare of the victim, the offender in turn can make reparation to the community. If mediation is used more widely, it may be possible to arrange services directly to the victim in suitable cases, provided that all concerned agree to it: this is being done, for example, in the Restitution Alternative program, Cumberland County, Maine. Although most people have something to offer as community service, it will not always be possible to provide work matched to everyone's abilities, in particular for those individuals damaged either physically (for example through brain damage by injuries or alcohol or environmental pollutants) or psychologically by their life's experience of rejection, institutionalization and other emotional scars. The Howard League has suggested (1977, pp.14–15) that a person like this can make amends for harm that he has done by voluntarily accepting opportunities for training, completing his education, developing social skills and self-confidence – while the community makes amends for deficiencies in his upbringing by providing these opportunities to make a new start. Help of this kind is already being offered through, for example, the day centres described in Chapter Five. The emphasis, however, is not on what is done to the offender but on what he does himself, and this principle may therefore be called 'making amends through self-rehabilitation.'

Natural Consequences

When a person does wrong there are consequences, apart from any harm to a victim, which cannot be ignored. Inevitably, other people react. If someone is caught in an act of dishonesty, he will for a time not so readily be trusted: at this level the response is personal and informal. For a more serious offence, people want a way to ensure that it will be more difficult for that person to commit it again for some time. He may be restricted from doing certain things, or supervised while he does them; if he used any instrument, it may be confiscated. These requirements are comparable to injunctions in the civil court. Lastly, it would be reasonable to require him to pay extra costs incurred as a result of his act.

To begin with restriction: everyone is familiar with the idea of disqualification from driving, but in some other instances the response could be regulated *more* than it often is now. If trust is betrayed by an employee or a professional person, such as a cashier, a local government official, a policeman or a lawyer, the present practice is for the court to punish him, but often less severely than would be usual for the offence, because he is also subject to unofficial punishments such as losing his job and pension rights, which can involve a substantial sum out of proportion to the offence. Rather than leave such things to the inconsistent practices of different employers it would be fairer if they were decided by a court; it would also be more reassuring to the public, since the decision would be publicly announced. The offender's disqualification from holding that job need not be life-long (though in practice once he had left it he would often find other employment and not return to it); the ban could be for a specified period, proportionate to the offence, during which he could be given the opportunity to regain the trust he had forfeited. If pension rights are taken away, this should be expressly ordered, as a means of securing compensation or reparation by the offender. Deprivation of the right to vote or to hold public office should similarly be a specific response to abuse of the electoral process, not an incidental concomitant of imprisonment. In some cases, such as a teacher who assaulted children, the ban would be applied not only to his own occupation but to related ones, including voluntary youth work.

This need not involve any change in the principle that when a doctor, for example, commits a fraud against the National Health Service, which also constitutes professional misconduct, it is for the Disciplinary Committee of the General Medical Council to deal with that aspect (*Laud* v. *General Medical Council, Times,* 8 March 1980); it would merely mean that the sanctions available to the court would overlap with those of the professional body. Where on the other hand the offence was unconnected with the person's job there is no reason why he should lose it: if he is to make financial amends there is every reason why he should keep it.

A second response, whether or not the offence was related to a person's job, is to place the offender under supervision for a time. The usual way of ensuring this is to require him to report at stated intervals; this does not of course prevent him from committing further offences in the meantime, but it alerts the authorities if he fails to make contact, and for many people probably acts as something of a psychological brake. Reporting need not always be to a probation officer, although he is well qualified to offer help and advice if necessary; it could also be to the police, or as suggested in Chapter Five to an employer, a responsible local citizen or voluntary organization. This raises issues of accountability, but they are not entirely new: there are precedents in the new Swedish law on supervision of young offenders (see Chapter Five), and in the relationship of voluntary organizations to the probation service in enforcing community service orders in England and Wales. After certain types of offence the supervisor would go to see the offender: there would be, for example, frequent inspection of the factory where toxic effluents or unsafe machinery had been found, or of the accounts of a company where there had been fraud or evasion of sanctions against an illegal régime. The closest supervision is surveillance, possibly combined with house arrest; it was imposed on a woman in California in 1979, for example, who was convicted of manslaughter of her husband. Care would have to be taken, however, that this did not become repressive in a different way: in some cases it could condemn a person almost to solitary confinement in his own house; and as always when new penalties are considered, it would be necessary to impose safeguards to prevent it from being used as a substitute for a *less* severe measure. Another variant on the theme is to require a person to keep away from a certain area; but it is difficult to enforce, and tends to result merely in extra charges if he is caught committing some new offence there. It can, however, be achieved obliquely by requiring him to report frequently at a place some distance away, where he would consequently have to live.

The ultimate consequence which a person must expect if he persistently and seriously harms other people is physical restraint. The measures just referred to all involve some degree of restraint; the drastic step of total deprivation of liberty should only be taken in strictly limited and closely defined circumstances: when the offender had already committed an offence of the greatest seriousness *and* the probability of his repeating it was high. This involves complex issues, referred to in Chapter Eight. In order to detain as many as possible of those who would otherwise commit very serious offences, and as few as possible of those who would not, methods of identifying them have to be devised. Then there is the question of deciding when they should be released: after a fixed period, or a re-assessment. Both the original decision and the decision to release depend on a further factor: some people will be dangerous only in certain circumstances, and if it is possible to avoid those circumstances in future by some ethically acceptable means short of detention, it should be done. The general points to be made here are that since the purpose of detention would be merely restraint and not punishment, the régime and conditions should be radically different from those in most present-day prisons; and that, since only restriction on liberty should be kept to a minimum, the state would be under an obligation to research into ways of identifying those who need not be detained and conditions on which detained persons could be released under supervision.

The same principle of temporary withdrawal of trust lies behind the proposal that implements used in the commission of an offence should be confiscated, for example the car in which a person drove when drunk, or the house in which he intimidated tenants in order to secure vacant possession. There are, however, problems in some of these superficially attractive ideas: obvious ones are that the car might belong to an employer or a hire purchase company; the house would need to be managed. There are also problems of equity, since the instrument in a less serious offence might be very costly; possibly this could be cancelled out by limiting the period for which it was forfeited. There is, moreover, a danger that measures intended as merely preventive would in practice be punitive, which it is the intention of these proposals to avoid.

A final proposal under the heading of consequences is that a person whose behaviour has brought about a court hearing should accept responsibility for the costs of the hearing; this is suggested by the Six Quakers (Arthur and others, 1979, pp.18–19). It could be appropriate for example in cases of unsuccessful attempts at crimes, or where the question of restitution did not arise. Payment of costs by the offender should however take second place to individual compensation to the victim, and would also have to be moderated where necessary to take account of the offender's earning capacity.

When the Voluntary Principle Is not Enough

The majority of defendants plead guilty; the majority of probation and community service orders are completed satisfactorily. It is therefore reasonable to suppose that measures based on a voluntary commitment to make amends could be agreed in a substantial proportion of cases. It is true that the consent, without which an offender cannot be placed on probation or community service, is not entirely free, since he knows that if he does not agree the alternative might be more unpleasant; nevertheless, the arrangement appears to work. Consent is also implied in the growing use of 'contracts', in which the probation officer undertakes to provide certain services, and the offender to use them. People will even sometimes go willingly to institutions if they accept that the purpose of these is to help them to rehabilitate themselves into society. This was successfully done with young offenders at the Hawkspur Camp as long ago as the 1930s (Arthur and others, 1979, p.21). Providing people with a refuge where they can go while they 'sort themselves out' can also have a valuable function in preventing not only crime but mental stress and disorder.

When the measure is agreed upon after mediation, there is in theory no need for a 'tariff'; since each case would be decided voluntarily by the participants, and as Aristotle pointed out a man cannot be unfairly treated with his own consent. It has been suggested by the Six Quakers that there should be no scale that 'aims at identical treatment for identical offences. We believe that true justice lies ... in treatment that is *equal* for everybody in the sense that everybody's needs are equally met. ... True justice in our view rests not in an equal distribution of pain, but in an equal satisfaction of needs, in the victim, in society, and in the offender himself' (Arthur and others, 1979, pp.41–42, emphasis in original). This might work in cases where agreement was reached by mediation, though it would be dependent on finding enough mediators conforming to the Quaker ideal of the person of natural authority, strong and secure within himself (*ibid.*, p.42) to preside at the hearings and encourage the participants to share this ideal of fairness – and such qualities are not too common. The argument in its 'strong' form is attractive as an ultimate ideal, and those who believe that no lesser compromise should be countenanced may skip the remainder of this section.

But others may regretfully feel, as I do, that an intermediate stage is necessary before our society is ready for the ideal. Where solutions had to be imposed without consent, wide variations in the settlements of comparable offences might be seen as arbitrary and lead to feelings of injustice: some sort of 'going rate' would have to emerge. I hope however that this will be seen as a step towards the ideal expressed by the Quakers, and not as undermining its attainment.

Let us consider how a tariff could be compiled which was generally felt to be fair, before turning to the question of enforcement. The starting point would have to be the seriousness of the offence for which amends were to be made. Surveys such as that by Sellin and Wolfgang (1964) suggest that there would be a tolerable degree of consensus in assigning levels of seriousness to particular acts. Research now in progress may throw more light on this. Next, the level of amends would have to be decided. This is more difficult: it may be agreed that a wounding is more serious than a petty theft, but that does not provide a clear indication of the amount of compensation or community service (or for that matter punishment) merited by each. If it were to be possible for either the offender or the court to choose between making amends through a payment, or service, or self-rehabilitation, a certain amount of arbitrariness could not be avoided, and there might be less consensus. One recent survey found that when two groups of students were asked to place various punishments in order of severity, one group ranked a fine of $50,000 between 12 and 18 months' imprisonment, the other between 10 and 15 *years*. The first group, similarly, thought that 10 years' probation was preferable to a prison sentence of only 6 months, while the other, which evidently under-valued the seriousness of prison, ranked it between 5 and 7 years' imprisonment (Sebba, 1978). Perhaps these variations simply underline the need for the construction of an acceptable tariff; and it may be that a certain amount of arbitrariness would be unavoidable. A basis would have to be found for converting, for example, a sum payable in compensation, or a period of community service performed on one day a week, to full-time attendance

at a day centre or residence in a hostel; and for ensuring as far as possible that the offender with money would not be able to buy his way
out of a more time-consuming way of making amends. One practical
problem is that it has been found in practice that the maximum work-
able period for a community service order in its present form is about
240 hours, which takes about a year to fulfil. Where the offence was
so serious as to call for a greater degree of reparation, could another
method be found, such as taking a lower paid but socially useful job?
In 1979, for example, a dentist was sentenced to 18 months' imprisonment for obtaining large sums from the National Health Service by
inventing fictitious patients. Such a sentence was a waste of everyone's time; how much more useful to require him to work for a period
in an area where there is a shortage of dentists. This would of course
require his consent and co-operation, so as to comply with the United
Nations' prohibition of forced labour, and to ensure that his patients
benefited as intended. It would be important also that offenders with
useful skills did not receive preferential treatment compared with
those who have none.

A further difficulty is that these proposals for changing the basis of
the system from punishment to making amends are being put
forward at a time when the scale of punishments in Britain and still
more in the United States is widely considered to be far too high;
those who have become used to this level of penal inflation may therefore feel that the scale of amends suggested is too low. But this is a
separate issue and does not affect the principles. If the level of
amends used in the example seems inadequate to deter, this is
because it is not intended to: for the reasons given in Chapter Eight,
deterrence is treated as an unreliable by-product, rather than as a
primary aim, and comes more from the offender's fear of being
caught than from the enormity of the sanction. Indeed, there would
be a positive gain for public protection: greater attention would be
given to more positive forms of crime prevention, which would be
suggested by the problem-solving type of hearing; and by discarding
the vain quest for deterrence through severity, society would also free
itself of the social problems which, as we have seen, can be *caused* by
the penal system. Again, if the level of amends seems inadequate by
current standards to denounce a particular offence, this is because
that function will no longer be fulfilled solely by the number of years
the offender is required to spend behind bars, but by a threefold
expression of seriousness and recognition of the harm suffered by the
victim: by the help given to the victim, the resources devoted to

dealing with the incident, and the assessment of the degree of amends to be rendered.

For these reasons, the examples to illustrate how these proposals might work will not be made too specific. There are dangers in doing so when propounding a new idea, since disagreement with this or that detail may lead some people to reject the whole. I hope, therefore, that those who are sympathetic to the principles may instead consider, like Harrington, that 'Truth is a spark to which objections are like bellows,' and will be able to suggest answers to particular problems. The proposals are in any case intended as an ideal to be worked towards, rather than a plan for immediate introduction. With these caveats, an outline can be given of the possible operation of the principles in practice.

ASSESSMENT OF SERIOUSNESS

If the victim and the offender could not agree, through mediation, on the amends to be made by the offender, the seriousness of his act would be assessed. This could be done either by placing offences in a few broad categories, as in California, or by grading them in more detail. For the sake of argument it will be assumed in the following examples that they are graded on a scale from, say, 1 to 1,000. Normally, this would be related to the actual harm suffered by the victim; but in some cases, such as attempts, the harm would be conceptualized as being done to the community. Care would be taken to ensure that non-violent offences were kept to the bottom of the scale, so that the greater public condemnation of offences endangering life and health, especially with firearms and explosives, could be clearly marked.

AMOUNT OF AMENDS

The amount of amends would be related to the assessment of seriousness and to the offender's earning capacity. It would be expressed as a number of day-payments, each of which was a fixed percentage of his disposable daily income. Alternatively it could be expressed as a period of time (regardless of income) or a combination of time and payment. For each point on the assessment of seriousness the appropriate amends might be a week's day-payments, or a day's community service. A week's attendance at a day centre, since it involves a greater restriction of liberty, might be worth two points.

At this point another possible objection is that the tariff has not entirely eliminated the two main elements of arbitrariness for which existing sentencing policy is criticized. One is the *relative* level of seriousness attributed to various offences. But there should at least be fewer anomalies in making this moral judgment in a coherent way rather than piecemeal as it is now: it could be decided on the basis of public opinion surveys, or by Parliament, and periodically revised. The other element is the *absolute* level: the calibration of the scale. If it is agreed that offences in group A are more serious than those in group B, what level of amends is commensurate with each? One possible basis has been suggested by Wilkins (1974): that the seriousness of the crime depends on its effect in forcing the victim to change his life-style (for example through loss of life savings, or physical injury). This might indicate that the offender should undertake as much in the way of making amends as would change his life-style to a comparable extent; but there would be difficulties if his own lifestyle was far below (or above) that of his victim, and moreover the concept comes close to being based on the principle of retribution. These complexities may lead some to feel that there is, after all, less scope for anomalies in the approach put forward by the Six Quakers, which is to seek fairness by trying to meet everybody's needs equally. Here, however, we shall continue to explore the implications of a scheme based on a tariff.

FORM OF AMENDS

The way in which amends are to be made could include financial reparation, community service, or amends through self-rehabilitation. Agreement about the appropriate form would normally be reached between the offender and his supervisor, but in some cases the court might be given power to order that a certain proportion must take a particular form.

NATURAL CONSEQUENCES: DISQUALIFICATION, PROHIBITION, AND SUPERVISION

The concept of natural consequences has been outlined earlier in this chapter. The court's assessment would also include the period in which the offender could work to regain the trust of the community, until when he would be under supervision, or disqualified from undertaking certain activities, or prohibited from exercising certain rights. In a few specified exceptionally serious cases this restriction of freedom would involve placement in an institution. Again, the time would be related to the degree of restriction of liberty: three weeks' ordinary probation supervision might be regarded as equivalent to two weeks' intensive supervision (perhaps with daily reporting), or compulsory residence at a probation hostel; or to one week in prison, or day centre and hostel concurrently. As with amends, the court could be given power to stipulate the proportion to be spent in certain ways, in carefully defined circumstances.

NATURAL CONSEQUENCES: COSTS

The costs of investigating the case would be assessed, in addition to the amends expected of the offender. Perhaps he could be required to pay the reward promised to staff for the detection of shoplifters; this can be done in West Germany, but with an upper limit of DM 50 (Huber, 1980). The two forms of payment would be kept distinct, with the amends taking precedence. As before, there would be provision for adjusting the amount to his means, making work available so that he could earn the money, or possibly converting the amount to non-financial forms as above. There would be an implicit obligation on the authorities not to incur costs disproportionate to the offence, and if they did so this should be a ground for appeal.

RECOMMENDATIONS TO THE COMMUNITY

Finally, the panel might make recommendations as to action that the community might take, either to assist the recovery of the victim, or to help the individual offender to make a new start, or to deflect others from committing similar acts in future.

An example of the application of these criteria might be a fairly serious but non-violent offender against property. His current offence is assessed at 200 points. In addition to restoring any goods still in his possession, he would be required to make a certain number of day-payments of compensation. After his previous offence daily reporting had proved insufficient to check his nocturnal activities, so he must now spend the first period in a probation hostel, by which he will 'work off' further points; subject to completing this satisfactorily, he can spend the next period on intensive supervision, and the last on ordinary probation. Another offender, after a similar offence, might agree on a different 'package' within the same total, because, let us say, he wants to catch up on his neglected education, or to overcome his compulsive gambling. Although he is homeless, he does not need the extra supervision of having to live in a probation hostel; he is helped to find ordinary accommodation, but undertakes to attend a day centre where he is offered appropriate help and if possible enabled to find a job. This allows him to make his day-payments of compensation; at first he will be under supervision, which will have to be intensive if his attendance at the day centre has been irregular. If he feels that any measure, such as the course he started at the day centre or the support of a probation officer, is helping him, he will of course be allowed to continue it voluntarily.

It is worth noting in passing that the principle of compensation could be applied to companies which inflict harm. A more constructive reaction than, say, imprisoning selected senior executives or imposing a corporate 'death penalty' by forcing the firm out of business, would be to follow the precedent set in the case of the Japanese Chisso Corporation. The company was prosecuted for having discharged mercury-containing waste into Minamata Bay, and thereby contaminating the fish living in its waters. People who had eaten this fish suffered paralysis, nervous disorders and even death, and some of their children were born deformed and mentally retarded. After agreeing to pay each victim an average of £20,000 compensation, and being confronted with a bill for dredging the bay, the corporation had a huge deficit; but the government decided to issue bonds to enable it to continue so that it could meet these liabilities.

Supposing that the offender has either agreed to a settlement, after mediation, or faces an order for amends and possibly further consequences; in either case the question has to be asked: what happens if he does not comply? To begin with, it does not seem too much to hope that compliance would benefit from the scheme's emphasis on securing voluntary agreement whenever possible, and by the fact that it would be based on amends rather than punishment. More people might regard evasion as mean rather than clever if payment were going to a victim, or a victims' fund (preferably a local one), instead of to the Exchequer, and this should be emphasized in the wording of forms and notices and the way the collectors were asked to approach their job. Support could be enlisted from public opinion. In West Germany, payments to charity or other non-profit-making organizations, particularly by under-21s, have a high yield (Council of Europe, 1976). Of course the system would not work in every case; but there is no reason to suppose that it would be less effective than the present one.

If however a person will not pay, there are various means of helping him or putting pressure on him to do so. Enforcement should be the responsibility of a separate enforcement office, as in Sweden and as recommended in this country (Committee on Enforcement,

1969). The office would arrange payment, which in some cases could be through an attachment of earnings order. For large amounts, the use of criminal bankruptcy could be further developed. There are some who do not pay mainly because their finances are in a muddle, which may have contributed to the offence. They could be helped by developing the little used system of money payments supervision orders. These are usually administered by the probation and after-care service, but this was done in only 3,977 cases in 1979 (Home Office 1980, p.39). A back-up of debt counselling and help with budgeting could be a social or educational service with a preventative role, by easing the pressures towards dishonesty. Someone who appears to be wilfully not paying can be brought to court to give an account of himself. Non-payment would be a separate offence. This would mean that when the offender failed to pay it would not be necessary to threaten imprisonment straight away: the first step would be the threat of prosecution. This is the method used by Inland Revenue to secure payment, and it is successful in a high proportion of cases. If the threatened or actual publicity of proceedings and newspaper reports were not effective, the court could check that the payment had been correctly assessed and was not beyond the offender's means, and order compulsory attachment of earnings, though this has not been found to be proof against determined non-payers.

Distraint on possessions is another possibility, though there is a risk that it will cause disproportionate hardship to other members of the family, especially if they are living near to, or below, the poverty line. It is also open to the objection that it relies, in the last resort, on the use of force. Ultimately it is possible to tell a person that if he will not work in the community to pay compensation, he must do so in prison; but there are three practical objections to this, and one of principle. The practical ones are that it is difficult to provide enough work of any kind in prison; that experience with the imprisonment of fine-defaulters suggests, as was seen in Chapter Five, that too often it is the 'can't pays' rather than the 'won't pays' who end up in prison; and that if a person is determined to resist regardless of the consequences there comes a point where the authorities have to desist if their enforcement measures are not to become oppressive. The state should refrain from going to the limit of its power over the individual, even when he is feckless or intransigent. This can easily be represented as weakness; in fact it is the more civilized policy of restraint. The objection of principle is that if the original act was not serious enough

265

to merit imprisonment, a person should not end up in prison for it. If he causes harm, is required to make amends, and wilfully refuses to do so, the moral blame lies with him. Society can go to certain lengths to uphold its values; but if it goes further and resorts to inhumane methods, it puts itself in the wrong and loses its moral authority.

One aid to enforcement would be incentives for prompt payment and punctual attendance: after a certain number of weeks, one week would be remitted. Even this could however be unfair in practice: capable, well-organized people would earn the maximum remission, while confused and inadequate ones might end up paying more or serving longer. In short, there is no entirely satisfactory solution, whether under the existing or the proposed system; there is a need to explore how it could better be done, and meanwhile make as much use as possible of the pressure of public opinion.

Amends by the Community

The scales of justice may be taken to symbolize a two-way responsibility: the blame or the making of amends should not be placed solely on the transgressor, but should be weighed against the contributory shortcomings of the community in which he was brought up and lives and has committed his harmful act. An early example of the community's acceptance of responsibility is the Riot Damages Act 1886, which provides that if the police fail to prevent a riot, citizens whose property is damaged can claim compensation. In an analogous way, the community, and especially its leaders, may be regarded as sharing responsibility if a fire has more disastrous results because of inadequate fire safety precautions; those in authority should not confine themselves to measures against any individual whose act or negligence caused the fire, but should do something towards making amends by enforcing the regulations more scrupulously in future. An important way in which the community should shoulder its responsibilities is by taking care of victims, whose needs have received little attention until relatively recently. A Home Office survey found that two in three victims of property offences and five in six assault victims described difficulties of finance, health and emotional distress (Vennard, 1976). For property offences, about three quarters were granted court orders for compensation to be paid by the offender; for assaults, only one third. Courts hardly ever made an order unless the police or (rarely) the victim applied for one. Many victims expressed shock at the fact that, in the court proceedings, no concern appeared to be given to their problems and feelings. If it were, Vennard suggests, this might help to overcome the victims' sense of injustice and consequent punitiveness. The community should offer financial and emotional help to victims, but also has responsibilities towards its members as a whole, including the offenders themselves.

The first official attempt to aid victims in Great Britain was the Criminal Injuries Compensation Scheme, established in 1964 after a campaign by a leading Howard League figure, Margery Fry. This has made a useful start, although it has several serious limitations. A relatively small proportion of those entitled to claim know of their right, and even fewer know how to apply (Vennard, 1976), though this position is no doubt improving. Compensation is not paid in cases where it would amount to less than £150. Where the victim and the person responsible for the injuries are living in the same household the minimum is £500, and even this was only introduced when the scheme was revised in 1979 (*Hansard* [H.C.], 23 July 1979, cols. 17–25), after recommendations by the Howard League (1977) and others; previously such cases were excluded altogether, apparently for fear that there would be collusion, or that the assailant might benefit from compensation paid to the injured spouse or child. The League also recommended that psychological injury should be included, for example the shock which some people suffer after being burgled. Everything should be done to make at least an initial payment quickly, and the amount of awards should be reviewed to make the basis for awards as generous as possible.

Where the offender is required to make amends but does not pay the full amount due to the victim, the state should make up the difference. In the case of crimes of violence this principle can be applied, but with offences against property problems arise because of the large numbers involved and the greater possibility of fraudulent claims. The great majority of property offences, however, involve small sums which will generally be in the offender's power to repay. It can be argued that commercial organizations can recover their losses either from their insurance policies or from the public through their pricing policies; individuals with incomes above the poverty level should also be able to protect themselves through insurance. An exception should however be made for victims with very low incomes, especially pensioners and those dependent on social security, who may not be able to afford premiums, or may have felt that their few possessions were hardly worth insuring. Unfortunately many victims of crime are themselves poor and disadvantaged.

But it is not just a question of money. Some victims have emotional and practical problems, and the community can express its concern by offering help and support. It is beginning to develop ways of doing so, either through general organizations such as victims' support schemes, or in specialized centres, for example for women assaulted by their husbands or for victims of rape. The first victims' support scheme was started in Bristol in 1974. An organizer obtains details of victims in the area every day from the police, and arranges for a trained volunteer to visit within 24 hours to offer comfort or assistance, if needed, in such matters as claiming compensation and arranging for repairs. The idea has caught on: there are now over 70 schemes offering help to some 18,000 people a year. They are affiliated to the National Association of Victim Support Schemes, which was established in 1980 with a government grant, and offers guidance on starting new schemes.

Women's Aid centres also developed during the 1970s. Their essence is to offer shelter to women and their children, so that they can escape from a violent husband without becoming homeless. By 1976 there were about 80 refuges in this country, with some 500 places in all, and three years later the number had doubled; but the House of Commons Select Committee on Violence in Marriage considered that there should be many more: one place for every 10,000 of the population. They too have a national organization: the National Women's Aid Federation. It has been suggested that men's houses are also needed: violent husbands are often as distraught as their wives and a potential liability, if not a danger, to the community; they also sometimes become homeless.

Several centres for assistance to rape victims have been started in this country. They consist of telephone services (those in London and Birmingham operate 24 hours a day) and appointments can generally be made for visits to the centre if required. Two examples from the United States are the Stop Rape Crisis Center, Baton Rouge, Louisiana (Whitcomb and others, 1979), and the Rape/ Sexual Assault Care Center, Des Moines, Iowa, both of which have been designated as Exemplary Projects by the Law Enforcement Assistance Administration. Common features of such schemes are advice about legal and medical matters, and campaigning for public education, to dispel myths and prejudices, and preventive measures on the basis of information supplied by victims. Although there is no pressure on the victims to report offences to the police or to give their names, more of them are doing so, and as it becomes known that there is a greater probability that an offender will be brought to court, there should be an increased deterrent effect.

All of these initiatives have grown up in the community to offer help when it is desperately needed. There is no reason why they should be taken over by the statutory social services, but they should receive state help to enable them to continue and extend their work. This should not, however, be unconditional: they should be required to state their aims clearly, and to be assessed independently. Their aims should include not merely making the existing system work better but suggesting ways in which it could be improved.

So much for the community's duty to victims. But it has another duty, which at first sight may seem paradoxical: to make amends to offenders. This is not a new insight: a century ago Mary Carpenter told a House of Commons Select Committee: 'If society leaves (offenders) knowingly in the state of utter degradation in which they are, I think it absolutely owes them reparation, far more than they can be said to owe reparation to it' (Manton, 1976, p.108). She was not placing the entire responsibility for their lawbreaking on society, but she was redressing the usual imbalance in which offenders bear the full brunt of blame for their reaction to circumstances not of their making. Not only that, but as we have seen the harmful acts committed by those who have already experienced the rough end of the educational, housing and social services are under the present system more likely to be detected and to attract harsh punishments than other kinds of harmful act committed by those who are better placed. Traditionally reformers have used this as the basis for a plea that the offender from a deprived background should not bear the full weight of punishment. A system based on making amends, however, affords him no such let-out. Like anyone else he can be required to face the consequences of his actions, and make good the harm he has caused, subject only to his ability to do so. Society in turn must recognize its failure to offer him a fair share of opportunity, not by letting him escape these consequences, but by doing what it can to make up for past deficiencies. The offender's willingness to make a new start is matched by society's willingness to offer him one.

Can these innovations have more than a token impact on an unregenerate society, and the attitudes of the people who comprise it? Can they counteract the influence of competition and acquisitiveness, in favour of collaboration, sharing and caring? Perhaps they can only make a beginning; and in what they do it is important that they should not merely disguise the excrescences of a structure that is unchanged underneath. But to wait until the social and economic system had been transformed into some ideal state would be to wait for ever. Economic reform, housing reform, educational reform and many others can help to bring that ideal nearer. Alongside these penal reform has a part to play, and one of the most fundamental tasks for penal reformers is to re-think their terms of reference. In the search for a society in which people harm each other as little as possible, and as much as possible of the harm is repaired, the radical question is whether a system that is primarily penal is the most effective and just that we can devise.

References

Chapter One (pp 19–29)

Advisory Council on the Penal System (1978) *Sentences of Imprisonment: A Review of Maximum Penalties*. (Chairman: Baroness Serota) London: HMSO.

Advisory Council on the Treatment of Offenders (1960) *Corporal Punishment,* Cmnd 1213. London: HMSO.

Canada: Sub-Committee on the Penitentiary System in Canada (1977) *Report to Parliament*. (Chairman: Mark MacGuigan) Ottawa: Ministry of Supply and Services.

Howard League for Penal Reform (1961) *Corporal Punishment: Fact versus Fiction,* London: The League.

Khan, Muhammad Zafrulla (1967) *Islam and Human Rights*. London: The London Mosque.

Lawton, Lord Justice (1975) *The Law and Public Opinion* (9th Riddell Lecture). London: Institute of Legal Executives.

McGee, Richard A. (1978) 'California's New Determinate Sentencing Act.' *Federal Probation,* vol. 32, no. 1, pp. 3–10.

Shaw, Bernard (1922) Preface to Sidney and Beatrice Webb, *English Prisons under Local Government*.

Chapter Two (pp 30–50)

Abse, Leo (1973) *Private Member*. London: Macdonald.

Bowker, L. H. (1978) *Victimization in Correctional Institutions: An Interdisciplinary Analysis*. Milwaukee, Wis: University of Wisconsin, School of Social Welfare.

Bowker, L. H. (1980) *Prison Victimization*. New York: Elsevier.

Canada: Sub-Committee on the Penitentiary System in Canada (1977) *Report to Parliament*. (Chairman: Mark MacGuigan) Ottawa: Ministry of Supply and Services.

Committee for the Defence of Political Prisoners in Israel (1978) *Prisons and Prisoners in Israel*. Tel Aviv: The Committee.

Corden, J. and others (1978) *After Prison: The Post-Release Experience of Discharged Prisoners*. University of York: Department of Social Administration and Social Work.

Davis, Alan J. (1968) 'Sexual Assaults in the Philadelphia Prison System and Sheriff's Vans.' *Trans-action,* December, pp.8–16.

Dickens, Charles (1842) *American Notes.* Chapter 7.

Field, J. (1848) *Prison Discipline.* 2nd ed., vol. I, quoted by Webb, S. and B. (1922), p.158.

Fitzgerald, M. and J. Sim (1979) *British Prisons.* Oxford: Blackwell.

Fox, Lionel W. (1934) *The Modern English Prison.* London: Routledge.

Gray, J. M. (1940) *A History of The Gambia.* Cambridge: Cambridge University Press.

Hobhouse, S. and A. Fenner Brockway (1922) *English Prisons Today.* Privately printed.

Holford, George (1821) *Thoughts on the Criminal Prisons of this Country.* cited in Webb, S. and B. (1922), p.57.

Home Office (1964) *The Sentence of the Court.* London: HMSO.

Home Office (1975) *Report on the Work of the Prison Department 1974.* Cmnd. 6148. London: HMSO.

Home Office (1977) *Prisons and the Prisoner: The Work of the Prison Service in England and Wales.* London: HMSO.

Home Office (1978) *Report on the Work of the Prison Department 1977.* Cmnd. 7290. London: HMSO.

Home Office (1979) *Report on the Work of the Prison Department 1978.* Cmnd. 7619. London: HMSO.

Home Office (1980a) *Prison Statistics, England and Wales 1979.* Cmnd. 7978. London: HMSO.

Home Office (1980b) *Report on the Work of the Prison Department 1979.* Cmnd. 7965. London: HMSO.

Home Office Research Bulletin (1978) 'A Survey of the South-East Prison Population.' *Research Bulletin* no. 5, pp.12–24.

Howard League for Penal Reform (1979) *Losing Touch: Restrictions on Prisoners' Outside Contacts.* London: The League.

Lockwood, Daniel (1980) *Prison Sexual Violence.* New York: Elsevier.

Martin, J. P. and D. Webster (1971) *The Social Consequences of Conviction.* London: Heinemann Educational Books.

Mayhew, Henry, and John Binney (1862) *The Criminal Prisons of London and Scenes of Prison Life.* London (new impression, Cass, 1968).

McVicar, John (1978), *in: Sunday Times Magazine,* 30 July 1978, p.17.

Morris, Pauline (1965) *Prisoners and Their Families.* London: Allen & Unwin.

Nagel, W. G. (1973) *The New Red Barn: A Critical Look at the Modern American Prison.* New York: Walker.

Nagel, W. G. (1977) 'On Behalf of a Moratorium on Prison Construction.' *Crime and Delinquency,* April, pp.154–172.

Prisons Committee (1895) *Report.* (Chairman: H. J. Gladstone) C. 7702. London: HMSO.

Rector, Milton G. (1977) 'Are More Prisons Needed Now?' *in:* John P.

Conrad and Milton G. Rector, *Should We Build More Prisons?* Hackensack, N. J.: National Council on Crime and Delinquency.

Shaw, Bernard (1924) *Saint Joan: A Chronicle Play in Six Scenes and an Epilogue*. London: Constable.

Stonham, Lord (1967) *Hansard* [HL]. May 10, col. 1430.

Tyler, Mary (1977) *My Years in an Indian Prison*. London: Gollancz.

Walmsley, R. (1972) *Steps from Prison: An Enquiry into the Need for Accomodation for Homeless Prisoners*. London: Inner London Probation and After-Care Service.

Webb, S. and B. (1922) *English Prisons under Local Government*. p.122. Privately printed.

Wilkins, Leslie (1974) 'To Do and Dare: The Necessity for Innovation.' *in:* NACRO, *The Prevention of Crime*. London: NACRO.

Chapter Three (pp 51–76)

Advisory Council on the Penal System (1968) *The Regime for Long-term Prisoners in Conditions of Maximum Security*. London: HMSO.

Banks, C. and S. Fairhead (1976) *The Petty Short-Term Prisoner*. (Howard League for Penal Reform) Chichester: Barry Rose.

Barry, J. V. (1958) *Alexander Maconochie*. Melbourne: Oxford University Press.

Bowker, Lee H. (1978) *Victimization in Correctional Institutions: An Interdisciplinary Analysis*. Milwaukee, Wisconsin: The University of Wisconsin, School of Social Welfare (mimeog.).

Boyle, J. (1977) *A Sense of Freedom*. Edinburgh: Canongate and London: Pan.

Canada: Sub-Committee on the Penitentiary System in Canada (1977) *Report to Parliament*. (Chairman: Mark MacGuigan) Ottawa: Ministry of Supply and Services.

Committee for the Defence of Political Prisoners in Israel (1978) *Prisons and Prisoners in Israel*. Tel Aviv: The Committee.

Dean, Malcolm (1978) 'An Open and Shut Case?' *Guardian,* March 28.

Fleisher, B. M. (1966) *The Economics of Delinquency*. Chicago: Quadrangle Books (quoted in Gladstone, see below).

Forde, R. A. (1977) Unpublished Papers on the Identification of Subversive Prisoners. Hull Prison, Psychology Unit. (quoted in Grayson, see below)

Foucault, M. (1977) *Discipline and Punish: The Birth of the Prison*. London: Allen Lane.

Gent, P. (1978) 'Behind Bars.' *Gay News* (144), June 1–14.

Gladstone, Francis (1979) 'Crime and the Crystal Ball.' *Research Bulletin* (Home Office Research Unit), (7), 36–41.

Glaser, D. and K. Rice (1959) 'Crime, Age and Unemployment.' *American Sociological Review,* vol. 24, pp.679–686.

Grayson, David (1979) *Unlocking the Facts: A Review of Prison Psycholo-*

gists' Research Which Has Had a Bearing on Managerial Decisions.* London: Home Office Prison Department, Director of Psychological Services.

Greenberg, D. F. (1977) 'The Dynamics of Oscillatory Punishment Processes.' *Journal of Criminal Law and Criminology,* vol. 68, pp.643–51.

Gunn, John, and J. Gristwood (1976) 'Twenty-seven Robbers.' *British Journal of Criminology,* vol. 16, no. 1, January, pp.56–62.

Haney, C., C. Banks and P. Zimbardo (1973) 'Interpersonal Dynamics in a Simulated Prison.' *International Journal of Criminology and Penology,* vol. I, pp. 69–97.

Home Office (1977a) *Prisons and the Prisoner: The Work of the Prison Service in England and Wales.* London: HMSO.

Home Office (1977b) *Report of an Enquiry into ... the Events at H.M. Prison, Hull* (by the Chief Inspector of Prisons, G. W. Fowler). H.C. 453. London: HMSO.

Home Office (1980a) *Prison Statistics England and Wales 1979.* Cmnd. 7978. London: HMSO.

Home Office (1980b) *Report on the Work of the Prison Department 1979.* Cmnd. 7965. London: HMSO.

Home Office Research Bulletin (1978) 'A Survey of the South-East Prison Population.' *Research Bulletin,* no. 5, pp.12–24.

Howard, John (1777) *The State of the Prisons in England and Wales.* Warrington. Reprinted, Abingdon: Professional Books (1977).

Howard Association (*c.* 1870) *Prison Facts.* London: The Association.

Howard League (1969) *Annual Report 1968/69.* London: The League.

Howard League (1979a) *Prisons as Part of the Penal System.* London: The League.

Howard League (1979b) *Losing Touch: Restriction on Prisoners' Outside Contacts.* London: The League.

Israel Committee *see* Committee for ... Prisoners in Israel.

Jackson, George (1970) *Soledad Brother.* New York: Coward McCann & Geoghegan and Bantam Books. London: Jonathan Cape and Harmondsworth: Penguin (1971).

Lawton, Lord Justice (1975) *The Law and Public Opinion.* (9th Riddell Lecture) London: Institute of Legal Executives.

McGurk, B. J. and others (1977) *A Study of the Variables Relating to Recidivism in Delinquent Boys.* (Directorate of Psychological Services Report 1–9) London: Prison Department.

McVicar, John (1974) *McVicar by Himself.* London: Hutchinson.

Marchenko, A. (1969) *My Testimony.* Translated by M. Scammell. London: Pall Mall Press.

Marriage. H. (1973) *Report of Prison Department Working Party on Dispersal and Control.* Appendix, C. (quoted in Grayson – see above).

Milgram, Stanley (1974) *Obedience to Authority: An Experimental View.* London: Tavistock.

Murton, T. and J. Hyams (1969) *Accomplices to the Crime: The Arkansas Prison Scandal.* London: M. Joseph.

New York State Special Commission on Attica (1972) *Attica: The Official Report.* New York: Bantam Books.

Orland, Leonard (1975) *Prisons: Houses of Darkness.* New York: Free Press.

Prescott, J. (1976) *Hull Prison Riot, August 31 to September 3, 1975:* Submissions, Observations and Recommendations . . . (mimeog.).

PROP (n.d.) *Don't Mark his Face: The Account of the Hull Prison Riot (1976) and its Brutal Aftermath by the Prisoners Themselves.* London: National Prisoners' Movement.

Probyn, Walter (1977) *Angel Face: The Making of a Criminal.* London: Allen & Unwin.

Read, P. P. (1978) *The Train Robbers.* London: Coronet Books.

Sinyavskii, A. (1976) '"I" and "They": An Essay on Extreme Forms of Communication under Conditions of Human Isolation.' *Survey, a Journal of East and West Studies,* vol. 22, no. 3/4, pp.278–287.

South African Embassy (1980?) *South Africa Manpower: White Paper on the Report of the Commission of Inquiry . . . A Political Backgrounder.* London: The Embassy.

Stockdale, Eric (1967) *The Court and the Offender.* London: Gollancz.

Stratton, Brian (1973) 'Who Guards the Guards?' London: North London Group of PROP.

Tyler, Mary (1977) *My Years in an Indian Prison.* London: Gollancz.

West, Donald J. (1963) *The Habitual Prisoner.* London: Macmillan.

West, Donald J. (1973) *Who Becomes Delinquent?* London: Heinemann Educational Books.

Wootton, Barbara (1967) *In a World I Never Made.* London: Allen & Unwin.

Zellick, Graham (1977) 'Legal Services for Convicted Prisoners?' *Howard Journal,* vol. 16, no. 2., pp.65–69.

Chapter Four (pp 77–95)

Adley, Robert, and others (n.d. 1979?) *Take It . . . or Leave It? An Independent Study of the Cause and Effect of the Increase in Shoplifting.* Privately printed.

Advisory Council on Drug Dependence (1968) *Cannabis.* London: HMSO.

Advisory Council on the Penal System (1970) *Non-custodial and Semicustodial Penalties.* (Chairman of sub-committee: Baroness Wootton) London: HMSO.

Advisory Council on the Penal System (1974) *Young Adult Offenders.* (Chairman: Sir Kenneth Younger) London: HMSO.

Bluglass, Robert (1978) 'Regional Secure Units and Interim Security for

Psychiatric Patients.' *British Medical Journal,* vol. 1, February 25, pp.489–493.

Bottoms, A. E. (1980) *The Suspended Sentence after Ten Years: A Review and Reassessment.* Leeds: University of Leeds, Centre for Social Work and Applied Social Studies.

Bottoms, A. E. and F. H. McClintock (1973) *Criminals Coming of Age: A Study of Institutional Adaptation in the Treatment of Adolescent Offenders.* London: Heinemann Educational Books.

COHSE (1979) *NHS Secure Units: A Policy Statement.* London: Confederation of Health Service Employees.

DHSS (1974) *Report of the Committee on One-Parent Families.* (Chairman: Sir Morris Finer) Cmnd. 5629. London: HMSO.

Dronfield, Liz (1980) *Outside Chance: The Story of the Newham Alternatives Project.* London: Radical Alternatives to Prison.

Flackett, J. (1974) 'Juvenile Offenders in the Community: Some Recent Experiences in the United States.' *Howard Journal,* vol. 14, no. 1, pp. 22–37.

Home Office (1971) *Habitual Drunken Offenders.* (Chairman: T. Weiler) London: HMSO.

Home Office (1973) *Shoplifting and Thefts by Shop Staff.* London: HMSO.

Home Office (1974) *Working Party on Vagrancy and Street Offences: Working Paper.* London: HMSO.

Home Office (1976a) *Report of the Working Party on Vagrancy and Street Offences.* London: HMSO.

Home Office (1976b) *Report on the Work of the Prison Department 1975: Statistical Tables.* Cmnd. 6542. London: HMSO.

Home Office (1977a) *Prisons and the Prisoner: The Work of the Prison Service in England and Wales.* London: HMSO.

Home Office (1977b) *Report on the Work of the Prison Department 1976.* Cmnd. 6877. London: HMSO.

Home Office (1979) *Criminal Statistics 1978.* Cmnd. 7670. London: HMSO.

Home Office (1980a) *Prison Statistics England and Wales 1979.* Cmnd. 7978. London: HMSO. See especially Tables 3.2, 4.1, 5.1.

Home Office (1980b) *Report on the Work of the Prison Department 1979.* Cmnd. 7965. London: HMSO.

Home Office Research Bulletin (1978) 'A Survey of the South-East Prison Population.' *Research Bulletin,* No. 5, pp.12–24.

Hotson, B. (1970) *Thefts from Gas and Electricity Prepayment Meters.* Cambridge: Institute of Criminology (unpublished).

House of Commons Expenditure Committee (1979) *The Reduction of Pressure on the Prison System. Vol. I – Report.* (Fifteenth Report, 1977/78. H.C. 662 – I.) London: HMSO.

Howard Journal (1978) 'Criminal Law Act 1977: Time to Think Again.' vol. 17, no. 1, pp.4–5.

Howard League for Penal Reform (1975) *Cautioning and Imprisoning of Prostitutes*. London: The League.

Howard League for Penal Reform (1977a) *Lawyers and the Treatment of Offenders*. London: The League.

Howard League for Penal Reform (1977b) *'Unruly' Children in a Human Context*. Chichester: Barry Rose.

Howard League for Penal Reform (1979) *Women and the Penal System*. London: The League.

Huber, Barbara (1980a) 'The Dilemma of Decriminalization: Dealing with Shoplifting in West Germany.' *Criminal Law Review*, October, pp.621–627.

Huber, Barbara (1980b) *Experiences with the Day-fine Method in West Germany*. Unpublished lecture at Warwick University, June 1980.

Justice (1980) *Breaking the Rules: The Problem of Crimes and Contraventions*. London: Justice.

Kent Social Services Department (1980) *Fourth Report of Kent Family Placement Project, 1975–1979*. Maidstone: The Department.

Latham, C. T. (1973) 'Enforcement of Fines.' *Criminal Law Review*, September, pp.552–559.

Legalise Cannabis Campaign (1979) *Trash Rehashed*. London: The Campaign.

Leigh, L. H. and J. E. Hall Williams (1980) 'The Prosecution Process in Denmark, Sweden and the Netherlands.' *Home Office Research Bulletin*, no. 10, pp.10–13.

McNicoll, A. (1979) 'The Case against the Decriminalization of Cannabis.' [With appendices comparing cannabis with alcohol and tobacco, and annotated bibliography.] *International Criminal Police Review*, no. 328, May, pp.126–136.

Mead, Margaret (1937) *Co-operation and Competition among Primitive Peoples*. New York: McGraw-Hill.

Millham, S. and others (1975) *After Grace – Teeth: A Comparative Study of the Residential Experience of Boys in Approved Schools*. London: Human Context Books, Chaucer Publishing Co.

Morris, Allison (1978) 'Diversion of Juvenile Offenders from the Juvenile Justice System.' *in:* N. Tutt, ed., *Alternative Strategies for Coping with Crime*. Oxford: Blackwell.

Morris, N. and G. Hawkins (1970) *The Honest Politician's Guide to Crime Control*. Chicago: University of Chicago Press.

New York City. Criminal Justice Co-ordinating Council *and* Vera Institute of Justice (1970) *In Lieu of Arrest: The Manhattan Bowery Project – Treatment for Homeless Alcoholics*. New York: Vera Institute.

O'Gara, M. (1981) 'Fuel Prepayment Meters.' (Letter) *LAG Bulletin*, March, p.71.

Rutherford, A. (1978) 'Decarceration of Young Offenders in Massachusetts.' *in:* N. Tutt, ed., *Alternative Strategies for Coping with Crime.* Oxford: Blackwell.

Sandford, J. (1974) *Smiling David: The Story of David Oluwale.* London: Calder & Boyars.

Scarman, Lord Justice (1978) 'Control of Sentencing: The Balance between the Judiciary and the Executive.' *in:* J. Baldwin and A. K. Bottomley, ed., *Criminal Justice: Selected Readings.* London: Martin Robertson.

Scottish Council on Crime (1975) *Crime and the Prevention of Crime.* Edinburgh: HMSO.

Serrill, M. S. (1975) 'Juvenile Corrections in Massachusetts.' *Corrections Magazine,* vol. 2, no. 2, November, pp.3–12, 17–20.

SETRHA (1979) *Secure but not Secured.* 2nd ed. Croydon: South East Thames Regional Health Authority.

Simpson, C. (1977) 'Community Ties and the Bail Decision.' *Justice of the Peace,* vol. 141, no. 14–15, April 2–9, 194–196, 212–213.

Sinclair, Andrew (1962) *Prohibition: The Era of Excess.* London: Faber.

Softley, P. (1978) *Fines in Magistrates' Courts.* (Home Office Research Studies, 46) London: HMSO.

Tulkens, H. (1979) *Some Developments in Penal Policy and Practice in Holland.* Chichester: Barry Rose.

Tyler, Mary (1977) *My Years in an Indian Prison.* London: Gollancz.

United Nations (1980a) *Deinstitutionalization of Corrections and its Implications for the Residual Prisoner.* Working Paper A/CONF. 87/7, 6th UN Congress on the Prevention of Crime and the Treatment of Offenders, Caracas, 1980. (80–16792) New York: UN.

United Nations (1980b) *The Implementation of the UN Standard Minimum Rules for the Treatment of Prisoners.* Working paper A/CONF. 87/11 6th Congress (as above).

United States. President's Commission on Law Enforcement and Administration of Criminal Justice (1967) *Task Force Report: Drunkenness.* Washington: U.S. G.P.O.

Vera Foundation (c. 1971) *Towards Justice for the Poor: The Manhattan Bail Project.* New York: The Foundation.

Walker, N. (1977) *Behaviour and Misbehaviour: Explanations and Non-explanations.* Oxford: Blackwell.

Wilkins, G. (1979) *Making Them Pay: A Study of Some Fine Defaulters, Civil Prisoners and Other Petty Offenders in a Local Prison.* London: NACRO.

Chapter Five (pp 96–114)

Advisory Council on the Penal System (1974) *Young Adult Offenders.* (Chairman: Sir Kenneth Younger) London: HMSO.

Advisory Council on the Penal System (1977) *The Length of Prison Sentences: Interim Report.* London: HMSO.

Advisory Council on the Penal System (1978) *Sentences of Imprisonment: A Review of Maximum Penalties.* (Chairman: Baroness Serota) London: HMSO.

Banks, C. (1964) 'Young Offenders.' *in: Current Legal Problems.* London: Stevens.

Beck, J. L. and P. B. Hoffman (1976) 'Time Served and Release Performance: A Research Note.' *Journal of Research in Crime and Delinquency,* vol. 12, no. 2, pp.127–132.

Beha, J. and others (1977) *Sentencing to Community Service.* Washington, D.C.: Law Enforcement Assistance Administration.

Belville, M. (1978) 'Break-in to Literacy.' *Probation Journal,* vol. 25, no. 4, December, pp.128–133.

van Bemmelen, J. M. (1968) 'New Ways of Punishment.' *in:* M. E. Wolfgang, ed., *Crime and Culture: Essays in Honour of Thorsten Sellin.* New York: Wiley.

Bottoms, A. E. and W. McWilliams (1979) 'A Non-treatment Paradigm for Probation Practice.' *British Journal of Social Work,* vol. 9, no. 2, pp.159–202.

Briggs, Dennie (1975) *In Place of Prison.* London: Temple Smith.

Briggs, Dennie and Nancy Hodgkin (1972) 'A Transitional Therapeutic Community for Young Violent Offenders: The New Careers Project at Vacaville.' *Howard Journal,* vol. 13, no. 3, pp.171–211.

Brody, S. (1976) *The Effectiveness of Sentencing: A Review of the Literature.* (Home Office Research Study no. 35) London: HMSO.

Bryant, M. and others (1978) 'Sentenced to Social Work?' *Probation Journal,* vol. 25, no. 4, pp.110–114.

Bullington, B. and others (1978) 'A Critique of Diversionary Juvenile Justice.' *Crime and Delinquency,* January, vol. 24, no. 1, pp.59–71.

Burney, E. (1980) *A Chance to Change: Day Care and Day Training for Offenders.* London: Howard League for Penal Reform.

Cheshire Constabulary (1980) *Juvenile Volunteer Scheme.* Chester: The Constabulary.

Cohen, Stan (1979) *Crime and Punishment: Some Thoughts on Theories and Policies.* London: Radical Alternatives to Prison (reprinted from *New Society,* 1, 15 and 29 March 1979).

Ditchfield, J. A. (1976) *Police Cautioning in England and Wales.* (Home Office Research Study 37) London: HMSO.

Draper, John (1979) 'IT: An Offer He Ought to Refuse?' *Community Care,* 19 April, pp.15–17.

Dunlop, Anne B. (1980) *Junior Attendance Centres.* (Home Office Research Study no. 60) London: HMSO.

Eichman, Charles J. (1966) *The Impact of the Gideon Decision upon Crime and Sentencing in Florida: A Study of Recidivism and Sociocultural Change.* Tallahassee: Florida Division of Corrections.

Folkard, M. S. and others (1976) *IMPACT: Intensive Matched Probation* and After-Care Treatment. Vol. II – The Results of the Experiment. (Home Office Research Study no. 36) London: HMSO.

Gibson, R. E. (1971) 'Periodic Detention Centres (Youth) in New Zealand.' *Australian and New Zealand Journal of Criminology*, vol. 4, no. 2, pp. 86–93.

Hammond, W. H. (1977) 'A Study of the Deterrent Effect of Prison Conditions.' *Howard Journal*, vol. 15, no. 3, pp.12–23.

Hammond, W. H. and E. Chayen (1963) *Persistent Criminals: A Study of all Offenders Liable to Preventive Detention in 1956.* London: HMSO.

Harding, J. (1978) 'The Development of Community Service.' *in:* N. Tutt, ed., *Alternative Strategies for Coping with Crime.* Oxford: Blackwell.

Heimler, Eugene (1967) *Mental Illness and Social Work.* Harmondsworth: Penguin.

Home Office (1980) *Report on the Work of the Prison Department 1979.* Cmnd. 7965. London: HMSO.

Home Office Research Bulletin (1978) 'A Survey of the South-East Prison Population.' *Research Bulletin,* no. 5, pp.12–24.

Hood, R. (1966) *Homeless Borstal Boys.* London: Bell.

Hood, R. and R. F. Sparks (1970) *Key Issues in Criminology.* London: Weidenfeld.

Ilderton Motor Project (1978) *First Report.* London: Inner London Probation and After-Care Service.

Marks, Harold (1979) *Education for Offenders: Provision and Needs.* London: NACRO.

Millham, S. and others (1978) 'Another Try: An Account of a New Careers Project for Borstal Trainees.' *in:* N. Tutt, ed., *Alternative Strategies for Coping with Crime.* Oxford: Blackwell.

NACRO (1978) *Annual Report 1977/78.* London: National Association for Care and Resettlement of Offenders. (See also subsequent reports.)

NACRO [1981] *Education for Offenders in the Community: Some Different Kinds of Projects.* (Education Information leaflet no. 1.) London: NACRO.

Pease, K. and W. McWilliams (1977) 'Assessing Community Service Schemes: Pitfalls for the Unwary,' *Probation Journal*, vol. 24, no. 4, pp.137–139.

Pease, K. and M. Sampson (1977) 'Doing Time and Marking Time.' *Howard Journal,* vol. 16, no. 2, pp. 59–64.

Pease, K. and others (1977) *Community Service Assessed in 1976.* (Home Office Research Study no. 39.) London: HMSO.

Richardson, Anthony (1965) *'Nick of Notting Hill.'* London: Harrap.

Shore, Peter (1980) *The Swindon Basic Education Unit: An Experiment in Educational Provision for Offenders.* London: NACRO.

Society of Roadcraft (1977) *A Report and Proposal ... to Provide ... Roadcraft Training.* Hailsham, East Sussex: The Society.

Stace, N. (1979) 'Periodic Dentention Work Centres.' *Australian and New*

Zealand Journal of Criminology, vol. 12, no. 2, pp.3–18.

Sweden (1977) *Supervision Orders.* (Committee on the Abolition of Youth Imprisonment) SOU 1977:83.

Tulkens, H. (1979) *Some Developments in Penal Policy and Practice in Holland.* London: NACRO.

Willcock, H. D. (1974) *Deterrents and Incentives to Crime among Boys and Young Men Aged 15–21 Years.* (SS 352) London: Office of Population Censuses and Surveys, Social Survey Division.

Wright, Martin (1980) 'Cutting Prison Overcrowding: Sources of Help and Hindrance.' *Crime and Delinquency,* vol. 26, no. 1, January, pp.10–21.

Chapter Six (pp 115–147)

Bernstein, B. (1976) 'The Federal Bureau of Prisons Administrative Grievance Procedure: An Effective Alternative to Prisoner Litigation?' *American Criminal Law Review,* vol. 13, no. 737, pp.779–799.

Bowker, Lee H. (1980) *Prison Victimization.* New York: Elsevier.

Boyle, J. (1977) *A Sense of Freedom.* Edinburgh: Canongate and London: Pan.

Bullock, Alan (1960) *The Life and Times of Ernest Bevin.* London: Heinemann, vol. I, p.271.

Burney, Elizabeth (1980) *A Chance to Change: Day Care and Training for Offenders.* London: Howard League for Penal Reform.

Committee of Inquiry into the United Kingdom Prison Services (1979) *Report.* (Chairman: Mr. Justice May) Cmnd. 7673. London: HMSO.

Committee on Mental Health Review Tribunal Procedures (1978) *The Procedures of the Mental Health Review Tribunals: A Discussion Paper.*

Corden, John (1976) 'Prisoners' Rights and National Insurance Contributions,' *Howard Journal,* vol. 15, no. 2, pp.13–30.

Council of Europe (1979) *Work Programmes, Education and Vocational Training: The Role of Social Workers ... in the Social Rehabilitation ... and Employment of Prisoners* (SOC (79)2-E). Strasbourg: The Council.

Cronin, Harley (1967) *The Screw Turns.* London: Long.

Denenberg, T. S. (n.d.) 'The Application of Labor-Management Dispute Procedures to Prison Inmate Grievances.' Proceedings of 29th Annual Meeting, Industrial Relations Research Association.

Farrington, D. P. and C. P. Nuttall (1980) 'Prison Size, Overcrowding, Prison Violence and Recidivism.' *Journal of Criminal Justice,* vol. 8, pp.221–231.

Fogel, David (1978) 'The Justice Model for Corrections.' *in:* J. C. Freeman, ed., *Prisons, Past and Future.* London: Heinemann Educational Books.

Gunn, J. and others (1978) *Psychiatric Aspects of Imprisonment.* London: Academic Press.

Hamiduzzafar, M. (1977) *Burewala: Correction without Tears.* Karachi: National Book Foundation.

Harding, John (1980) *An Investigation into the Current Status and Effectiveness of Juvenile and Adult Restitution Programmes in the United States of America.* Exeter: Devon Probation and After-Care Service (unpublished).

Hepburn, J. R. and J. H. Laue (1980) 'Prisoner Redress: Analysis of an Inmate Grievance Procedure.' *Crime and Delinquency,* vol. 26, no. 2, April, pp.162–178.

Home Office (1966) *Report of the Inquiry into Prison Escapes and Security* by Admiral Earl Mountbatten of Burma. Cmnd. 3175. London: HMSO.

Home Office (1977a) *Prisons and the Prisoner: The Work of the Prison Service in England and Wales.* London: HMSO.

Home Office (1977b) *Review of Criminal Justice Policy 1976.* London: HMSO.

Home Office (1977c) Report of an Inquiry into ... the Events at H.M. Prison Hull (by the Chief Inspector of Prisons, G. W. Fowler). H.C. 453. London: HMSO.

Howard, John (1792) *Prisons and Lazarettos: Vol. 1.– The State of the Prisons in England and Wales.* 4th ed. Reprinted: Montclair, N.J.: Patterson Smith, 1973.

Howard League for Penal Reform (1974) *Ill-founded Premises: The Logic of Penal Policy and the Prison Building Programme.* London: The League.

Howard League for Penal Reform (1979a) *Losing Touch: Restrictions on Prisoners' Outside Contacts.* London: The League.

Howard League for Penal Reform (1979b) *Prisons as Part of the Penal System: Prison Administration and the Reduction of Overcrowding.* London: The League.

Howard League for Penal Reform (1979c) *Supervision and Control of Young Offenders: Comments on the Green Paper.* London: The League.

Howard League for Penal Reform and others (1975) *Boards of Visitors in Penal Institutions.* (Chairman: Earl Jellicoe) Chichester: Barry Rose.

Kane, R. (1980) 'But what would you do with....?' *Abolitionist,* Autumn, no. 6, pp.20–21.

Keating, J. R. and others (1975) *Grievance Mechanisms in Correctional Institutions.* Washington, D.C.: U.S. National Institute of Law Enforcement and Criminal Justice.

King, Roy D. and Rod Morgan (1980) *The Future of the Prison System.* Farnborough, Hants.: Gower.

Klare, H. J. (1960) *Anatomy of Prison.* London: Hutchinson.

McCarthy, W. E. J. and N. D. Ellis (1973) *Management by Agreement.* London: Hutchinson.

McGillis, D. and others (1976) *Controlled Confrontation: The Ward Grievance Procedure of the California Youth Authority.* Washington, D.C.: National Criminal Justice Reference Service.

McVicar, J. (1974) *McVicar by Himself.* London: Hutchinson.

Marnell, Gunnar (1974) 'Penal Reform: A Swedish Viewpoint.' *Howard Journal,* vol. 14, no. 1, pp.8–21.

Marnell, Gunnar (1981) 'Treatment of Long-term Prisoners: The Swedish Approach,' *in:* D. A. Ward and K. F. Schoen, ed., *Confinement in Maximum Custody: New Last-resort Prisons in the United States and Western Europe.* Lexington, Mass.: Lexington.

Mathiesen, T. (1974) *The Politics of Abolition.* London: Martin Robertson.

Nagel, William G. (1973) *The New Red Barn: A Critical Look at the Modern American Prison.* New York: Walker.

National Association of Attorneys General (1974) *Prisoners' Grievance Procedures.* Raleigh, N.C.: The Association.

New York State Special Commission on Attica (1972) *Attica: The Official Report.* New York: Bantam Books.

Pope, P. J. (1976) 'Prisoners in Maximum Security Prisons.' *Prison Service Journal,* no. 22, pp.2–5.

Pope, P. J. and T. C. N. Gibbens (1979) 'Medical Aspects of Management Problems in Maximum Security Prisons.' *Medicine, Science and the Law,* vol. 19, no. 2, pp.111–117.

Priestley, Philip (1978) 'Release Courses: A New Venture for Prison Officers.' *Prison Service Journal,* no. 30, pp.3–6.

Prison Rules (1964) Statutory Instrument: 1964, No. 388.

Shaw, Stephen (1980) *Paying the Penalty: An Analysis of the Cost of Penal Sanctions.* London: NACRO.

Short, Renee (1979) *The Care of Long-term Prisoners.* London: Macmillan.

Tucker, Gillian (in press) 'Prison, Parole, Prediction: A Critical Analysis.'

Chapter Seven (pp 148–170)

Advisory Council on the Penal System (1974) *Young Adult Offenders.* (Chairman: Sir Kenneth Younger) London: HMSO.

Advisory Council on the Penal System (1978) *Sentences of Imprisonment: A Review of Maximum Penalties.* (Chairman: Baroness Serota) London: HMSO.

Allinson, Richard S. (1979) 'LEAA's Impact on Criminal Justice: A Review of the Literature.' *Criminal Justice Abstracts,* vol. 11, no. 4, pp.608–646.

Amnesty International, Howard League and National Council for Civil Liberties (1977) *A Dossier Concerning Treatment of Prisoners during and after a Disturbance at Albany Prison in September 1976.* London.

Bacon, Sylvia (1975) *The Standard Setting Process as a Method of Achieving Community Participation in Crime Prevention.* Statement . . . at the Fifth United Nations Congress on the Prevention of Crime and the Treatment of Offenders, Geneva. (mimeog.)

Blackmore, J. B. (1978) 'Minnesota Community Corrections Act Takes Hold.' *Corrections Magazine,* March, pp.45–56.

Briggs, Dennie (1975) *In Place of Prison.* London: Temple Smith.

CCPACC (1978) 'The Diminished Use of Probation Orders.' (Statement by Central Council of Probation and After-Care Committees) *NAPO Newsletter,* no. 164, November, p.3.

Committee of Inquiry into the U.K. Prison Services (1979) *Report.* (Chairman: Mr. Justice May) Cmnd. 7673. London: HMSO.

Community Corrections (1980) 'Probation Subsidy: "Behaviour Modification for Bureaucracies".' *Community Corrections,* 19 December, pp.19–22.

Dickson, Rachel (1976) 'The Voluntary Associate.' *Probation Journal,* vol. 23, no. 4, December, pp.121–2.

Flackett, John (1974) 'Juvenile Offenders in the Community: Some Recent Experiences in the United States.' *Howard Journal,* vol. 14, no. 1, pp.22–37.

Hazel, Nancy and Rosemary Cox (1976) *First Report of the Special Family Placement Project.* Maidstone: Kent Social Services Department.

Hine, Jean and others (1978) 'Recommendations, Social Information and Sentencing.' *Howard Journal,* vol. 17, no. 2, pp.91–100.

Home Office (1977a) *Prisons and the Prisoner: The Work of the Prison Service in England and Wales.* London: HMSO.

Home Office (1977b) *A Review of Criminal Justice Policy 1976.* London: HMSO.

Home Office (1980a) *Criminal Statistics England and Wales 1979.* Cmnd. 8098. London: HMSO. Table 6.19.

Home Office (1980b) *Report on the Work of the Prison Department 1979.* Cmnd. 7965. London: HMSO.

House of Commons Expenditure Committee (1978) *The Reduction of Pressure on the Prison System. Vol.1. Report.* (Fifteenth Report, 1977–78, H.C. 662–I) London: HMSO.

Howard League for Penal Reform (1976) *The Economics of Penal Policy: The Courts' Responsibility.* (Howard League Annual Report 1975–76).

Howard League (1979a) *Losing Touch: Restricting Prisoners' Outside Contacts.* London: The League.

Howard League for Penal Reform (1979b) *Participation in Prisons: The Need for a New Style and Structure of Management.* London: The League.

Howard League for Penal Reform (1979c) *Supervision and Control of Young Offenders: Comments on the Green Paper, 'Youth Custody and Supervision'.* London: The League.

Lerman, P. (1975) *Community Treatment and Social Control.* Chicago: University of Chicago Press.

Morgan, Rod (1979) *Formulating Penal Policy: The Future of the Advisory Council on the Penal System.* London: NACRO.

Morris, C. (1978) 'The Children and Young Persons Act: Creating More Institutionalization.' *Howard Journal,* vol. 16, no. 3, pp.154–158.

Morris R. M. (1980) 'Home Office Crime Policy Planning: Six Years On.'

Howard Journal, vol. 19, no. 3, pp.135–141.

NELP (1978) *Information vs. Crime:* ... papers given at a one-day conference on a proposed information centre on crime prevention and treatment of offenders. London: North East London Polytechnic.

NILECJ (1979) *Exemplary Projects: A Program of the Institute of National Law Enforcement and Criminal Justice.* Washington, D.C.: LEAA.

National Prisoners' Movement (PROP) (1978) *Don't Mark his Face: The Account of the Hull Prison Riot (1976) and the Brutal Aftermath by the Prisoners Themselves.* London: PROP.

PROP (1979) *Wormwood Scrubs: Special Report.* London: PROP, the National Prisoners' Movement.

Rose, Gordon (1961) *The Struggle for Penal Reform: The Howard League and its Predecessors.* London: Stevens.

Rutherford, Andrew (1978) 'Decarceration of Young Offenders in Massachusetts: The Events and their Aftermath.' *in:* N. Tutt, ed., *Alternative Strategies for Coping with Crime.* Oxford: Blackwell.

Smith, Robert (1972) *A Quiet Revolution.* Washington, D.C.: U.S. Department of Health, Education and Welfare.

Sugden, Geoff, and Lib Skinner (c. 1978) *The Pro's and the Ex-cons: A Record of our Experiences...* London: Hargrave House Project.

Sweden (1979) *This is National Council for Crime Prevention.* Stockholm: the Council.

Train, C. J. (1977) 'The Development of Criminal Policy Planning in the Home Office.' *Public Administration,* pp.373–384.

Wootton, Barbara (1978) *Crime and Penal Policy.* London: Allen & Unwin.

Chapter Eight (pp 171–208)

Advisory Council on the Penal System (1978) *Sentences of Imprisonment: A Review of Maximum Penalties.* (Chairman: Baroness Serota) London: HMSO.

American Friends Service Committee (1971) *Struggle for Justice: A Report on Crime and Punishment in America.* New York: Hill & Wang.

Andenaes, J. (1975) General Prevention Revisited: Research and Policy Implications.' *in:* National Swedish Council for Crime Prevention (1975) *General Deterrence: A Conference on Current Research and Standpoints.* Stockholm.

Asquith, Lord Justice (1950) 'The Problem of Punishment.' *The Listener,* vol. 43, 11 May, p.821.

Baxter, R. and C. Nuttall (1975) 'Severe Sentences: No Deterrent to Crime?' *New Society,* 2 January, pp.11–13.

Bedau, H. A. (1980) 'Punishment as the Expression of Moral Indignation.' Lecture to British Society of Criminology, 28 May 1980 (unpublished).

Beyleveld, D. (1978) *The Effectiveness of General Deterrents against Crime:*

An Annotated Bibliography of Evaluative Research. Cambridge: Institute of Criminology.

Beyleveld, D. (1979) 'Deterrence Research as a Basis for Deterrence Policies.' *Howard Journal,* vol. 18, no. 3, pp.135–149.

Blom-Cooper, L. (1965) 'Preventible Homicide.' *Howard Journal,* vol. 11, no. 4, pp.297–308.

Board of Control (1947) *Pre-frontal Leucotomy in a Thousand Cases.* London: HMSO.

Bottomley, A. K. (1979) *Criminology in Focus.* Oxford: Martin Robertson.

Bottoms, A. E. and W. McWilliams (1979) 'A Non-treatment Paradigm for Probation Practice.' *British Journal of Social Work,* vol. 9, no. 2, pp.159–202.

Bowers, W. J. and G. L. Pierce (1980) 'Deterrence or Brutalization: What is the Effect of Executions?' *Crime and Delinquency,* vol. 26, no. 4.

Boyle, J. (1977) *A Sense of Freedom.* Edinburgh: Canongate and London: Pan.

Brody, S. (1976) *The Effectiveness of Sentencing: A Review of the Literature.* (Home Office Research Study no. 35) London: HMSO.

Brody, S. (1978) 'Research into the Aims and Effectiveness of Sentencing.' *Howard Journal,* vol. 17, no. 3, pp.133–148.

Burnett, M. (1978) *The Delinquent's Challenge: Trust Me if You Dare.* Chichester: Barry Rose.

Calvert, E. Roy (1936) *Capital Punishment in the Twentieth Century.* 5th ed. revised by Theodora Calvert. London: Putnam.

Carasov, Victor (1971) *Two Gentlemen to See you, Sir: The Autobiography of a Villain.* London: Gollancz.

Chauncey, R. (1975) 'Certainty, Severity and Skyjacking.' *Criminology,* vol. 12, no. 4, pp.447–473.

Committee . . . to Consider Authorized Procedures for the Interrogation of Persons Suspected of Terrorism (1972) *Report.* Cmnd. 4901. London: HMSO.

Cornish, D. R. and R. V. G. Clarke (1975) *Residential Treatment and its Effects on Delinquency.* (Home Office Research Study no. 32) London: HMSO.

Fogel, David (1978) 'The Justice Model for Corrections.' *in:* J. C. Freeman, ed., *Prisons Past and Future.* (Howard League for Penal Reform) London: Heinemann Educational Books.

Gostin, Larry O. (1977) *A Human Condition: The Law Relating to Mentally Abnormal Offenders – Observations, Analysis and Proposals for Reform.* Vol. 2. London: MIND.

Grahame, K. (1908) *The Wind in the Willows.* London: Methuen.

Hart, H. L. A. *Prolegomenon to the Principles of Punishment.* Presidential address to the Aristotelian Society, 19 October 1959.

Home Office (1980) *Prison Statistics England and Wales 1979.* Cmnd. 7978. London: HMSO.

Home Office and others (1980) *Young Offenders*. Cmnd. 8045. London: HMSO.

Howard League for Penal Reform (1974) *Control by Consent: Towards a Penal Philosophy*. London: The League.

Howard League for Penal Reform (1975) *Procedure and Resources for Mentally Abnormal Offenders*. London: The League.

Jefferson, Tony and J. Clarke (1974) 'Down These Mean Streets: The Meaning of Mugging.' *Howard Journal*, vol. 14, no. 1, pp.37–53.

Kesey, K. (1962) *One Flew over the Cuckoo's Nest*. London: Methuen, Pan.

Manton, Jo (1976) *Mary Carpenter and the Children of the Streets*. London: Heinemann.

Martin, J. P. and D. Webster *The Social Consequences of Conviction*. London: Heinemann Educational Books.

Martinson, R. (1974) 'What Works: Questions and Answers about Prison Reform.' *Public Interest*, no. 35, Spring.

Mays, J. B. (1970) *Crime and its Treatment*. London: Longman.

Morgan, P. (1978) *Delinquent Fantasies*. London: Temple Smith.

Morris, Norval and F. Zimring (1969) 'Deterrence and Corrections.' *Annals of the American Academy of Political and Social Science*, vol. 381, pp.137–146.

Newton, Anne M. (1978) 'Prevention of Crime and Delinquency.' *Criminal Justice Abstracts*, vol. 10, no. 2, p.251.

Norris, M. (1979) 'Offenders in Residential Communities: Measuring and Understanding Change.' *Howard Journal*, vol. 18, no. 1, pp.29–43.

Palmer, T. (1975) 'Martinson Revisited.' *Journal of Research in Crime and Delinquency*, vol. 12, no. 2, pp.133–152.

Parker, Tony and R. Allerton (1962) *The Courage of his Convictions*. London: Heinemann.

Pease, K. and J. Wolfson (1979) 'Incapacitation Studies: A Review and Commentary.' *Howard Journal*, vol. 18, no. 3, pp.160–167.

Pike, L. O. (1876) *A History of Crime in England*. London: Smith, Elder.

Prisons Committee (1895) *Report*. (Chairman: H. J. Gladstone) C.7702. London: HMSO.

Probyn, Walter (1977) *Angel Face: The Making of a Criminal*. London: Allen & Unwin.

Radzinowicz, Sir Leon and Joan King (1977) *The Growth of Crime: The International Experience*. London: Hamish Hamilton (Harmondsworth: Penguin, 1979).

Romig, Dennis (1978) *Justice for our Children: An Examination of Juvenile Delinquent Rehabilitation Programs*. Lexington: D. C. Heath.

Rose, Gordon (1961) *The Struggle for Penal Reform: The Howard League and its Predecessors*. London: Stevens.

Ross, H. L. (1973) 'Law, Science and Accidents: The British Road Safety Act of 1967.' *Journal of Legal Studies*, vol. 2, no. 1.

Schwartz, B. (1968) 'The Effect in Philadelphia of Pennsylvania's Increased

Penalties for Rape and Attempted Rape.' *Journal of Criminal Law, Criminology and Police Science,* vol. 59, pp.509–515.

Shaw, Bernard (1922) Preface to Sidney and Beatrice Webb, *English Prisons under Local Government.*

Shinnar, R. and S. Shinnar (1975) 'The Effects of the Criminal Justice System on the Control of Crime: A Quantitative Approach.' *Law and Society Review,* vol. 9, pp.581–611.

Sommer, R. (1976) *The End of Imprisonment.* New York: OUP.

Steer, David (1980) *Uncovering Crime: The Police Role.* (Royal Commission on Criminal Procedure, research study no. 7) London: HMSO, quoted in *Times,* 11 November 1980.

Tarling, R. (1979) 'The "Incapacitation" Effects of Imprisonment.' *Home Office Research Bulletin,* no. 7, pp. 6–8.

Temple, William (1934) *Ethics of Penal Action.* (Clarke Hall Lectures, 1) London: Clarke Hall Fellowship.

Thomas, D. A. (1979) *Constraints on Judgment.* Cambridge: Institute of Criminology.

Trasler, Gordon (1976) 'Reflections upon the Use of Custody.' *Howard Journal,* vol. 15, no. 1, pp.6–15.

Van Dine, S. and others (1979) *Restraining the Wicked: The Incapacitation of the Dangerous Criminal.* Lexington: D. C. Heath.

Von Hirsch, A. (1976) *Doing Justice.* New York: Hill and Wang.

Walker, N. (1969) *Sentencing in a Rational Society.* London: Allen Lane.

Walker, N. (1979) 'The Efficacy and Morality of Deterrents.' *Criminal Law Review.* March, pp.129–144.

West, D. J. and D. P. Farrington (1977) *The Delinquent Way of Life.* London: Heinemann Educational Books.

Wilson, J. Q. (1975) *Thinking about Crime.* New York: Basic Books.

Wootton, Barbara (1963) *Crime and the Criminal Law* (Hamlyn lectures). London: Stevens.

Wootton, Barbara (1978) *Crime and Penal Policy.* London: Allen & Unwin.

Wright, Martin (1977) 'Nobody Came: Criminal Justice and the Needs of Victims.' *Howard Journal,* vol. 16, no. 1, pp.22–31.

Chapter Nine (pp 209–239)

Alderson, J. (1978) *Communal Policing.* Exeter: Devon and Cornwall Constabulary.

Alderson, J. (1979) 'Ethics and Utility of Communal Policing.' (Lecture to Howard League annual general meeting) *Police,* vol. 12, nos. 3–4, November–December, pp.16–18, 20; 8.

Alexander, C. (1964) *in:* W. R. Ewald, ed., *Environment for Man.* Bloomington, Indiana: Indiana University Press.

Ben-Veniste, R. (1971) 'Pornography and Sex Crime.' *in:* Commission on Obscenity and Pornography, 1971 (see below)

Castle R. and A. Kerr (1972) *A Study of Suspected Child Abuse.* London: NSPCC.

Clarke, R. V. G. and P. Mayhew (1980) *Designing out Crime.* London: HMSO.

Cohen, Stan (1979) *Crime and Punishment: Some Thoughts on Theories and Policies.* London: Radical Alternatives to Prison (reprinted from *New Society*, 1, 15 and 29 March).

Commission on Obscenity and Pornography (1970) *Report.* New York: Random House and Bantam Books.

Commission on Obscenity and Pornography (1971) *Technical Report. Vol. 7:* Erotica and Antisocial Behavior. Washington: U.S. G.P.O.

Council of Europe (1978) *Newsletter on Legislative Activities,* no. 30, January/February. Strasbourg.

Council of Europe (1980) *Criminological Aspects of the Ill-Treatment of Children in the Family.* (Fourth Criminological Colloquium, Strasbourg, 1979.) Strasbourg: The Council.

Cross, P. A. (1978) *Vandalism: A Police Study Based on British and American Experience.* Birmingham: West Midlands Police.

Donovan, J. (1978) 'The Possibility of Being: New Youth Projects.' *in:* Ingham and others, 1978 (see below).

Eysenck, H. J. and D. K. B. Nias (1978) *Sex, Violence and the Media.* London: Temple Smith.

France (1981) Ministère de la Justice: circulaire du 7 février 1981 rélative à ... la loi no. 81–82 du 2 février 1981 renforçant la sécurité et protégeant la liberté des personnes. *Journal Officiel de la République Française,* 14 février, pp.1547–1558.

Gunn, J. (1976) 'Sexual Offenders.' *British Journal of Hospital Medicine,* January, pp.57–65.

Harding, Richard (1979) 'Firearms Use in Crime.' *Criminal Law Review,* December, pp.765–774.

Hedges, Alan and others (1980) *Community Planning Project: Cunningham Road Improvement Scheme. Final Report.* London: Social and Community Planning Research.

Home Office (1979) *Report of the Committee on Obscenity and Film Censorship.* (Chairman: Bernard Williams) Cmnd. 7772. London: HMSO.

Ingham, Roger and others (1978) *'Football Hooliganism': The Wider Context.* London: Inter-Action Inprint.

Jacobs, Jane (1961) *The Death and Life of Great American Cities.* Harmondsworth: Penguin, 1965.

Jeffrey, C. Ray (1971) *Crime Prevention through Environmental Design.* Beverly Hills: Sage.

Johnson, Pamela Hansford (1967) *On Iniquity: Some Personal Reflections Arising out of the Moors Murder Trial.* London: Macmillan.

Kutschinsky, B. (1971) 'Towards an Explanation of the Decrease in Registered Sex Crimes in Copenhagen.' *in:* Commission on Obscenity and Pornography, 1971 (see above).

Levin, Bernard (1970). *The Pendulum Years*. London: Pan.

McGrath, W. T. (1978) 'The Public's Responsibility in Criminal Justice.' Third Canadian Conference on Applied Criminology, Ottawa, 1978.

McIntosh, M. (1971) 'Changes in the Organization of Thieving.' *in:* S. Cohen, ed., *Images of Deviance*. Harmondsworth: Penguin.

Mayhew, P. and others (1976) *Crime as Opportunity*. (Home Office Research Series no. 34) London: HMSO.

Mayhew, P. and others (1979) *Crime in Public View*. (Home Office Research Series no. 49) London: HMSO.

NACRO and SCPR (1978) *Vandalism: A Pilot Project*. London: National Association for the Care and Resettlement of Offenders.

NILECJ (1977) *An Exemplary Project: Community Crime Prevention Program, Seattle, Washington,* by P. Cirel and others. Washington, D.C.: U.S. G.P.O.

NSPCC (1979) *Annual Report 1978*. London: National Society for the Prevention of Cruelty to Children.

Newton, Anne (1978) 'Prevention of Crime and Delinquency.' *Criminal Justice Abstracts,* vol. 10, no. 2, p.254.

Pease, K. (1979) *Reflections on the Development of Crime Prevention Strategies and Techniques in Western Europe, excluding Roman Law Countries*. (Report to the United Nations Centre for Social Development and Humanitarian Affairs.)

Périer-Daville, D. (1981) 'Les décisions du Conseil constitutionel rélatives à la loi Sécurité et Liberté.' *Gazette du Palais,* 13–14, février, pp.2–6.

Phillipson, C. M. (1971) 'Juvenile Delinquency in the School.' *in:* W. G. Carson and P. Wiles, ed., *Crime and Delinquency in Britain*. London: Martin Robertson.

Pickett, J. (in Press) 'The Management of N.A.I. to Children in the City of Manchester.' *in:* M. Borland, ed., *Violence in the Family*. Manchester: Manchester University Press.

Rolph, C. H. (1962) *The Police and the Public: An Enquiry*. London: Heinemann.

Scottish Council on Crime (1975) *Crime and the Prevention of Crime*. Edinburgh: HMSO.

Shaw, Bernard (1919) *Heartbreak House*. London: Constable.

Spence, James, and A. Hedges (1976) *Community Planning Project: Cunningham Road Improvement Scheme. Interim Report*. London: Social and Community Planning Research.

Stebbing, L. Susan (1939) *Thinking to Some Purpose*. Harmondsworth: Penguin.

United Nations (1981) *Consideration of Reports ... under Article 40 of the Covenant. Addendum: Netherlands*. (Human Rights Committee, CCPR/C10/Add.3.

United States National Advisory Commission on Criminal Justice Standards and Goals (1973) *Community Crime Prevention.* Washington, D.C.: U.S. G.P.O.

Walsh, D. P. (1978) *Shoplifting: Controlling a Major Crime.* London: Macmillan.

Wilson, H. (1980) 'Parents Can Cut the Crime Rate.' *New Society,* 4 December, pp.456–458.

Chapter Ten (pp 240–270)

Arthur, J. and others (1979) *Six Quakers Look at Crime and Punishment.* London: Quaker Social Responsibility and Education.

Blom-Cooper, L. (1977) 'The Criminal Justice System: Myth or Reality.' London: Howard League for Penal Reform.

Chinkin, Christine M. and Robin C. Griffiths (1980) 'Resolving Conflict by Mediation.' *New Law Journal,* 3 January, pp.6–8.

Christie, Nils (1977) 'Conflicts as Property.' *British Journal of Criminology,* January, pp.1–15.

Colson, Charles W. and D. H. Benson (1980) 'Restitution as an Alternative to Imprisonment.' *Detroit College of Law Review,* Summer, pp.523–598.

Committee on Enforcement of Judgement Debts (1969) *Report.* (Chairman: Mr. Justice Payne) Cmnd. 3909. London: HMSO.

Council of Europe (1976) *Alternative Measures to Imprisonment.* Strasbourg: The Council.

Galaway, B. (1977) 'The Use of Restitution.' *Crime and Delinquency,* vol. 23, no. 1, pp.57–67.

Home Office (1980) *Probation and After-Care Statistics England and Wales 1979.* London: Home Office.

Howard League for Penal Reform (1977) *Making Amends: Criminals, Victims and Society – Compensation, Reparation, Reconciliation.* Chichester: Barry Rose.

Huber, Barbara (1980) 'The Dilemma of Decriminalization: Dealing with Shoplifting in West Germany.' *Criminal Law Review,* October, pp.621–627.

Hulsman, L. H. C. (1973/4) 'Criminal Justice in the Netherlands.' *Delta,* vol. 16, no. 4, pp.7–19.

Hulsman, L. H. C. (1976) '"Civilizing" the Criminal Justice System: Strategies to Reduce Violence in Society.' Lecture to annual general meeting of Howard League (unpublished).

Hulsman, L. H. C. (1978) 'Criminal Policy: Strategies and Evaluation – How to Create Room for Alternatives?' (unpublished).

McGillis, D. and J. Mullen (1977) *Neighbourhood Justice Centers: An Analysis of Potential Models.* (National Institute of Law Enforcement and Criminal Justice.) Washington: U.S. G.P.O.

Manton, Jo (1976) *Mary Carpenter and the Children of the Streets.* London: Heinemann.

Paterson, Basil A. and others (1978) 'An Alternative to Criminal Justice Process.' *New York Law Journal*, vol. 177, no. 7, pp.1, 24.

Sebba, L. (1978) 'Some Explorations in the Scaling of Penalties.' *Journal of Research in Crime and Delinquency,* vol. 15, no. 2, July, pp.247–265.

Sellin, T. and M. E. Wolfgang (1964) *The Measurement of Delinquency.* New York: Wiley.

Softley, P. and R. Tarling (1977) 'Compensation Orders and Custodial Sentences.' *Criminal Law Review,* December, pp.720–722.

Softley, P. (1978) *Compensation Orders in Magistrates' Courts.* Home Office Research Series no. 43) London: HMSO.

Tallack, William (1900) *Reparation to the Injured; and the Rights of the Victim of Crime to Compensation.* (Paper for Quinquennial International Prison Congress, Brussels, 1900) London: Werheimer, Lea.

Vennard, J. (1976) 'Justice and Recompense for Victims of Crime.' *New Society,* 19 February, pp.378–380.

Vera Institute of Justice (1979?) *Mediation and Arbitration as Alternatives to Prosecution in Felony Arrest Cases: An Evaluation of the Brooklyn Dispute Resolution Center (first year).* New York: The Institute.

Wahrhaftig, P. (1981) 'Dispute Resolution Retrospective.' *Crime and Delinquency,* vol. 27, no. 1, January, pp.99–105.

Whitcomb, Debra, and others (1979) *Stop Rape Crisis Center: Baton Rouge, Louisiana, An Exemplary Project.* Washington, D.C.: National Institute of Law Enforcement and Criminal Justice.

Wilkins, Leslie (1974) 'To Do and Dare: The Necessity for Innovation.' *in:* NACRO, *The Prevention of Crime* (annual conference, 1974).

Index

293